OX 07/15

RTS 2/19

To renew this book, phone 0845 1202811 or visit
our website at www.libcat.oxfordshire.gov.uk
You will need your library PIN number
(available from your library)

**OXFORDSHIRE
COUNTY COUNCIL**
SOCIAL & COMMUNITY SERVICES
www.oxfordshire.gov.uk

The publisher gratefully acknowledges the generous support of the Fletcher Jones Foundation Humanities Endowment Fund of the University of California Press Foundation.

HITCHCOCK ON HITCHCOCK

HITCHCOCK ON HITCHCOCK

Selected Writings and Interviews
Volume 2

———

Edited by

Sidney Gottlieb

UNIVERSITY OF CALIFORNIA PRESS

University of California Press, one of the most distinguished university
presses in the United States, enriches lives around the world by advancing
scholarship in the humanities, social sciences, and natural sciences. Its
activities are supported by the UC Press Foundation and by philanthropic
contributions from individuals and institut⸍
visit www.ucpress.edu.

University of California Press
Oakland, California

© 2015 Sidney Gottlieb.

For permissions, please see page 269.

Library of Congress Cataloging-in-Publica

Hitchcock, Alfred, 1899–
   Hitchcock on Hitchcock: selected writin⸍
Volume 2 / edited by Sidney Gottlieb.
      p.   cm.
   "Bibliography of writings by Hitchcock": p.
   Includes bibliographical references and index.
   ISBN 978-0-520-27958-2 (cloth : alk. paper)
   ISBN 978-0-520-27960-5 (paper : alk. paper)
   ISBN 978-0-520-96039-8 (e-book)
   1. Motion pictures.   2. Motion pictures—Production and direction.
   3. Hitchcock, Alfred, 1899–   —Interviews.   I. Gottlieb, Sidney.
   II.Title.
   PN1994.H53   1995
   791.43'0233'092—dc20   94–31624

Manufactured in the United States of America

24   23   22   21   20   19   18   17   16   15
10   9   8   7   6   5   4   3   2   1

In keeping with a commitment to support environmentally responsible
and sustainable printing practices, UC Press has printed this book on
Natures Natural, a fiber that contains 30% post-consumer waste and meets
the minimum requirements of ANSI/NISO z39.48–1992 (R 1997) (*Permanence of Paper*).

CONTENTS

HITCHCOCK AT WORK

HITCHCOCK SPEAKS

ACKNOWLEDGMENTS

I am deeply grateful to Patricia Hitchcock O'Connell and Leland Faust, representing the Hitchcock Estate, for their gracious support of this project and their permission to reprint the material herein. I also want to thank Daniel Halpern, Makoto Imai, R. Allen Leider, and F. Anthony Macklin for facilitating further permission to reprint the material herein that they had a hand in. At the University of California Press, Mary Francis was to me what she has been to scores of others, a tireless collaborator, and I have been sustained by her encouragement and efficiency and taken full advantage of her patience. And this second volume of *Hitchcock on Hitchcock* also bears the imprint of my University of California Press editor for the first volume, Ed Dimendberg, whose good advice then continues to be good advice now.

This book would not have been possible without the generous support and tangible assistance of numerous people who sent me copies of articles that they had discovered or that I was looking for but could not find. Charles Barr and Christopher K. Philippo in particular were constant sources of material as well as information, advice, and encouragement. I also got valuable items and help from Wayne Beach, David Bordwell, Stephane Duckett, David Henry, Alain Kerzoncuf, Nathalie Morris, Patrick McGilligan, Michael Walker, James M. Vest, and Nancy Vest. In addition, James Vest translated two interviews specifically for this volume and made important suggestions and corrections that I integrated into my commentary on these interviews. My work on the Hitchcock-Truffaut material benefited greatly from numerous exchanges with Janet Bergstrom, as well as her own very important essay on that subject. Renata Jackson looked over my introductions, and Robin Whitaker read the entire manuscript and both helped remove innumerable errors and infelicities and offered valuable advice and support.

Much of my research was conducted at the New York Public Library, the Film Study Center at the Museum of Modern art, the British Film Institute, and the Margaret Herrick Library at the Academy of Motion Picture Arts and Sciences. I am grateful to the librarians and research associates at those institutions for their help. And Christopher Philippo has been a particularly good guide for me in navigating the new online research environment that we truly can't live without. I wouldn't have been able to find the time to work on such a long-term project without the long-term help of Andrew Miller, Jim Castonguay, and Debbie Danowski, my colleagues at Sacred Heart University, who in their terms as our department chairperson arranged my teaching schedules and departmental responsibilities in ways that allowed me to do other things as well and coordinated much needed and much appreciated sabbatical leaves, without which two decades of work on this project would have stretched far into a third.

I have always relied on the kindness of friends, and there is little that I do related to Hitchcock that isn't somehow grounded in my admiration for and friendship with Richard Allen, Charles Barr, Thomas Leitch, and David Sterritt, all of which goes far beyond this thing of ours, Hitchcock studies. Closer to home, literally, I am fortunate beyond words to have Chris Sharrett and Rick Grigg as intellectual models, good buddies, and formidable allies in our shared pursuit of the sublime and the ridiculous, Hitchcockian and otherwise.

INTRODUCTION

Some years ago when I proposed publishing a volume of selected writings by and interviews with Alfred Hitchcock, I admit that I felt the need to be somewhat defensive. Several key challenges needed to be addressed: about whether Hitchcock should be taken seriously not only as a filmmaker (Robin Wood's famous question had been answered affirmatively, in ways persuasive to most people, by that time) but also as a commenter on films and filmmaking; about whether there was much of interest and substance beyond what was already easily available (especially in what was sometimes considered Truffaut's "definitive" book); and about whether any claim that Hitchcock's pronouncements on film merited extensive consideration was fatally undermined by the fact that they were often presented as glib publicity efforts, were sometimes not easily identifiable as written by Hitchcock himself, and were frequently repetitious, familiar, and prepackaged.

While I was prepared to champion Hitchcock, in fact he didn't and doesn't really need my help, other than as a facilitator in making his often evanescent and inaccessible but frequently thoughtful, revealing, and extremely valuable comments more easily available. The material ultimately published in *Hitchcock on Hitchcock: Selected Writings and Interviews,* volume 1 (1995), speaks for itself and defends itself quite capably from the above challenges. And as it turns out, so does the material I have gathered for this second volume of *Hitchcock on Hitchcock.* I think that a strong case could be made for a comprehensive edition (in print or digital format) of all of Hitchcock's writings and interviews, however repetitive and uneven in quality and usefulness such a collection might be: old-school scholarship presents a legitimate model (not just a fetish object) of carefully prepared editions of even the marginalia of significant authors (five thick volumes for Coleridge, for example), and T. S. Eliot's quip about the value of even Shakespeare's (as yet unearthed) laundry lists applies just as well to our cinematic Shakespeare. But the material available for a second volume of *Hitchcock on Hitchcock* is far more than the result of a gleaning or a second pressing. New articles by Hitchcock displaying his lifelong reflections on his art and career continue to be discovered, and we have reached a point where these pieces added to ones regrettably left out of the first volume for reasons of space, not quality and level of interest, make up a substantive new collection.

In assembling and shaping this volume, I was guided by a few principles. The pieces are (with only a few exceptions) reprinted in their entirety and range from the very short to the very long. But we are quite lucky to have, for example, even a few hundred words on Hitchcock's thoughts from the late 1930s on the use of color film, and the rambling prolixity of the transcript of his production conversation with a technical collaborator on *Stage Fright* (c. 1950) and of his comments to Bryan Forbes and a particularly lively and well-informed audience at the John Player Lecture in 1967 is worth preserving and studying in full detail. I have aimed to cover Hitchcock's entire career and have included items from each of the decades from the 1920s to the 1970s. It happened fortuitously that there is a reasonable balance in the number of items from each decade, but my primary objective was to include material that is valuable no matter what period it came from. I am particularly pleased to be able to include so much from the very early period, and the numerous pieces here from the 1920s help fill in a pivotal part of Hitchcock's career not well covered in the initial volume. Although his writings from the 1950s and 1960s are well represented in that volume, the selections here address in much more detail his television work, the maintenance of his persona, and his awareness of new developments in contemporary cinema and the strains of responding to them. Repetition—among the pieces in this new collection and in the two volumes taken together—is inevitable, but there is also much diversity. The two volumes work well together in giving a full view of continuity and change in Hitchcock's ideas on film and sense of his persona and career. We get a deepened sense of the forging of the carefully defined Hitchcock "brand" but also of the play of the more than occasional Hitchcock variations as he presents himself and his ideas on cinema.

In order to allow for as full a view as possible, I define "writings and interviews" somewhat loosely. These include, as in the first volume, articles with his byline (taking this as a sign of "authorship" broadly defined), "as told to" pieces, and straightforward interviews with back-and-forth exchanges (although even these are undoubtedly edited and reshaped), as well as journalistic articles reporting on Hitchcock but containing interspersed direct quotations. I chose not to include several kinds of articles, even though they came out under Hitchcock's name and are often substantive and interesting. For example, I do not include samples of the many articles that focus exclusively or primarily on food, weight, and his family life, topics perhaps worth investigating as part of the shaping of his public persona and as revealing his personal habits and interests but of lesser importance than his comments on cinematic topics. And while I had originally hoped to include at least one example of "graphic" Hitchcock, perhaps something like "'Have You Heard?' The Story of Wartime Rumors" (*Life*, July 13, 1942, 68–73), which is mostly a pictorial rather than a written narrative that ties in nicely with some of his other wartime work in the early 1940s, space would not allow for this. Perhaps some future coffee table book illustrating Hitchcock's life and work will reprint a sample of one or another of these surprisingly numerous pieces showing Hitchcock's application of visual storytelling to the print medium and playful cameo appearances even outside his films.

But there is space here for a variety of pieces often from unexpected sources that contain valuable information about Hitchcock at work and occasionally at home and at play. I have not gone as far as Dan Auiler in his invaluable *Hitchcock's Notebooks* (which, like *Hitchcock on Hitchcock,* deserves a second volume) in attempting to "illustrate" Hitchcock by gathering samples of the wide range of his tracks in letters, memos, production notes, sketches, comments on screenplays, and other such documents, but I have reprinted several pieces normally not classified as "writings," including, as mentioned above, a transcription of a production meeting that gives much insight into how visual imagination takes material form and a legal document that expresses Hitchcock's notion of himself as an auteur in the context of an industrywide battle over property rights to films. And while "A Lesson in PSYCHO-logy" is a summary of instructions to distributors, not a discursive essay, its detailed description of the marketing and "staging" of *Psycho* is—especially given Hitchcock's recurrent attention to film as a blend of art and commerce—an important complement to his many comments on the making of *Psycho.*

I also take a somewhat unconventional approach to "raw" material from an interview to allow for the inclusion of an excerpt from what surely deserves full publication in the near future: a transcription of the original three-way conversation (the recordings indicate the extent to which Helen Scott was somewhat more than a mere translator) that was subsequently radically edited and reshaped to form Truffaut's "Hitchbook." What we hear on the recordings is strikingly different from what we read in the text. We know the legend but should have access to the facts. I should add that in this case, they do not challenge the legend—the printed version is not a misrepresentation or a misleading fabrication—but they deepen (much is left out) and sharpen (some is blurred) our image and understanding of Hitchcock, a claim that I believe is substantiated by examining the section from the original conversation that I include herein, restoring comments on Hitchcock's grooming and directing actresses and also a fascinating exchange on Truffaut's *The 400 Blows* that did not make it into the book that we all know.

As with the first volume of *Hitchcock on Hitchcock,* I have organized the material chronologically within thematic sections. The five headings are broad and inevitably overlapping—"Stories and Suspense," "Pure Cinema and the Hitchcock Touch," "On Directors and Directing," "Hitchcock at Work," and "Hitchcock Speaks"—and determining where a particular item should be placed was sometimes difficult, especially because Hitchcock's comments are often far-ranging and don't lend themselves to simple categorization. But I have tried to group together pieces that have a demonstrable affinity, and indeed intriguing links among the articles give each section at least some kind of coherence and unity. This is a book that can be dipped into and read in whatever order seems useful for the reader, but following the thematic groupings often highlights Hitchcock's extended discussions of key topics, showing both continuity and sometimes development, even changes in and revisions of some of his ideas. I'm not sure that many reversals or contradictions are to be found here: Hitchcock was consistent and thought out his ideas very carefully before expressing them and putting them into practice. But reading through all the articles and interviews collected herein reveals that alongside the often bold, provocative, and frequently repeated summary statements of his key ideas are complex reexaminations and thoughtful qualifications of what might otherwise be taken as overstated credos. A full and close study of his observations on his art is eye-opening: Hitchcock is a master of suspense but of surprise as well. For all his emphasis on pure cinema as visual montage, he is also quite attentive to the resources of sound effects, the tone as well as the content of voices, and music. Alongside memorable statements about his disinterest in story and logical coherence are numerous indications of his commitment to cinema as a storytelling medium and his scrupulous attention to consistency, accuracy, and narrative unity. The master manipulator of audiences is also shrewdly knowledgeable about how audiences can contribute to the shaping of a film, and his anticipation of their response is built into his production work and design. While "photographs of people talking" was a shorthand statement of what he envisioned as the death of cinema, he frequently discusses how he found creative ways to make photographs of people talking highly cinematic (e.g., the famous kissing sequence in *Notorious;* numerous anguished conversations in *Vertigo;* and dramatic verbal confessions everywhere in his films), and he repeatedly reveals the importance of good dialogue and of how witty his films are verbally as well as visually. Perhaps not surprisingly, the true Hitchcock Touch has depth and details that emerge vividly in the view afforded by the vast body of his comments on films and filmmaking.

To say the least, Hitchcock speaks very well for himself throughout the volume. Nevertheless, I include introductions to each section that in some cases give extensive summaries and analyses of the individual pieces, not because they are opaque or require any special pleading, but because they benefit from a kind of contextualizing and close reading that they don't always get. The occasion of a Hitchcock article or interview is usually self-explanatory—often the release of a new film— and the subject matter is typically directly related to his current project or some aspect of his well-known but constantly cultivated image. But I try to call attention to not always obvious instances in which these documents are a key part of his biographical record and offer interesting insight into his state of mind and his sense of the state of his career and of cinema in general. This record is dynamic rather than static: alongside numerous repetitions and "plagiarisms of himself" that critics tend to focus on, there is a much more complex dialogue with himself that emerges in the echoes and variations in the pieces collected here, some of which I trace. And while Hitchcock's reference point is most often himself, this is not his sole subject and concern. I try to highlight key examples of how his comments are often contributions to broader discussions, in film circles and at large, of public issues, such as the fate of British cinema, the advent and impact of new media technology, contemporary values and morals, and debates about violence, censorship, and the uses of art in modern society, especially during an age of anxiety. Finally, my premise throughout many years of work on this volume is that Hitchcock's writings and interviews, like his films, are often characterized by clear statements, bright surfaces, simplicity, strong voices, and vivid directness, but also indirection and misdirection, subtlety, nuance, complexity, shadowy depths, and undertones. First glances reveal the former, but close attention is necessary to reveal and make sense of the latter, and it is this kind of attention that I attempt to apply in the various close readings I include in the section introductions. I am in no danger of confusing one of Hitchcock's essays on his films for the film itself, nor am I trying to suggest that Hitchcock's essays and interviews are fully "well wrought urns" that justify any critical and interpretive ingenuity that can be applied to them. But I do try to illustrate the often unexpected riches and delights that, to return to the inevitable refrain, come from taking Hitchcock's writings and interviews seriously.

As in the first volume, the articles and interviews reprinted here are transcribed directly from the texts as they were first published. I include original publication information for each piece. Obvious errors are corrected silently, and in the rare instances when the original text is unclear or otherwise defective, I include my best guess at whatever letters or words are missing. Spelling is Americanized, and I regularize punctuation, the use of quotations marks, and the presentation of film titles. I have also standardized details of layout and design, eliminating unnecessary line spaces, indentations, and section titles, and adding prefixes in interviews when necessary to identify who is speaking. Many of the pieces were originally accompanied by interesting and informative illustrations, captions, and headnotes, but it has not been feasible to include them in this volume. Finally, I include a brief selected bibliography at the end, which does not do justice to how much I have relied on the enormous amount of valuable writing on Hitchcock that is available but at least lists the works that I mention specifically in my introductions and also several articles in which I reprint key pieces by Hitchcock included in this volume (and one that is not) with detailed commentaries.

STORIES AND SUSPENSE

INTRODUCTION

Before he was in a position to make films, Hitchcock wrote stories that, not surprisingly, are recognizably Hitchcockian in tone and subject and are also remarkably cinematic. "Gas" (reprinted in the first volume of *Hitchcock on Hitchcock*), a story he published in the *Henley Telegraph,* a magazine put out by the company he worked for after he left St. Ignatius school, is often taken as a template for many of his future works, with its imperiled woman, evocation of sadism, detailed description of the experience of fear, and twist ending: it's all been a dream, prompted by anesthesia in a dentist's office. But subtleties and complexities exist here as well. For all that he talked later in his career about avoiding clichés, this story is based on them. He sets the mood in "Gas" with a shorthand reference to Grand Guignol and a subsequent piling up of conventional details. Ultimately it is a story based on clichéd stories, not experiences—in fact, it is a dramatization of a woman steeped in stories and drama that overheat her imagination and color her sense of the world around her. The clichés of the story turn out to be part of a conscious examination of how clichés fill one's mind and shape one's experiences. It is a study in hysteria originating in possession by lurid art.

But "Gas" is only the first of seven stories that Hitchcock published in the *Henley Telegraph.* The remaining stories were unearthed and reprinted, with a full commentary, by Patrick McGilligan (30–46), and I include them herein. McGilligan calls the second story, "The Woman's Part," "especially cinematic" (26) and relates its frame-within-a-frame structure, theatrical setting and imagery, and unstable sense of truth and reality to numerous later Hitchcock films. It is worth adding that this story, like the first, is also an early Hitchcockian exercise in the subjective point of view, with the twist at the end coming from the revelation of how limited and distorting this point of view is. The title of the story is particularly significant, referring not only to the literal subject matter revealed at the end—that the narrator's wife is an actress playing a role on stage—but to the way that the husband is feminized, identifying with the woman he watches as he himself is a passive victim observing events around him that he cannot direct. The story is a preliminary sketch of a disempowering rather than an empowering gaze, an important but often overlooked motif for Hitchcock, especially in films like *Rear*

Window and *Vertigo,* arguably his most profound analyses and dramatizations of "the woman's part" played by both a man and a woman.

"Sordid" is a rather simple tale of drama and deception, once again, like "Gas," showing the contrast between the stories we tell and the often far more mundane truth that lies behind them. The revelation at the end explains the otherwise inscrutable title by turning it into a pun: as McGilligan explains (27), it is indeed a sorry sight to realize how routinely we accept an extravagant legend that upon closer examination proves to be completely fabricated, betrayed by the "words" that compose our tales about the "swords." One of Hitchcock's main concerns in the stories he told is the lesson of unreliable narration: stories are inescapably captivating but also misleading and problematic in numerous ways. The *Henley* pieces vividly illustrate that Hitchcock was an inveterate storyteller and one whose recurrent concern was the very subject of storytelling itself.

Little good can be said about "And There Was No Rainbow," which is at best a trifling bit of attempted light humor at the expense of a "poor Romeo," his friend who is far from the "brainy man" he seems to be and whose silly man-to-man advice almost gets him cuckolded, and the woman in question, who must be faulted for being susceptible to the advances of both of these two boobs. This is a comically grim view of men, women, and eros, but there is no need to take it overly seriously: plenty of far more substantial evidence in Hitchcock's later work will support our sense of his comically grim view of men, women, and eros.

This one comedic dud in the series is followed, however, by two more appealing bits of humor that Hitchcock published in the next issue of the *Henley Telegraph.* "What's Who?" may be closer to music hall silliness than Ionesco and Pirandello, but it nicely captures the escalating dizziness that occurs when a group of actors enter the vortex of impersonating one another and release the genie that inevitably arises from the unanswerable questions "who's you?" and "what's me?"—the presiding genie, as it turns out, of many of Hitchcock's later films. And "The History of Pea Eating" is perhaps the most assured and literary of the *Henley* pieces, effectively adopting a kind of Swiftian satiric drollery in showing how a penchant for immodest proposals and misguided experiments characterize modern man as *Homo ridiculoso.*

These first six pieces do not prepare us for the last in the series, published just before Hitchcock left the company for a job at British Famous Players-Lasky. There's no way of knowing whether or not "Fedora" is based on a real woman actually seen by Hitchcock, but his description of her and fantasies about her future career and the men she will profoundly affect (there is perhaps a little Pygmalion in him as he envisions different shapes she may take, although for other men, not him) are deeply felt and effectively conveyed. And this sketch is not only a story about his desires and ambitions for "worldly greatness" as well as romance but also a musing on stories in general. The fact that "every person has a plot . . . and every plot is the same" entails the responsibility to express and explore that plot, a task that Hitchcock was in the process of turning into his vocation.

The discovery of a manuscript in Hitchcock's own hand dating probably from the very early 1920s gives us a good glimpse of the next stage in his storytelling career. "Good-night, Nurse!" is not a fully fledged tale intended for print but an outline of a plot, a treatment evidently aimed at attracting the attention of a studio as a possible film project. It focuses on a young man (Felix) who wants to satisfy both his romantic and financial needs and can do so only if he escapes from his plan to elope with a Spanish dancer (Juanita), using her to spoil the reputation of his cousin (Egbert) so that he will be disinherited by their uncle, leaving Felix as the heir. Egbert marries Juanita, but rather than tarnishing his reputation this marriage leaves his uncle grateful, because he himself had been trapped "in the clutches" of the Spanish dancer. In a final twist, things work out well for everyone but Felix: Egbert becomes confirmed as the new heir, and the uncle ends up with Mary, his nurse, the woman Felix had hoped to marry. It is easy to imagine "Good-night, Nurse!" printed on the last dialogue title card, literally describing the ending but also perfectly expressing Felix's feelings as he mouths this common term of exasperation. One wonders what Hitchcock had in mind that led him to believe such a story might open any doors for him: he must have imagined that there was a substantial demand for eccentric and exotic characters, as well as farce and erotic intrigue driven by implausibility and coincidence—qualities that after all pulled Jazz Age audiences to Feydeau and DeMille, among many others. And it is curiously coincidental that around the same time Hitchcock was working as the title designer for a film titled *The Spanish Jade* (directed by John Robertson, 1922) he was writing a sketch featuring a woman who could figuratively be called a Spanish jade, although as yet there is no further demonstrable link between these two projects. In any event, this early manuscript perhaps illustrates not so much Hitchcock's skill at or particular interest in romantic comedy as his effort at this time to become as versatile as possible in his quest to make himself the kind of person who would someday be allowed to make films.

Hitchcock continued to write stories long after he was well established as a filmmaker, and I include several examples of his later efforts. "Death in the Crystal Ball," which purports to be based on a real experience that he had with his family more than a decade earlier, takes place in one of his favorite settings, an amusement park, home to the unconscious and the uncanny. (It was published while he was working on *Strangers on a Train*, which similarly concludes with a shocking death witnessed by "hundreds of witnesses" who "shrieked in horror.") This story is structured quite literally as a variation on the classic example Hitchcock used to define suspense (the hidden bomb, set to go off at a time that we know), but in this case not just the audience but the protagonist as well—he himself—is told the exact time that a horrible event will happen. We are all left to nervously await the arrival of 6:07, which indeed brings a catastrophe that is both expected and shocking, a useful reminder that while Hitchcock always highlighted the differences between suspense and surprise, as well as his preference for the former, he nevertheless used both effects, often in tandem.

"The Wise Man of Kumin" is similarly structured as a tale of suspense but is also a reflexive meditation on that dramatic device. A Chinese leader lives his life beneath a heavy chandelier dangling from a frayed rope, a condition made even more perilous by the rumbling of the train that passes by every day. The ruler's imperviousness to this constant danger is taken as unshakable bravery, and his reputation protects his kingdom from attack by neighboring warlords hesitant to challenge such a fearless ruler. Only years after the man's death is it revealed that living a life of suspense is a strategic ruse: the chandelier will in fact never fall because it is supported by a steel wire. The twist ending lays bare the truth behind the appearances that constantly mislead us and perhaps looks forward to *Family Plot,* Hitchcock's most fully developed presentation and demystification of the occult. The wink at the end of that film (also associated with a chandelier, as in "The Wise Man of Kumin") does not challenge the power of the occult but reveals that it rests on something mundane rather than mystical: the expert manipulation of suspense, a talent shared by fortune-tellers, the wise man of Kumin, and the wise man of Hollywood, Alfred Hitchcock.

The final story I include is not the most artful but is in some respects the most compelling, in part because of what may be an undercurrent of oblique topical references to Hitchcock's real, not just fantasy, life. "The Chloroform Clue" is a detailed retelling of what Hitchcock calls "one of the strangest stories I have ever encountered," that of Edwin and Adelaide Bartlett and Reverend George Dyson. Edwin invited Dyson into the household to educate Adelaide and then apparently encouraged their intimacy and watched approvingly as the two carried on romantically in his presence. After settling his estate on his wife and naming Dyson the executor of his will, Edwin became increasingly sick, and he died not long afterward, poisoned by chloroform, which Adelaide had procured. While the sensational trial that followed reaffirmed the "grave suspicion" of her role in the death, the mystery of how she might have administered the chloroform was unresolved, so she was acquitted, much to the approval of the courtroom audience, which "burst into cheers and applause."

Hitchcock introduces this story as an example of how much he is "fascinated by tales of murder," "suspense," "sudden death," and "most unusual love stor[ies]," all qualities of his newly released film at that time, *I Confess.* It's not surprising that in summarizing the story to Truffaut he notes, "I often thought it might make a good picture" (206). But numerous aspects of the story relate it to a scenario that Hitchcock was perhaps not just envisioning but living through. The snapshot of the husband-wife relationship—"The Bartletts' marriage . . . had been entirely platonic.

Except for one occasion which resulted in a stillborn child, they lived together as friends and nothing more"—is uncomfortably close to the way that Hitchcock often described his life with Alma (although with one key difference: their one sexual act, as he told it, led to the birth of their daughter, Patricia). And the insistence that Adelaide and Dyson's act was specifically not "illicit" but one conducted "in the presence of her husband" and with his awareness parallels Patrick McGilligan's speculation of what may have characterized Hitchcock's own domestic as well as working environment in the late 1940s and early 1950s, with Whitfield Cook joining Alfred and Alma as the third Hitchcock (415 and elsewhere). McGilligan confidently states that Alma and Cook had a sexual relationship, and while lacking hard evidence about what Hitchcock knew and didn't know, he repeatedly suggests that it is at least plausible that the ongoing cordiality of the three Hitchcocks may have been based not on the director's obliviousness but on his approval and willingness to "sympathetically allow the flirtation to progress" (427). The information provided by McGilligan helps explain why the Bartlett story was even more of a touchstone for Hitchcock than the cases of Crippen and Christie, which he also frequently mentioned. It is less about violent death than complex domestic relationships, and its reference points are not only historical but also contemporary and personal: a "true mystery" in unexpected ways, the Bartlett story is in its essence arguably Hitchcock's story as well.

While in his interviews and writings Hitchcock often took great pleasure in telling stories about his films, he also frequently made clear how important the element of story was in them but did so in carefully qualified ways. In "Hitchcock on Stories," he notes that work on a film begins with the search for a story, and he briefly defines the kind of stories that are most suitable. His general advice is that a story must be unified and focused but also capacious enough to allow for the addition of the other ingredients that drive a film: "glamour, suspense, romance, charm, drama, emotion, and so forth." But he calls attention to a kind of tension between story and cinema, warning that while story is necessary for a film, it can also be a distraction, especially in his chosen genre: there is some palpable irony in his comment that "murder mysteries are not often great successes on the screen . . . because they demand too much acute concentration." Hitchcock is of course famous for telling the story of the MacGuffin, but here he comes close to saying that story in general is itself a MacGuffin: extremely valuable and captivating but basically a pretext. The key challenge, if not paradox, is that story should get and keep things going, catching the attention of the audience, but not get in the way or dominate. Even at this point relatively early in his career (these comments were published in 1937), Hitchcock was preparing a response to what he identified somewhat later as his archenemy, the "plausibles." At the core of his defense against misapprehension and criticism, from audiences enraptured by narrative and always on the lookout for lapses in his works, is perhaps a

Hitchcockian version of René Magritte's well-known painting *The Treachery of Images* (1928–29), picturing a pipe and the caption (in French) "This is not a pipe." In discussing his productions in numerous interviews and articles, Hitchcock repeatedly announced in one way or another, "This is not a story: it's a film." The real work of cinema is not "logical," which in this present essay as elsewhere he associates with clear and linear narration, but "visual," presumably not limited to the demands of faithful representation of people, things, and actions. Story is not abandoned or disrespected, but it is put in its proper place, included but subordinated in his definition of and plea for pure cinema: "It is no use telling people; they have got to SEE." For all its brevity, "Hitchcock on Stories" effectively conveys a fundamental truth: Hitchcock was always a storyteller but always aware of "the Treachery of Story."

It may seem a bit jarring to move from a short essay describing the dangers of overattentiveness to one that praises that capability, but in "Lights! Action!—but Mostly Camera" Hitchcock avoids contradicting himself by shifting his ground from the audience, which must be protected from being distracted, to a particular kind of protagonist whose talent and vocation revolve around "his ability to observe the minute details." In this brief introduction to a volume of detective fiction, Hitchcock defines the detective as the exemplary "seer," someone with "heightened perception" that puts him in a position to track the eruption of the "abnormal" into the "normal" and "know the whole story," which would otherwise remain inscrutable.

The terms he uses to describe the talents of the detective reveal why Hitchcock has a particular interest in this figure: the detective is characterized by a "camera spirit," "camera sense," and "camera eye," insofar as the camera "tells" and "records" the truth. And his ability to notice and record details is complemented by an active mental capacity to process them, recognizing what is different and significant in an otherwise "normal" setting, and not only "recording the extraordinary" but assembling it into a "series of plates" that "form a picture that gives the truth." The detective is, in short, not just a camera but a director, and Sherlock Holmes, Father Brown, Sir John Menier, L. B. Jefferies, and Alfred Hitchcock, to name only a few of the many in this clan, are mirror images of one another who face the same problem and task: "The component parts of the story are there; the job is to make a picture of them." "Lights! Action!—but Mostly Camera!" is on the surface a modest homage to a beloved genre and archetypal character, but it is also a provocative sketch of how a fundamentally cinematic process—"camera perception," he calls it, "the making of one moving picture of the disjointed negatives"—constructs the stories that solve crimes, compose films, and ultimately explain, as well as we can, the world around us.

Hitchcock continues to talk about his interest in crime fiction and mysteries in Beth Twiggar's profile of him, "Hitchcock, Master Maker of Mystery." His primary reference point is *Suspicion,* his latest film, and this article is valuable because of his extensive comments on the various endings he considered before narrowing down the twenty they discussed to two and finally deciding on the one he eventually went with. Conspicuous by its absence is any mention of not being allowed to end with Johnny revealed as a murderer because the studio or the audience wouldn't allow such a thing to happen to a character played by Cary Grant. Instead Hitchcock focuses on a far more sophisticated notion of what the audience needs and expects and also what his sense of cinematic form requires. "Logic" dictated that he consider an ending in which Johnny brings Lina a glass of milk that may or may not be poisoned and "that she should drink it and put him to the test." But when they filmed and screened this version, it turned out to be completely undramatic: "Trial audiences booed it, and I don't blame them." And ending with Johnny as the murderer, while "psychologically right and esthetic as all get-out," would similarly have led Hitchcock to commit an unpardonable cinematic crime: because of the Hays Office's directive to punish wrongdoers, it would "take an anti-climactic reel or two to turn him over to justice. That's no good."

He resolved this dilemma and in general shaped his film by relying on the model of the short story, which emphasizes speed, "psychological value," "richness of character" established in a brief period of time, and perhaps especially important in this case, a twist ending. The actual literary source that he used for the film is not the best specific example to cite here: *Before the Fact,* by Francis Iles, is a full-length novel, not a short story, and ends without a twist, leaving no doubt that Johnny is a murderer. But what Hitchcock acknowledges in this article is the extent to which he was guided, in *Suspicion* and elsewhere, by the overall tradition of a certain kind of short story that appealed to him, and he presents a memorable instance of how this enabled him to resolve a particularly critical cinematic problem. The short story is, as he states directly, the "nearest parallel to the feature motion picture as an art form" and influenced Hitchcock's conception and practice of pure cinema.

In the middle of his career Hitchcock was associated with spy stories, and it is not surprising that he found numerous opportunities to clarify his relationship to this popular tradition. Hitchcock never named Eric Ambler as one of his influences in this area, but his deeply felt kinship with Ambler comes across in nearly every line of the introduction he wrote for a volume collecting four of Ambler's spy novels. He praises Ambler for exactly those qualities that he wanted noticed and respected in his own works: the avoidance of clichés while operating in a convention-laden genre; the use of ordinary characters in extraordinary situations; an emphasis on identification; and an overriding sense of nightmarish realism in the context of familiar landscape, villains, and events, recognizably drawn from "the material of reality." Hitchcock is often thought of as "apolitical," but he is very alert to the topicality of Ambler's writings and the way his characters and plots "ring true" in their presentation of the ongoing threat of "fascist intrigues and the greed of big business," elements that we should be alert to in Hitchcock's films as well. But whether or not topical realism is a vehicle of political analysis for Hitchcock, it is unquestionably a way to get to the heart of what he, like Ambler, is ultimately after: the composition of "a hypnotically fascinating study in fear"—*Journey into Fear* is the title of one of Ambler's novels and also a strikingly apt descriptive summary of most of Hitchcock's oeuvre—and "the creation of suspense." His comment that the latter is "after all the whole purpose and the first convention of the spy novel" is perhaps the most succinct statement he ever made about what defines this genre and why it is so attractive, for him and for us.

He makes an even broader claim about the "the quality of suspense" in the introduction he wrote with this title for a volume of stories that he was credited with editing. Speaking as an enthusiastic fan and as the appointed spokesperson because he is so "closely identified" with it, he boldly states, "Suspense is the significant element in all stories" and turns what would otherwise be a craft into an art. We get enormous pleasure not so much from the "embellishments" of character and setting as from "the thread of the story itself," which "draws" us from one paragraph to the next. Suspense is the bedfellow of our innate and powerful cognitive desire: "You want to know how it will turn out. That is Suspense."

The particular type of suspense that Hitchcock is interested in, of course, involves danger, and he uses examples of the stories in his volume to illustrate various ways this element can be presented. He explains in detail the options of either "shar[ing] with his reader and his characters the nature of the danger which threatens" or withholding this information, "allow[ing] the reader to guess the nature of the danger and watch the characters of the story move to meet it with blissful and terrifying unconcern." The stories collected here show that each of these approaches is viable, although we know that he prefers the former. He also predictably emphasizes the importance of establishing a close identification of the audience with a character "so that the interest in the story grows more intense as the Suspense built upon that character's fate grows more urgent and keen." What is particularly interesting and valuable in this introduction, though, is the way that Hitchcock portrays what I would call his distinctive alchemy of suspense: suspense terrifies and reveals the horrors and vulnerabilities of life but is ultimately associated with pleasure and survival. He repeatedly affirms that suspense—in the stories he has collected here and the kind of films "in which I have specialized as a director"—yields delight, because we engage with the individual pieces as appealing narratives but also as "cherished friends" brought together in a "kind of meeting" by the editor. When stories are told, emotions are generated, lessons are learned, and relationships and communities are formed. The powerfully therapeutic aura of suspense is encapsulated in Hitchcock's use of Scheherazade as the presiding archetype. Her own story is as significant as the ones she tells, and for Hitchcock the message of her story is simple and powerful: suspense saves.

While I have been presenting Hitchcock as a thoughtful theorist of his chosen genre, he is also its agent, and he plays both roles in "The Film Thriller." For all his dedication to defining, practicing, and in many respects colonizing suspense, acting as its perpetual spokesperson was sometimes a bit wearisome, and when asked for yet another round of comments on the subject he begins his brief essay by admitting, "Even the word 'suspense' bores me. It has become hackneyed with too much use." He is well aware that audiences feel this too, and his response is twofold, alternately comical and serious. To lighten the tone he adopts a persona that will become very familiar a decade later from his television series: that of a reluctant pitchman, mocking his product and the whole enterprise of pitching a product. He talks about suspense nostalgically, recalling a time before he too became "hardened" to its effects, gives an early version of what will soon become his familiar protest that "it was only a picture" as part of a defense against the discomforts of suspense, and jokingly acknowledges the resistance to one of his sequences in *Foreign Correspondent,* when Joel McCrea was about to be pushed off a tower, the impatient audience seemed to demand, "Please get it over with. We can't bear the waiting." Hitchcock describes this as a kind of "reverse English," but despite his joking, this is a potentially damaging rejection of a conventional feeling he relied heavily on and worked hard to cultivate, perhaps stated best, as he may have recalled, by of all people Gwendolen in *The Importance of Being Earnest,* when at a particularly tense moment she says, "This suspense is terrible. I hope it will last" (act 3, scene 3).

Fearful that Gwendolen perhaps no longer speaks for us all, Hitchcock feels the need to revitalize and rebrand his product. He redefines suspense by widening its territory: in this case to include the entire "business of preparing an audience for the greatest amount of enjoyment from any given incident or situation." Freeing suspense from being applied "merely to melodrama or mystery" may be a useful way to separate it from the clichés that trivialize the subject and numb its audience. He also reminds us that despite clichés and desensitization, the mysterious power of suspense persists: we may never understand exactly why we "sit breathless" in its presence, but this kind of thrilling spectacle "has always been, and doubtless it always will be." Finally, and most important, he vows to approach suspense with a sincere new dedication to improve the product, and he uses the aptly titled *Spellbound*—a word meant to describe the protagonist and the spectator of the film—as an example of his turn to multilayered suspense stories, in which he "complicated one suspensive happening with another." The old models for suspense loom large in this essay—a train and car racing side by side toward a crossing, a man in danger of being stabbed, and especially a circular saw approaching the head of a heroine—but Hitchcock also has his eye on the future of suspense, which lies in envisioning new and more complex models where fears and problems multiply. We know from Hitchcock's subsequent work that his promise of a "new and improved" product was not just a pitchman's plea.

The interview that concludes this section goes off in many directions, but as the title "It's the Manner of Telling" suggests, it repeatedly zeroes in on stories and what to do with them. Hitchcock seems to take great delight here in giving extraordinarily detailed descriptions of what happens in key sequences in *Family Plot* in particular but also in *Sabotage, The Wrong Man, The Birds,* and *Frenzy.* Although there are some perfunctory and mechanical turns to rote pronouncements throughout the interview, many of his anecdotes, reminiscences, and reflections are precise and persuasive illustrations of his approach to the art of storytelling. He takes a comprehensive approach in discussing the kinds of stories that he favors, examining theme, character, structure, and technique. His brief summaries of his recurrent subjects—"the innocent man who gets involved in bizarre situations"; one or another variation on human vulnerability in a predictably unpredictable and dangerous world—are useful even though they confirm what we probably already know about his films. Focusing on characters in *Family Plot* gives him the opportunity to coin the phrase "uncaught criminal"—the applicability of this phrase to almost everyone in his films reveals something important about his conception and portrayal of human nature and the human predicament—and also prompts interesting comments on a recurrent figure in his films: a leading man who is a blend of menace and humor. In an earlier era such a part would be played by a star like Cary Grant but now goes to a character actor like Bruce Dern, whom Hitchcock clearly admires. *Family Plot* also helps Hitchcock illustrate that his preferred cinematic plot is complex and nonlinear: this film, perhaps typical of Hitchcock's works, is carefully structured around how "two stories meet" and "contrapuntal behavior patterns and characters."

Finally, throughout the interview he backs up his assertion that the "manner of telling" is of paramount importance by giving a useful overview of his particular manner. He repeatedly emphasizes the significance of humor in his films, still a somewhat neglected aspect of Hitchcock's artistry, which complements what might otherwise be "heavy-handed melodrama" in his tales and also adds an element of sophistication. He predictably raises the topic of visual storytelling and illustrates this technique with a detailed description of a sequence from a film by one of the great masters of "pure cinema" who, as surprising as it may seem, merits deeper examination as a model for and influence on Hitchcock: Chaplin. And when the talk turns to suspense, as it must, Hitchcock recalls yet once more the bomb and the boy sequence in *Sabotage* but updates it with a reference to a very complicated and effectively suspenseful sequence in his latest film (Blanche's imprisonment behind a brick wall in *Family Plot*) and also introduces a new context for the discussion: the blunt confession that "I believe in playing with the audience, definitely, especially with suspense" reminds us that storytelling for Hitchcock involves far more than the telling of a tale.

THE *HENLEY TELEGRAPH* STORIES

The following stories were all originally published in the *Henley Telegraph*, from June 1919 to March 1921. They were reprinted with commentary in Patrick McGilligan, *Alfred Hitchcock: A Life in Darkness and Light*, 30–46, preserving original spelling and punctuation. The first of Hitchcock's stories, "Gas," printed in the June 1919 *Henley Telegraph*, was reprinted in the first volume of *Hitchcock on Hitchcock* and is not included here.

THE WOMAN'S PART

"The Woman's Part" was originally published in the *Henley Telegraph*, September 1919.

"Curse you!—Winnie, you devil—I'll———Bah!" He shook her off, roughly, and she fell, a crumpled heap at his feet. Roy Fleming saw it all.—Saw his own wife thus treated by a man who was little more than a fiend.—His wife, who, scarcely an hour ago had kissed him, as she lingered caressingly over the dainty cradle cot, where the center of their universe lay sleeping. Scarcely an hour ago—and now he saw her, the prostrate object of another man's scorn; the discarded plaything of a villain's brutish passion.

She rose to her knees, and stretched her delicate white arms in passionate appeal toward the man who had spurned her.

"Arnold, don't you understand? You never really cared for her. It was a moment's fancy—a madness, and will pass away. It is I you love. Think of those days in Paris. Do you remember when we went away together, Arnold, you and I, and forgot everything. How we went down the river, drifting with the stream as it wound its way like a coil of silver across the peaceful pasture lands. Oh, the scent of the hay and lilac blossoms that morning! The songs of the birds, the joy of watching the swallows sweeping across the river before us—Arnold, you have not forgotten? It was the first day you kissed me.—Hidden in that sheltered sweetness where only the rippled sunbeams moved upon the myrtle-tinted stream—Arnold, you have not forgotten?"

The man crossed the room, and leaned upon a table, not far from where she crouched, gazing down at her with a look from which she shrank away.

"No," he said bitterly, "I have never forgotten!"

Still kneeling, she moved nearer, and laid a trembling hand on his knee:— "Arnold, don't you understand? I must leave England at once. I must go into hiding somewhere—anywhere—a long way from here. I killed her, Arnold, for your sake. I killed her because she had taken you from me. They will call it murder. But if only you will come with me, I do not care. In a new country we will begin all over again—together, you and I."

Roy Fleming saw and heard it all. This abandoned murderess was the woman who had sworn to love and honor him until death should part them. So this was— yes, and more than that. But Roy made no movement.

Was he adamant? Had the horror of the scene stunned him?

Or was it just that he realized his own impotence?

The man she called Arnold raised her suddenly, and drew her to him in a passionate embrace.

"There is something in your eyes," he said fiercely, "that would scare off most men. It's there now, and it's one of the things that make me want you. You are right, Winnie. I am ready. We will go to Ostend by the early morning boat, and seek a hiding place from there."

She nestled close to him, and their lips met in a long, sobbing kiss.

And still Roy Fleming gave no sign—raised no hand to defend his wife's honor—uttered no word of denunciation—sought no vengeance against the man who had stolen her affections. Was it that he did not care? No—not that, only— don't you realize? He was in the second row of the stalls!

SORDID

"Sordid" was originally published in the *Henley Telegraph*, February 1920.

"It's not for sale, sir."

Through a friend I had heard of a Japanese dealer in Chelsea, who had a remarkable collection of English and Japanese antiques, and, being a collector, I had made my way to his shop to look over his curious work.

The sword, a fine heavy specimen, with a chased blade and elaborate handle, was not very ancient, perhaps about twenty years old—but it had attracted me.

"I will give you a good price."

"I am sorry, but I do not wish to sell."

There must have been something unusual about it, and so I became more fascinated and determined to obtain the sword. After much expostulating and protesting, he agreed to sell on the promise that I would purchase other things in the near future.

"There is some history connected with this, is there not?" I asked.

"Yes, there is, and if you have time I will tell it to you."

At the time of the Russo-Japanese War, Kiosuma, his son, was an ambitious lieutenant in the Imperial Japanese Army. It chanced that once Kiosuma was charged with the despatch of documents to a destination back in Japan which took him near his home. On the journey he failed to notice that he was being followed by two men—Russian Agents.

His home was about an hour's journey short of his ultimate destination so he decided he would call there first.

As he alighted from the train, a feeling of delight enveloped him when he thought of the surprise that he would give his parents. He made his way up the hill of the little village beyond which his parents lived, his path lying through a wood. He quickened his step with the excitement of anticipation, until—almost within sight of his house—he heard a step behind him. Turning he saw an arm raised, then came oblivion—

It was night when he regained consciousness, and as he struggled to his feet he endeavored to collect his dazed thoughts.

Then he remembered—the papers!

What should he do? With the papers gone—!

He staggered towards his house, the lights of which were discernible through the trees, and was met by his father.

"O son, from whence came thou?"

Kiosuma proceeded to explain with difficulty.

The brow of his father darkened, his eyes narrowed, and his face grew to that of a mask.

"Oh, unworthy one! Thou hast betrayed the trust of the great Nippon. Where now is thy honor?"

"But my father, they have not the code!"

"Thou dare to excuse thyself! Take the sword—thou knowest the only course."

Slowly, but fearlessly, Kiosuma proceeded to his room. He laid a white sheet on the floor, and placed a candle at each corner, then having robed himself in a white kimono, he knelt down and cast his eyes upwards.

He raised the sword, with the point to his heart and—

. . .

I took the sword home and in the firelight continued to examine my purchase while I pondered over the strange tale of the afternoon.

I noticed that the handle was a little loose; perhaps it unscrewed. I tried it with success, and detached the blade.

Lowering it to the firelight I studied the unpolished surface and read—

Made in Germany, 1914!

AND THERE WAS NO RAINBOW

"And There Was No Rainbow" was originally published in the *Henley Telegraph,* September 1920.

Robert Sherwood was "fed up"; of that fact there was not the least doubt. Time hung heavily, for he had exhausted his source of amusement and had returned from whence he had started—the club. He did not know what to do next: everything seemed so monotonous. How he had looked forward to these few days' rest! And now—well, there it was! He was fed right up!

While he was thus engaged in reviewing his present circumstances, in strolled his pal, Jim. Now, Jim was married, so he was in a position to sympathize with him. Jim's life contract had not been the ultra-modern—where you repent and eventually divorce at leisure. It simply happened that Jim had struck lucky, and he was content.

"Hullo, Bob, old fruit!"

"Hullo, Jim!"

"You don't look in the pink. Anything wrong?"

"Oh, I'm tired—and fed up!" And Bob unfolded his little drama.

"Why, I know the solution. What you want is a girl!"

"A girl?"

"Yes: a nice young lady—someone with whom you can share all your little joys and sorrows—and money!"

Bob shook his head. "No, that's no good; I'm not built that way. Besides, I don't know any girls."

"Listen to me. All you have to do is to go up to one of the suburbs—say, Fulham— and keep your eyes open around the smart houses. When you have struck your fancy, just go up and—oh, well, you know what to say! Simply pass the time of day, etc."

Bob got up. "I'll think about it. Can't do any harm, and in any case it'll pass an hour."

"Good man!" exclaimed Jim. "Let me know how you get on."

· · ·

It was pouring heavily, and, in consequence, Bob swore. If he had any special antipathy it surely was relations (all of the old and crusty sort) and duty visits. The latter was a demand of the present occasion, and he made haste to get the ordeal over. But the rain teemed down heavier, and, being without an umbrella, he slipped into a nearby doorway. Some minutes had passed without any abatement of the rain, when a cloaked figure made its way up the garden path towards the refugee.

"Oh!" exclaimed the newcomer, startled.

"Excuse me," said Bob, "but I am sheltering from the rain. I hope you don't mind."

"Not at all," she replied, inserting her key in the lock. "Oh, dear," she cried, "I can't get the key to turn."

"May I try?" volunteered Robert. Receiving assent, he continued the good work, but was equally unsuccessful. "The only thing to do is to force the door," he said.

"Oh, is there no other way?"

"I'm afraid that's the only solution. I find that one of the wards of the key has been broken off. You must have dropped it."

"I did—this afternoon, after I had closed the door. Well, as force is the only remedy, do you mind trying?"

A few heaves with his shoulder proved sufficient to send the door flying open.

"Thank you so much," she said. "In return for your kindness may I ask you to come in and sit down until the rain ceases?"

Bob hesitated for a moment; then he remembered Jim's advice, and assented, with thanks. Once inside, he lost no time in getting acquainted, and the end of thirty minutes saw the pair intensely interested in each other. Brainy man, Jim (thought Bob), to put me on a stunt like this. I shall never be able to thank him enough! He'll be glad to hear of my progress.

At the end of an hour he was all but engaged. Then came the sound of footsteps up the path.

"My husband" she gasped. "What shall I do? You must get out of the window—hide—or do something—quick!"

"Oh—hell!" groaned poor Romeo. "Here's a go!" To her he said quickly: "Switch out the light, and I'll slip out of the door when he enters!"

She sprang to the switch and the room was plunged into darkness.

But almost simultaneously her husband opened the door and turned on the light, finding Bob at his feet, ready to escape.

"Bob!"

"Jim!"

"You d—n fool!" he shouted. "I said Fulham—not Peckham!"

WHAT'S WHO?

"What's Who?" was originally published in the *Henley Telegraph*, December 1920.

"Now," said Jim, "the proposal I have to put forward is a novel one!"

We yawned.

Jim was the producer of our local amateur theatricals, you see, and beyond that description it is not in my power to make further comment. Jim is twice my size.

"In the next show each of you three," he continued, "will impersonate each other!"

I gasped.

"Now you, Bill," he said to me, "will be him"—pointing to Sid; "and Sid will be Tom, and Tom you. Then when—"

"Wait a minute," interposed Tom, "let's get this clear. Now I'm Sid—"

"No, you're not, you're me!"

"Well, who's you?"

"You are, you fool!"

"You're all getting into a muddle. Let me explain further," said Jim.

"Doesn't need any explanation," I replied, "it's all as clear as Tom—"

"What do you mean?" interrupted he. "If you're going to get personal about it, I'll chuck up being you before we start."

"All right then, you be Sid, and I'll be you."

"But!" yelled Sid, "you said you were me!"

"Well, so I am."

"You're not, you're him!"

"Look here," broke in Tom, "let him be you, and you be me, and I'll be him."

"Shut up!" screamed Jim above the din. "Why don't you all stick to my first arrangement?"

"All right, then," commenced Tom. "I'll be Sid."

"No you won't. I'll be Sid."

"But just now you said you were me."

"Shut up, he's you."

"Well, who's me?"

"I don't know."

"Why, Sid is, of course," put in Jim. "Now let's start."

"When—"

"Wait," said Tom, "I can't be him; he's bandy."

"Who's bandy?"

"You are, you fool."

"I'll punch your nose!"

"Don't start to scrap—"

"Well, he—"

"Look at what—"

"I'm not, you idiot—"

Jim fainted.

THE HISTORY OF PEA EATING

"The History of Pea Eating" was originally published in the *Henley Telegraph,* December 1920.

Modern science, with its far-reaching effects on the life of the community, has yet one more problem to solve to further the progress of the world—that of eating peas. Considerable speculation has been given to the methods employed in the early ages, and we read of the prehistoric man who simply buried his face in the plate of peas and performed practically an illusion by his act of demolishing the vegetables without the use of his hands.

One must admit, however, that this method may be described as crude, for one can hardly imagine the modern corpulent gentleman attempting the same feat, because of the danger of his excessive "adiposity" reaching the floor before his face reached the plate.

We are told that Sir Roger D'Arcy, in the early Middle Ages, found no great difficulty in the problem. All he did was to attach to the headpiece of his armor a double piece of elastic in the form of a catapult. He simply placed a pea between the piece of leather attached to the elastic and aimed towards his open mouth. But even this method brought inconvenience, for it was soon discovered that there were many gentlemen with a bad aim, and often a duel resulted from the fact that Sir Percy had badly stung the wife of Baron Edgar over the other side of the room. It is believed that an Act was instituted prohibiting the use of this method without a license, and one had to pass a test to secure the necessary permission to adopt this very ingenious style of feeding.

These restrictions were responsible for the falling off in the popularity of peas, and after a time, they were practically non-existent as an edible vegetable. Many years later, however, their revival brought a great interest to the now famous pea-eating contests, the details of which reveal a further method of manipulation. It appears that each competitor was required to balance a certain number of peas along the edge of a sword, from which he was to swallow the pea, without spilling any. Of course, in very exciting matches the contestants' mouths and faces were often cut. It is believed that the performance of sword swallowing was evolved from this feat, and that very large-mouthed people of today are direct descendants from the champions of that period.

As is well known, many estimable people still practice this method on a smaller scale.

Still further styles of deglutition were tried in late years, and the modern boy's pea-shooter recalls the employment of pages to shoot the peas in My Lord's mouth. Bad aim, of course, was reflected with dire results to the page.

We have yet to discover a really useful and satisfactory method of pea eating. A recent inventor evolved a process by which a pipe was placed in the mouth and the peas drawn up by pneumatic means. But in the trials the inventor unfortunately turned on the power in the reverse direction, with the result that the victims tongue is now much longer than hitherto.

Another person suggested that they might be electrically deposited, but the idea of the scheme was so shocking that it was not considered.

One of the most sensible ways which is at present in the experimental stages is receiving the attention of a well-known market gardener, who is endeavoring to grow square peas so as to eliminate the embarrassing habit which peas have of rolling off the cutlery. It is to be hoped that the experiment will prove successful.

In order to help on this very important scientific development, suggested methods from our readers will be welcomed, and forwarded to the proper authority. Please direct any suggestions to The Manager, THE HENLEY TELEGRAPH.

FEDORA

"Fedora" was originally published in the *Henley Telegraph,* March 1921.

A play of a year or two back provided a situation of a little man seeking the goal of worldly greatness. In order that we should return home with a feeling of satisfaction, the author allowed the hero to attain his object, but not without the usual obstacles experienced by all great men. His earliest efforts included self-education, and I can clearly remember his model line for an exercise in handwriting. It was, "Great things grow from small." I believe this obvious aphorism was the pivot of the whole plot, and also of all our plots. Because every person has a plot (I don't mean allotment) and every plot is the same.

I don't know if you have ever seen a puny young nanny goat alone in a field in a rainstorm. If so, you have seen Fedora. Fedora is the heroine of this disquisition. She is small, simple, unassuming, and noiseless, yet she commands profound attention on all sides. People stop to observe her, and I believe it to be on record that one of the policemen on point duty at the Bank has held up the traffic—all for Fedora. You suggest she is beautiful—no, not definitely—I say not definitely, because I hold out hopes. Her appearance:—"Starting with the top," as the guide book says, there is an abundance of dark brown hair, under which peeps out a tiny perky face consisting of two greeny brown eyes, an aquiline nose (usual in these eases), and a faded, rosebud lipped mouth. Her figure is small, possessing some of that buoyance of youth when walking with the aid of a pair of unassuming legs, or, shall I say, to get away from the suggestion of artificiality, inconspicuously regular.

"Great woman labor leader hits out . . ." Can that be? I had hoped for better, but no worse. Perhaps an actress? I can see a storm of emotion exploding in the face of a helpless, juvenile lead . . . the fury of a woman scorned. Then the vociferous applause from all, except her victim. What will be his feeling? Perhaps he will be overcome by her dazzling personality. Dare he ask her to be his . . . wait, if our Fedora is to marry, surely she shall be a real wife, a worthy figure of womanly charm and grace—this, of course, depends upon the realization of my hopes. Let me suggest the wife of the Mayor. Shall I put it, as it were, the power behind the chair.

"My dear George the tram service lately has been disgusting, you must see that . . ."

"Yes, my dear. I will mention . . ." At functions she will be the recipient of bouquets from the daughter of the local contractor.

Sometimes, I imagine, she will write brilliant novels, profound essays and learned works. But it is all mere conjecture on my part. Whatever may be . . . but I am no prophet, neither is she. Time will tell.

"GOOD-NIGHT, NURSE!"

"Good-night, Nurse!" is printed from a manuscript signed by A. J. Hitchcock, undated but c. 1922–23.

The reason for the depressed look on the face of Felix Dayton was due, he told his fellow club members, to the fact that he was to elope the following evening. And those members who knew Juanita Luiz—the Spanish dancer of temperament— realized that Felix had something that needed some shaking off.

Juanita Luiz held the secret of "perpetual youths" and Felix Dayton, part-heir to his uncle's estate, seemed good enough to settle upon.

Late the following evening find Felix and Juanita arriving at an old Tudor inn on the Bath Road. Felix finds that one of the guests is leaving for the north and is waiting for a car which is picking him up. This fact gives Felix an idea to escape from Juanita. He contrives to lock the man in his room, and take his place in the car. He is horrified, however, when the car has sped from the hotel, to find an arm creep around his neck, in the dark, and a voice softly say "Darling, isn't it wonderful—our eloping." He switches on the interior light and sees the face of a fair girl, who is screaming at finding a strange man by her. The car slows up & Felix dashes out across the fields.

Several days later, we find Felix back in his rooms reading two letters—one from Juanita threatening proceedings for breach of promise and the other from his cousin Egbert with the news that his uncle is ill. This latter fact provides him with an incentive to pay a visit.

Arriving at his uncle's house in Mayfair he finds his cousin well installed as the "favourite" and recently engaged to his uncle's nurse with whom he fell in love in the space of a couple of days. The uncle looks on this match with favor.

When Felix is introduced to the nurse he is dumbfounded to find that she is the "girl in the car." An exchange of signals prevents the recognition of the meeting. She later explains that she abandoned the folly of running away, and warns him that his uncle is not at all pleased with Felix's mode of living, and this fact may be reflected in his will.

Faced with the possibility of being disinherited, and also of the fact that he had "fallen" for the nurse, he plans to re-establish himself in his uncle's favor, and "side-track" Egbert in his "affair" with the nurse.

Felix makes tracks for the flat of Juanita, and pleads that his uncle has disinherited him, and the money will go to his cousin Egbert. Juanita becomes interested in Egbert, and Felix slyly suggests that they will be in the Park on the morrow morning.

Felix calls on Egbert, and they take a stroll and eventually meet Juanita.

The latter "vamps" poor simple Egbert, and the result of the morning's work is an appointment for Egbert to take Juanita to the "Midnight Follies."

Felix persuades Mary—the nurse—to accompany him to the Follies, when he will reveal Egbert's duplicity.

The effect of these events proves to establish Felix in Egbert's place both in regard to his uncle and the nurse, Mary.

His uncle declares that Egbert shall be made to stand by his promise to Mary, and not play fast and loose with her. Felix informs him that this cannot be so, because he has learnt that Egbert was secretly married to Juanita yesterday. At this news his uncle is delighted, much to Felix's surprise, for he explains that he was himself in the clutches of Juanita and now that Egbert has married her, it has put an end to a trouble that has caused him to be unwell. He declares that he will not only compensate the nurse handsomely, but will give Egbert a marriage settlement beside making him his heir. Felix nearly faints at such a result of his labors.

Anyhow, he consoles himself that Mary the nurse will be a good consolation prize. He asks her on what day she would like to be married. She suggests he asks his uncle. "Why," he returns. "Because, I am going to marry your uncle!" she replies.

HITCHCOCK ON STORIES

"Hitchcock on Stories" was published in *World Film News* 2, no. 1 (April 1937), 17, citing its original publication in *News Chronicle,* no date given.

We want to find a story. We meet and talk. We read the reviews—we have no time to read the whole books. We pore over notices of plays. We discuss every possible type of story—and that brings me to the first prime requisite for a film story.

It must blend two things which seem almost mutually exclusive: it must hang on one single central idea which must never get out of the minds of the audience for one single solitary minute, either consciously or subconsciously; and it must offer scope for the introduction of a number of elements, which you have read about every single picture that has ever been produced: glamour, suspense, romance, charm, drama, emotion, and so forth.

The formula for making a picture is to find a single problem which is sufficiently enthralling to hold the attention of the people who are watching the play unfold, and yet not sufficiently difficult to demand uncomfortable concentration.

The reason murder mysteries are not often great successes on the screen is because they demand too much acute concentration: the audience is keyed up to watching for clues, listening for clues, trying to glean from every line of dialogue some light into the mystery.

The true motion picture formula is to state in the first reel your single central theme which must be a problem. It may be of the simplest: "Boy meets girl; boy falls for girl; boy quarrels with girl; boy and girl come together again."

There the problem is: Will they be reconciled? And the corollaries are: How long before they are reconciled? How will they be reconciled? . . .

The difficulty of writing a motion picture story is to make things not only logical but visual. You have got to be able to see why someone does this; see why someone goes there. It is no use telling people; they have got to SEE. We are making pictures, moving pictures, and though sound helps and is the most valuable advance the films have ever made they still remain primarily a visual art.

There are very few—astonishingly few—people who can write a screen story. There are no chapter-headings; no intervals between the acts. The fading in and fading out are so quick that they do not give the audience time to discuss and work out and think over what they have seen and why they have seen it.

LIGHTS! ACTION!—BUT MOSTLY CAMERA!

"Lights! Action!—but Mostly Camera!" was originally published as the introduction to *The Pocket Book of Detective Stories,* ed. Lee Wright (New York: Pocket Books, 1941,) v–vi.

Detective fiction is distinguished from all other types of crime fiction by its insistence upon the normal. The abnormal event—theft, arson, murder—is explained in terms of the material, the natural, the logical. Crime is the stone thrown into a quiet pool. It is the oddly colored thread woven into a colorless pattern.

The detective is the diagnostician. It is his business to study the ripples on the surface of the pool and to find the disturbing stone, his job to pick the elusive thread from the tapestry.

This insistence on the normal adds the illusion of reality. It is a piquant and subtle accompaniment to extraordinary behavior. Murder in a madhouse is a probability; therefore not so mysterious nor exciting, when it happens, as murder at the greengrocer's. One expects horrors from a monster created by Frankenstein. It is a more subtle titillation of the nerves to get them from an insignificant and respectable householder who is whimsically devoted to canaries.

And it is this surrounding lack of color that makes the test of a detective's greatness. The measure of his genius is to be found in his sensitivity to the abnormal, his ability to observe the minute details that are out of focus.

This sensitivity is the common denominator of the great detectives of fiction who have been assembled in this volume. Each had heightened perception—whether visual, tactile, or aural—that delivers to his brain an insistent warning. "This thumbprint is impossibly placed," says the camera eye of Sherlock Holmes. "This chair has been moved," says the camera touch of Max Carrados. "This sentence is a lie," says the camera spirit of Father Brown. And the imperishable record has been made and stored away until it can be fitted into the picture.

Each time the abnormal occurs, this camera sense registers and eventually the series of plates) developed and stored in the brain—forms a picture that gives the truth.

For the camera tells the truth. It is an implacable record of what really happened. Those who see the picture—and observe all its details—must inevitably know the whole story.

Such is the game here offered to the reader. He knows, as the detective knows, everything that can be seen, everything that can be heard. The challenge to his camera eye is in the recording of the extraordinary. The challenge to his wits is in the making of one moving picture of the disjointed negatives.

It is essentially a director's problem. The component parts of the story are there; the job is to make a picture of them.

Certainly it is a problem familiar to me. And this intimacy has given me a genuine admiration, a fellow craftsman's appreciation, of the sure directions assembled here.

These great detectives are unique, they are intensely individual. They range from the deceptively stolid tenacity of Inspector French to the Gallic and mercurial intuitiveness of Hercule Poirot. Some are eccentric, some ordinary; some naive, some sophisticated. Here are professionals and amateurs, rich dilettantes and hard-working police officials.

But one quality they have in common—the one essential quality—camera perception.

HITCHCOCK, MASTER MAKER OF MYSTERY

Beth Twiggar

"Hitchcock, Master Maker of Mystery," by Beth Twiggar, was originally published in the *New York Herald Tribune,* December 7, 1941, section 6, 3.

Alfred Hitchcock shook his head and chuckled. The director, who is famous as a master builder of suspense in mystery films, had just been asked about his success in that line. Had he always been interested in crime fiction? Was he a follower of police records?

"No," he said. "As a matter of fact, I've always been afraid of policemen. I never see one without a potent urge to flee. I don't know why, and of course I never do run away, but the fright's there just the same. Strange, isn't it?"

Suspicion, a Hitchcock picture, is now in its third week at Radio City Music Hall. The film is based on *Before the Fact,* a novel by Francis Iles, and through it runs the sustained high pitch of excitement which is the English director's trademark. Hitchcock had planned to be in New York at this time anyway, but the continued presence of his latest in the city makes the holiday especially pleasant.

"No," he repeated, "I don't think you'll find any predilection to the mysterious in my life. Outside the studio I've no bent toward things sinister, and certainly no wish to consort with the police. It would distress me to enter a station, let alone read a record. As to making mystery films, I fell into it because I had always believed in swift action for all pictures. The culmination of speed, of course, is the crime tale.

SHORT STORY A PARALLEL

"To my mind the nearest parallel to the feature motion picture as an art form is neither theater nor the novel but the short story. In a play there are intermissions. There are lapses of minutes to weeks in the reading of a novel. But short stories and films are taken in all at one sitting. There are no breaks to give the audience digestion time. The plot in both cases must spin directly to a climax, and speed is essential to directness. Implicit, indeed. So the short story and the screen play have unity and speed in common, and one thing more—each, in my opinion, requires a twist ending.

"For instance, all through *Suspicion* belief piles up in the wife's mind and the audience's that the husband is a murderer. The written novel had time for soliloquy and brooding. So when the husband is proved actually to be a murderer it is psychologically right and proper. But that conclusion wouldn't do in a film or a short story. Build him up as a killer with all the tricks of the trade and then say yes, he is a killer, and the audience would ask a weary "So what?" Aesthetically the novel's outcome is perfect. In a picture it would be simply flat. No, it's got to have a twist.

"There was more than one problem in filming the windup to *Suspicion*. We discussed about twenty conclusions, shot two, and then chose the one that seemed best. I think we ran into every difficulty Hollywood had to offer.

"I knew as soon as I read *Before the Fact* that there'd have to be a different ending. I asked myself the question I always ask before going to work on a picture: Is it worth making? Obviously, the answer was yes. The story had such definite psychological value and such richness of character in a fast-moving plot that it struck me as well worth a public showing—even with a different finish.

"It is axiomatic in Hollywood that unhappy endings breed commercial failures. There are exceptions, of course. *Wuthering Heights,* for example. But that, like *Gone With the Wind,* was a story well known to the public. They wouldn't have tolerated any tampering. Bette Davis can play tragic endings and get away with them. She is the rare star who is expected to suffer, and audiences go to see her with handkerchiefs ready. But even with Bette Davis in a well publicized play like *The Little Foxes* the grimness had to be brightened by a happy little couple who escaped from it all. Ordinarily, Hollywood is right. People flock to the pictures for relaxation and pleasure. They don't want to emerge all bowed down with sadness.

THE FINAL PROBLEM

"In *Suspicion* we had a story that led naturally to an unhappy finale. But the play itself was unknown, so that we did not have an audience predisposed to a sorrowful closing. Cary Grant is familiar as a light comedian, and Joan Fontaine is remembered mainly as the heroine of the happily ending *Rebecca*. It is doubtful that those two would be accepted as figures in a tragedy.

"But supposing we had forgotten all that and made the husband a murderer—then we'd have had the Hays office to deal with. The code demands that a murderer face punishment by law. All right. The man poisons his wife and it's psychologically right and aesthetic as all get-out. But it will take an anti-climactic reel or two to turn him over to justice. That's no good.

"Toward the end of the film Grant brings Miss Fontaine a glass of milk which she believes to be poisoned. It seemed logical to me that she should drink it and put him to the test. If he wished to kill his devoted wife, then she might well want to die. If he didn't, fine and good; her suspicions would clear away and we'd have our happy ending. We shot that finish. She drained the glass and waited for death. Nothing happened, except an unavoidable and dull exposition of her spouse's innocence. Trial audiences booed it, and I don't blame them. They pronounced the girl stupid to wilfully drink her possible destruction. With that dictum I personally do not agree. But I did agree that the necessary half-reel of explanation following the wife's survival was really deadly.

"Well,"———. Hitchcock smiled. "Those troubles are over now, for better or worse. By the run, I judge it's for better! And the troubles were never as bad as they might have been. I'd greatly prefer to have a story stall at the end than in the middle. There won't be any such difficulties with my next—I trust. What's it to be? A "chase" yarn, something on the order of *Foreign Correspondent*. Only, it will have an American scene, the pursuit going from West to East, passing through Radio City Music Hall itself and perhaps ending in the Statue of Liberty. I can't say much about it now, largely because I don't know much. There are just a few pet scenes shaping up in my mind. That's how a film always begins with me."

INTRODUCTION TO *INTRIGUE: FOUR GREAT SPY NOVELS OF ERIC AMBLER*

Originally published as the introduction to Eric Ambler, *Intrigue: Four Great Spy Novels* (New York: Knopf, 1943), vii–viii.

Perhaps this was the volume that brought Mr. Ambler to the attention of the public that make best-sellers. They had been singularly inattentive until its appearance—I suppose only God knows why. They had not even heeded the critics, who had said, from the very first, that Mr. Ambler had given new life and a fresh viewpoint to the art of the spy novel—an art supposedly threadbare and certainly cliché-infested.

Consider his characters. His heroes are anything but heroic, nor are they startlingly wise, or even daring. They are ordinary, rather pleasant people. One is a newspaperman, another an engineer, a third a writer; they are just men who want to stay out of trouble and live comfortably. In only one of these four novels does the hero *do* anything; in the others, things are done to him.

The result must be obvious: it becomes possible for the reader to identify himself with these heroes in a way that is wholly impossible in the typical thriller. What happens to the journalist, for example, could easily have happened to you. You are riding in a train. A stranger asks you to carry a wallet or a portfolio for him across the approaching border. It is a small service and you agree because you will be paid well for it and you are stone broke. From that moment half a dozen men are trying to assassinate you.

Or take the case of the writer in that amazing novel, *A Coffin for Dimitrios*. You hear of a sudden death by violence and there is a hint of mystery in the background. Now, have you not at some time or other read a news story which made you say to yourself: "I wish I knew what led up to this"—because the news story does not tell you? Since you are a busy and respectable citizen you don't do anything with your curiosity. But if you are a writer, you are not respectable and there are times when you are not very busy. And so it is possible for you, if you wish to, to satisfy your curiosity. This particular writer began to trace the background of the sudden, shabby death of Dimitrios. From that moment he was the object of intense interest on the part of at least one criminal, and his idle search through the police records of Europe led him steadily and unconsciously to a rendezvous with a pistol.

The reader identifies himself with Mr. Ambler's heroes in still another way. His heroes suffer precisely the sort of emotions that you yourself would suffer in similar circumstances. *Journey into Fear* is the story of a man afraid. He is afraid because someone took a shot at him for no reason that he could readily grasp and he was now informed that the same man would take another shot at him and this time he would try not to miss. The following one hundred and forty-five pages compose a hypnotically fascinating study in fear. If you were that man—an engineer with an attractive wife and a pleasant home and a low handicap at golf—you would be afraid too. But do you realize that in the traditional spy novel you would not be afraid? You would be very busy trying to turn the tables on your unknown assailant—and, of course, the result would be a trite story with no genuine suspense.

So much for Mr. Ambler's "heroes." Consider the subsidiary characters. The "villains" are a strange and motley crew indeed. There are big business men and bankers; the cheap scum of the low cafés of the ancient Continental cities; the professional, suave, well-heeled gangsters whom we have learned to recognize as the incipient chiefs of Gestapos and fascist conspiracies. In brief, they are not only real people, they are actually the kind of people who have generated violence and evil in the Europe of our time. And the wise men—the clever ones, the ones who solve or help to solve the riddles in these stories—they are not the traditional old-school-tie officers of British Military Intelligence. In two of these novels they are Soviet agents operating in Italy and Austria just before the outbreak of the war; in the other two they are Turkish political police. Again, people you can believe in—above all, the kind of people who really were clever in the corrupt and stupid years of the past decade.

Which leads to a consideration of the kind of material that Mr. Ambler deals with. It is the material of reality. The crimes grow out of fascist intrigues and the greed of big business; they grow out of a Europe run down, decadent, dirty, rotten, ripe for war and revolt. Mr. Ambler is a young man who knows his Europe, understands the politics and the finance of that Europe. His stories ring true: you read them and you say to yourself: "Why, this is the kind of thing that happens all the time."

If by this time I have not persuaded you that Mr. Ambler is a phenomenon, then I must say a few words about what is after all the whole purpose and the first convention of the spy novel—the creation of suspense. These novels grip you and hold you, and they do so in very simple ways. For example, in *A Coffin for Dimitrios* you are drawn into a quite interesting story involving extraordinary characters. You read the narrative the way you would read any other novel. You follow the writer tracking down the history of Dimitrios from Istanbul, where he actually saw the almost mythical Greek corpse, to Smyrna, where the past begins. He pays a White Russian refugee to bribe a government official into letting him copy a certain dossier. The Russian delivers the essential document, but the Russian has been drinking, and he is drunk enough now to admit that three months before someone else had given him money to obtain the same dossier. . . . A shadow has fallen across the page. You are aware, at last, that this novel is not merely a portrait of a macabre character. You know that something unexpected and explosive will happen soon.

It would be difficult, if at all possible, to think of anyone else writing spy novels today who combines those distinctive and admirable qualities. The truth is that Mr. Ambler's works stand pretty much alone on their special shelf. They have, indeed, elevated that shelf to a rather sophisticated level. But not so sophisticated that anyone who enjoys spy novels—or, if you prefer, novels of international intrigue—could fail to be absorbed and excited by them. I hope that those who have not yet encountered these stories will be rewarded now.

THE QUALITY OF SUSPENSE

"The Quality of Suspense" was originally published as the introduction to *Suspense Stories Collected by Alfred Hitchcock* (New York: Dell, 1945), 3–6. When the volume was reprinted in 1947 with a different selection of stories, this introduction was revised extensively, with some paragraphs omitted and new paragraphs added, including ones on the "snapper ending" and the "action-suspense story."

All of my life I have possessed a profound interest approaching fascination for the quality of Suspense—a fact which probably will not be surprising to the thousands of movie-goers who have been kind enough to share my enthusiasm for stories which have this quality.

When this enthusiasm for Suspense became so closely identified with my name that a publisher was prompted to invite me to edit a volume of Suspense stories, I faced the difficulty of defining and limiting the quality upon which I had presumed myself to be something of an authority.

As a matter of fact, Suspense is the significant element in all stories. It is the plot device which has made the craft of story-telling an art from the beginning of time. Reciting the terrors of the hunt, primitive man held his cowering audience spellbound in the dim light of his cave with the Suspense of his tale. Scheherazade saved her pretty throat from the headsman's ax for a thousand and one nights by Suspense. She was clever enough to end the narration of her story each evening at a point of high suspense, and the Khalif, eager to learn what was going to happen next, could not resist postponing her execution another 24 hours.

Happily this stratagem repeated time after time saved not only the clever head of this Oriental beauty, but also preserved for us the delights of the thousand and one tales we know as the Arabian Nights. Perhaps it also gave modern magazine publishers a profitable inspiration for continued stories told in installments and "Continued in Next Month's Issue." Certainly the commercial advantages of Suspense were recognized in the early movie serial which left Pauline in peril until "Next Week's Episode," and in the modern radio soap operas which bid listeners "tune in tomorrow to hear what poor Mary will do." All the world enjoys waiting with bated breath to learn what will happen next.

Don't you, as a reader of stories, often find your pleasure in the plot—in what is going to happen? Characters, background and all the other elements of color and interest are certainly important, but fundamentally, they are embellishments. It is the thread of the story itself which draws you from the opening paragraph to the next page, and the next, and the next to the story's end. You want to know how it will turn out. That is Suspense.

But what is the difference between Suspense in the familiar boy-meets-girl plot, and Suspense in a story like "Suspicion," which was based on the superb novel *Before the Fact,* by Francis Iles, and *The Thirty-Nine Steps,* by John Buchan? In this difference lies the essence of the quality of Suspense in which I have found so much pleasure as a reader, and in which I have specialized as a director of motion pictures. It has been the yardstick for selection of the stories you'll read in this volume.

Principally, this difference lies in the fact that Suspense is here accompanied by Danger—danger mysterious and unknown, if possible. Or, if the danger is known—then as inexorable or as insurmountable peril as may be imagined. In all stories, it is well if the ideal tale of Suspense be built around a character with whom the reader may identify himself so that the interest in the story grows more intense as the Suspense built upon that character's fate grows more urgent and keen. Two of the stories printed in this volume are particularly adroit examples of this type of Suspense. If any writer has more successfully achieved the identification of his reader with a character in his story than Ralph Milne Farley has in "The House of Ecstasy," it has not been my good fortune to read it. And if more dramatic Suspense can be wrung from the attack of a universally cherished ideal by a rather horrible old cynic than you'll find in Stephen Vincent Benét's "Elementals," the writer who does so will have surpassed one of the greatest story-tellers of our time.

No stereotype formula restricts the ingenuity of plot of our favorite stories. They may involve the basis and perhaps sordid conflicts of man against man before a background of modern realism, as in James M. Cain's "The Baby in the Icebox." They may involve man as a struggling atom against the overwhelming odds of Nature's irresistible forces as in Captain Outerson's "Fire in the Galley Stove," Carl Stephenson's "Leiningen vs. the Ants," or Hanson Baldwin's "R.M.S. Titanic." The last, incidentally, is not fiction at all but a journalistic report of high order about the famous disaster of a palatial ocean liner caught by ice-floes on its maiden voyage. You'll agree with me, I think, that although it is a factual account it bows to few of the imaginative works in the quality of its Suspense.

An author may choose to share with his reader and his characters the nature of the danger which threatens, as in the stories I have just mentioned. On the other hand, he may choose to allow the reader to guess the nature of the danger and watch the characters of the story move to meet it with blissful and terrifying unconcern, as in Margery Sharp's "The Second Step." I predict that your flesh will shudder and crawl *more* when you reconsider this story after reading it, than it did while you were reading it.

Again, as in Ambrose Bierce's "An Occurrence at Owl Creek Bridge," the author saves the full crushing import of his plot until the last minute and delivers it just when—but you'll see what I mean. "The Liqueur Glass," "Blue Murder," and

"Flood on the Goodwins" are a little like that too, in the best tradition of spy and mystery stories—but in these the reader rather expects the solution to be saved until the end.

Speaking for the moment of staggering conclusions, you may expect a real treat in "The House of Ecstasy" I have already mentioned, and in Frank Stockton's classic "The Lady or the Tiger?" If any tales come from the top drawer of Suspense stories, these two certainly may claim that honor on the strength of their endings alone. You may be tempted, as I was for a moment, to be indignant upon reading them. But remember—we are supposed to be addicts of Suspense, and when an author gives it to us in full portion as Stockton and Farley have—we get only what we have been asking for!

It is natural enough, man being a story-teller by nature and stories themselves embodying Suspense as an essential, that certain tales of Suspense have been transmitted by word of mouth so universally that they have virtually achieved the status of folklore. Many never achieve print unless some connoisseur, like the late Alexander Woollcott, who loved such yarns, selects one for publication, usually in an effort to trace its origin. Albert Payson Terhune's short summary, "The Blue Paper," is one of the most fascinating of these tales, and by virtue of its plot and conclusion, it is included in this collection as an unquestionable classic of suspense. Another writer (besides those mentioned by Mr. Terhune) who has written a story using the plot of "The Blue Paper" is Ralph Straus. Straus called his, quite justifiably—and as an unusually merciful warning to the reader—"The Most Maddening Story in the World." Straus's "The Room on the Fourth Floor" has been included here as an excellent treatment of another theme of near-folklore familiarity.

It occurs to me that I have done less than a scholarly job as an editor of this collection of Suspense Stories. Quite frankly, I can't feel the least bit apologetic. I had no intention of being a learned editor presenting you with an anthology of "Suspense Stories of All Nations" or an "Evolution of the Tale of Suspense from Scheherazade to Superman." As you may have guessed by now, I am more of a reader than an editor. I can't even say that these are my favorite Suspense stories, for I have many favorites and space here to include but a few. If these please you, I may gather a few more together one of these days—not as an editor enlightening or educating you—but as myself introducing a number of cherished friends of mine to you. I believe you'll like them all the more for that kind of meeting, and that they'll be ever afterward numbered among your "friends" too!

THE FILM THRILLER

"The Film Thriller" was originally published in F. Maurice Speed, *Film Review 1946–47* (London: McDonald and Co., 1947), 22–23.

I have been asked to write a few words on suspense pictures, and I shall have to open these sage observations by remarking that even the word "suspense" bores me.

It has become hackneyed with too much use. Anyway, suspense doesn't apply merely to melodrama or mystery. You can very well utilize suspense in a love story. In fact, you had very well better if you want the audience to hang around long enough to see reel seven.

For myself, in place of "suspense pictures," I much prefer the words—my own coinage—"seat-clingers." I'm not too proud of them, but they have none of the connotation which used to attach to the words "cliff-hangers" when applied to serials.

With this in mind, we should be able to talk a little about suspense without being pontifical. Even a funny gag is no good unless you work up to it with suspense of some sort. Suspense becomes merely the business of preparing an audience for the greatest amount of enjoyment from any given incident or situation.

Suspense is sometimes achieved in a very obvious manner. Race a train and an automobile side by side toward an intersection and you may feel fairly sure that they won't talk about looking for the candy counter until the intersection has been passed.

Another obvious example is to have the audience provided with information not available to the characters, as when you have a man about to be stabbed in the back by another man, the audience sees but the victim does not. Suspense results from the audience wishing to warn its friend, the character who is about to be stabbed.

Sometimes this has reverse English, so to speak. In *Foreign Correspondent,* we put Joel McCrea on a tower and told the audience in so many sections that he was going to be pushed off. Out of inability to take it, the audience began to want the bad thing to happen. It was as if they said, "If he is to be pushed off, please get it over with. We can't bear the waiting."

In *Spellbound,* which co-stars Ingrid Bergman and Gregory Peck and which I directed for Vanguard Films, we complicated one suspensive happening with another. We have a hero who thinks he has committed murder, and we concern ourselves for a while with the matter of extricating him from this belief. But we couple his fear that he has committed murder with an added fear that he may do the same thing to the heroine of the story. When he seems to be getting free from one problem we confront him with another.

Let me say now that the thing which makes an audience sit breathless as the heroine's head approaches the circular saw is no more understood by me than it is by you. It has always been, and doubtless it always will be. No circular saw has ever yet cut off the heroine's head, yet we can use this situation, or its equivalent, many times over—and do.

Shall I confess that I myself remember, in past years and before I became hardened, and emotionally muscle-bound, being very apprehensive about what was going to happen to the heroine? I suppose the makers of the pictures which held me breathless would have called what I was undergoing suspense.

I used to whisper reassurances to myself that it was only a picture, just as you do, and that it was somebody else's picture at that. This helped somewhat.

Today, if I am ever tempted to think that something terrible is going to happen to the heroine, and that I ought to be concerned about it, I am usually able to tell myself not to worry about the poor actress, very likely she's at home quietly divorcing her husband. You may try this if you like. I haven't a patent on it.

We see improvement, in this matter of suspense, on every hand, of course. In the old days of melodrama they used to bring the saw-mill in out of the blue—no excuse for it, it was just there when the heroine's neck needed cutting.

We are more realistic now. It is an age of enlightenment and taste. We make the heroine the daughter of a lumberjack.

DEATH IN THE CRYSTAL BALL

"Death in the Crystal Ball" was originally published in *Coronet* 29 (December 1950): 38–39.

In the summer of 1939, I went with my family to Hastings, near London, for a vacation. On a warm summer's day, my daughter Patricia and I walked through the noisy amusement park which draws shrieking youngsters from all over the south of England.

We had already passed the tent of "Carlotta, the Crystal-Ball Gazer," when Patricia insisted we go back and have our fortunes told.

The setting was similar to a typical motion-picture version of a fortune teller's carnival booth. In the center of the shabby tent was a table bearing a large crystal ball. Carlotta, a pretty gypsy, read Patricia's fortune first. It was a routine, optimistic one.

Then she looked into the glass ball and read my fortune. All was serene in my future. I had nothing to worry about.

I paid her and we were just leaving when she called. "Sir, ever since I have told futures I have never told anyone bad news. Always I have kept that to myself. But there is something so terrible in your future that I must tell you. Maybe . . . somehow . . . you can avoid it. I pray you can."

"I see a clock and the time is exactly 6:07. The day is today. And after that time I see nothing. Just darkness. I hear the shrieks of a terrible accident. I do hope you'll be careful . . . that you'll try to avoid this awful thing that's in the crystal ball."

I was moved—not so much by what she had said as by how she had said it. Pat started to cry. With false optimism, I cheered her and we went on our way through the crowds of fun seekers. But the day was spoiled for me.

We arrived at our summer home about 5:30. By this time Pat had forgotten Carlotta and her prediction, and I left her with her mother while I retired to my study.

I was nervous. I told myself all this was foolish. The clock on my desk said 6 o'clock. Nervously, I played with my letter opener on the desk while the hands of the clock went to 6:05, then 6:06, and perspiration wet my palms.

Finally, it was 6:07. Nothing happened. But this was just pre-climax. I looked at my pocket watch to check, and the clock on my desk was five minutes fast. Again I sat in mounting uneasiness, watching the hands on my watch. 6:05. Again 6:06, and I sat waiting for something to happen.

Then I watched spellbound while the second hand went around and it was 6:07. Another 30 seconds. Nothing happened. 6:08 passed. I breathed again. The supposed danger was over!

I went down to dinner and told my wife of my experience. She joshed me. We all laughed.

Next morning at breakfast, Patricia put the London *Daily Mail* by my plate. At first glance I saw the story. "Gypsy Fortuneteller Killed in Freak Accident" was the headline. It went on:

"Last night on the scenic railway at Hastings, Carlotta, a crystal-ball gazer, was killed in a freak accident. She was riding in the back seat of a scenic-railway car going down a huge dip at 60-mile-an-hour speed. Ahead of her a loosened electric wire sagged, and the speed and wind held her rigid in her seat. She saw the wire but couldn't slump down—the suction was too great. The wire hit her under her chin and decapitated her. Hundreds of witnesses shrieked in horror—many fainted . . ."

With trembling hand I reached for the phone. There was one little detail I had to know—and yet I was afraid of what the answer might be. When the newspaper editor told me, it was the most frightening moment of my life.

Carlotta had died at exactly 6:07 o'clock!

THE WISE MAN OF KUMIN

"The Wise Man of Kumin" was originally published in *Coronet* 30, no. 2 (June 1951): 38–39.

The object that caught my eye and fascinated me so that I could scarcely concentrate on Chung, ruler of this little village of Kumin in China, was the tremendous bronze chandelier. It hung by a frayed hemp rope suspended over his head, from the very center of the high-domed room.

The chandelier, constructed of thousands of pieces of bronze fitted in a mosaic, caught every gleam of candlelight. It seemed to sway slightly, for it must have weighed half a ton. And yet it was held only by the thin worn rope.

I was almost tempted to catch my guide's blouse and say, "Watch out! It's going to fall!" but I was brought back to the business at hand as my guide bowed low and began to talk in rapid native dialect. He was asking permission for me to use Chung's quaint little community as the site of a movie.

After the guide finished his explanation, there was a pause. Then Chung unfolded his hands, gave me a long look, and answered with considered pauses.

Suddenly, in the midst of his conversation, there came a rumble and roar like that of an earthquake. I started, jumped back, and almost pulled the guide off balance, trying to snatch him from disaster. The big dog at Chung's feet leaped from under the teetering chandelier and ran, terror-stricken, to hide.

This time I actually shouted: "Watch out! It's going to fall!" but the old ruler bravely continued his slow speech, not even glancing upwards.

Then I realized, as the rumble and roar continued, that the daily train was passing behind the building and its vibration had almost broken the chandelier loose. As the roar of the train subsided, the chandelier, like a slowing pendulum, gradually reduced its swing and seemed to come to rest.

When the old man had finished his speech, he again folded his hands in his lap and closed his eyes. My guide motioned, and we retreated from the building. Once we were outside, I asked: "Why does Chung sit under that swaying chandelier? Doesn't he know his life is in danger every minute?"

My guide shrugged with fatalistic indifference. "He is a very brave and wise man. Twenty years ago, when a neighboring army planned to invade, they sent an emissary to give Chung a chance to surrender without bloodshed. When the emissary was brought before Chung, he too noticed the chandelier. Chung's answer to the demand for surrender was a sharp no. The emissary was so impressed with Chung's courage that he instructed his tribe not to make war, knowing that a group with so fearless a leader could not be defeated."

"What did Chung say to me?" I asked the guide.

"Again he doesn't want the village invaded. I am sorry."

Many times in succeeding years I thought of the brave Chung. But it was seven years later that I again had occasion to visit Kumin. I had heard that Chung had died "a natural death" so I decided to talk to the new leader.

Once again my guide led me into the dim building, and once again I looked at the gigantic chandelier, swaying on its even more frayed rope. This time, below it in the carved stone chair, sat a much younger, beardless man. To my amazement, he was an American.

I told him my reason for being there, and without the aid of the guide, he said, "Certainly you may use Kumin. We would be honored."

As we talked further, I said: "I can understand how a Chinese man, imbued with the beliefs of his ancestors and his Oriental religion, would risk his life to sit here and rule, risking death every minute. But how can you do it?"

The American arose, took me aside, and spoke quietly: "I was once a public-health inspector in the U.S. Thirty years ago I came here and fell in love with this community. And 30 years ago I was hired by Chung to run a steel wire down the center of the thin rope that supports the chandelier."

THE CHLOROFORM CLUE

My Favorite True Mystery

"The Chloroform Clue: My Favorite True Mystery" was originally published in the *American Weekly*, March 22, 1953, 18–20.

I always have been fascinated by tales of murder. As a boy in London I read avidly of Poe, Emile Gaboriau, and Sir Arthur Conan Doyle. The first picture I directed, in 1926, was *The Lodger,* a silent version of Marie Belloc Lowndes's gripping story of Jack the Ripper. Since then, a majority of the 48 films I have made, including my latest, *I Confess,* for Warner Brothers, have been concerned with suspense or sudden death.

In the annals of true crime, one of the strangest stories I ever encountered was that of Edwin and Adelaide Bartlett. It has many of the elements of a great film play. Packed with drama, it was a puzzling mystery and a most unusual love story. And in this case Death was the leading actor.

Poisoned by a draught of chloroform, Edwin Bartlett died on the night of Dec. 31, 1885, in his house in Pimlico, a section of London. Adelaide, his wife, had been with him throughout the entire evening. Later it was learned that she had a bottle of chloroform in her possession. A chain of circumstantial evidence was built against her. She was indicted and brought to trial.

Was Adelaide Bartlett guilty of the wilful murder of her husband? That was the question.

The opening phases of the drama began 10 years earlier, on April 9th, 1875, when Thomas Edwin Bartlett, an Englishman, married a French girl named Adelaide Blanche de Tremoulle. The bride was not yet 20 years old. She was decidedly attractive, with thick, straight brows, full curving lips, and a delightful figure. Edwin was a prosperous grocer about 30 years of age.

It was soon evident that this was to be no ordinary marriage. Indeed, it was said of Bartlett: "He had most peculiar views about matrimony." For one thing, he had an almost reverential regard for advanced learning. As a result, Mrs. Bartlett was immediately packed off to a boarding school, where she remained for two years, and came home to her husband only on holidays.

She spent the following year at a convent in Belgium. So it was not until 1878, three years after they took their marriage vows, that the Bartletts took up permanent residence together.

They had their troubles. In December 1881, Mrs. Bartlett was delivered of a stillborn child. Her labor had been difficult, and she had suffered great pain. When she was recovering, she said to Annie Walker, the midwife who attended her: "I shall never have any more children. Never!"

All through this period, Bartlett was a very busy man. A hard worker, he was up and about his business early, and did not return home until evening. As a result, he was quite successful. And Mrs. Bartlett was quite lonely.

Then in June, 1885, all this was changed. The Bartletts became acquainted with the Reverend George Dyson, the minister of a near-by Wesleyan chapel. He soon became a regular caller at the Bartlett home. Mrs. Bartlett's lonely days were over. And the pace of the drama picked up.

George Dyson was then about 27 years of age. He had mild, spaniel eyes, and he wore a long mustache, which drooped in a somewhat dejected manner. Not striking in appearance, he was nevertheless a man of some culture and learning. And Mr. Bartlett seems to have been attracted to him.

"My wife has had considerable schooling," Mr. Bartlett said. "But I should like her to take up her studies again. If you could find the time to instruct her I would be most grateful."

Dyson could—and did. He began to visit Mrs. Bartlett daily, and it was soon obvious that his "instructions" were not entirely confined to history and mathematics. It was noted that he never brought study books. And a maid reported: "I used to see them sitting on the sofa or on the floor. Once they had the window curtains pinned together and she was lying with her head against his knee."

Was an illicit romance being carried on behind the back of an unknowing husband? Apparently not. Mr. Bartlett, it seems, was not only aware of what went on, but he approved it.

George Dyson was later to say: "Yes, I have kissed Mrs. Bartlett. In the presence of her husband, and in his absence. He was always aware of our relations. We had no secret understandings."

At the end of August, the Bartletts journeyed to Dover for a vacation, and Dyson was invited to visit them. Since he was not a man of means, his fare was paid by Mr. Bartlett. Then in October, the couple moved their residence to Claverton Street in Pimlico, a section of London, and their young friend was thoughtfully provided with a season railway ticket from his home in Putney to Waterloo Station, London. Thus their usual—or shall we say "unusual"—mode of life continued.

During this time, Dyson seems to have been aware that their relations had reached a dangerous degree of intimacy. "Why does your husband throw us together in this manner?" he asked Mrs. Bartlett.

Her answer contained startling information. "Edwin is not well," she told him. "He is aware that he will not have a long life. He has affection for you and he trusts you. He knows that you will be my friend when he is gone."

Dyson also voiced some of his fears to Mr. Bartlett. "I must tell you that I am growing very attached to Adelaide. Perhaps it would be better for me to discontinue my friendship."

"But why?" asked Bartlett. "You have always helped her and benefitted her."

"It disturbs me in my work," said Dyson.

"It should not. I have every confidence in you, and I want you to be her friend. In fact I have just made a new will, leaving my entire estate to Adelaide, free of any restrictions. I have named you as my executor."

So . . . Mr. Bartlett's property had been bequeathed to his wife. And, in a sense, his wife had been bequeathed to his best friend.

Now events began to move rapidly to a climax. On December 8th, Edwin Bartlett fell ill. A Dr. Leach was called and he discovered a blue line around Bartlett's gums which, he said, pointed to mercurial poisoning.

"Have you taken mercury in any form?" Dr. Leach asked his patient.

"Perhaps it was in a pill I took a few days ago. I was not aware of its exact contents."

During the next two weeks Bartlett's physical symptoms responded to treatment. His teeth were found to be badly decayed, and Dr. Leach ordered some of them removed. But still the patient did not fully recover his health.

Adelaide Bartlett now appeared to be worried. "Doctor," she said, "Mr. Bartlett's friends will accuse me of poisoning him if he does not get out of the house soon."

As a result, a consultant, Dr. Dudley, was called in. But he could find no cause for alarm, nor did he suggest any change of treatment.

On December 21st, George Dyson left town to visit his father, and stayed with him over Christmas. He returned to London on the 26th, and found his friend, Bartlett, somewhat improved and in apparent good spirits.

Dyson called again the next day, and was met at the door by Mrs. Bartlett. She was just on her way to post a letter. Dyson accompanied her.

"George," she said, "buy me some chloroform."

"Good heavens! What for?"

"Edwin has been having violent paroxysms, and I need it to soothe and quiet him. Annie Walker, the nurse, used to get it for me, but now she has gone abroad to America."

"Then you must ask Dr. Leach to supply it."

"No. He does not know that I am skilled in the use of chloroform. He would be afraid to entrust it to me."

"Well . . ."

"I will need a large bottle. The liquid evaporates rapidly."

So Dyson agreed. He bought four small bottles in three different shops. He poured the contents into a larger medicine bottle, and he gave it to Mrs. Bartlett.

On December 31st, Edwin Bartlett had one more tooth extracted. Later he seemed improved in health and in spirits. When the landlady brought his evening meal, he said, "Well, Mrs. Doggett, I think the worst is over. The doctor has ordered me to take a trip to the seaside. I'm sure I'll be getting better soon."

At four o'clock the following morning—New Year's Day—Mrs. Bartlett came pounding down the stairs to knock on the Doggetts' door and cry: "Please come at once! I think my husband is dead!"

He was indeed. Dr. Leach was summoned and was somewhat puzzled. He could find no apparent cause of death.

Crying bitterly, Mrs. Bartlett asked, "Will there have to be an inquest?"

"I am not prepared to say," Dr. Leach answered. "But it is definite that we must have a post-mortem examination."

George Dyson came on the following day and spoke to Mrs. Bartlett. He was quite perturbed. "Did you use the chloroform I gave you?"

"No," she replied.

But Dyson's fears were not easily calmed. He took the small bottles in which he had bought the chloroform and threw them into some shrubbery. The next day, when he heard the results of the post-mortem, he hurried to Mrs. Bartlett's side.

"The autopsy shows that death was caused by chloroform," he told her. "I am a ruined man! I must make a clean breast of the whole affair."

Mrs. Bartlett raged at him. "Then you might as well charge me outright with having given Edwin the chloroform."

"I have no choice," said Dyson, whose thoughts seemed to be centered entirely on himself.

In the meantime, Dr. Leach was quite pleased by the post-mortem results. "I have good news," he told Mrs. Bartlett in his consulting room. "If a secret poison had been found, then there is no doubt that you would have been accused of giving it to him. Now this will set your mind at rest."

"On the contrary," said she, with deep concern. "I wish that anything but chloroform had been found."

Dr. Leach then heard a strange story. The Bartletts' marriage, she told him, had been entirely platonic. Except for one occasion which resulted in a stillborn child, they lived together as friends and nothing more.

Bartlett had wanted it that way. It had pleased him to surround her with male acquaintances. He had encouraged her friendship with George Dyson, and he urged them to become affectionate. In effect, he had "given" her to Mr. Dyson.

Then in the later stages of his illness, she said, Edwin Bartlett had tried to assert his rights as a husband. She had repulsed him. "That would not be fair to me," she told him, "or to the man to whom I am practically affianced."

Bartlett had made further advances, and she had secured some chloroform with which to resist him. She had planned to sprinkle it on a handkerchief, wave it in his face and put him peacefully to sleep.

"But my conscience bothered me," she said. "I gave Edwin the bottle and told him the whole story. He did not scold me. He put the chloroform on the mantelpiece and turned over and went to sleep. The next morning he was dead."

At the coroner's inquest, George Dyson, true to his promise, told his story. This evidence was so incriminating that Mrs. Bartlett was charged with wilful murder. And Dyson was found to have been an accessory before the fact. Both were arrested.

The ensuing trial was a sensation. The newspapers reported it in complete detail. Partisanship ran high; you were either "for" or "against" the accused.

Proceedings were hardly begun before the attorney general exploded a bombshell. He addressed the court: "We propose to offer no evidence against George Dyson."

A thrill rippled through the onlookers. Dyson stepped down. He walked out of the court a free man, and without a backward glance at the woman he had once loved.

Sir Charles Russell, the attorney general, now began to build his case. It finally resolved to this: Edwin Bartlett's death by chloroform could only have been one of three things, a suicide, an accident, or a murder.

Suicide was ruled out for lack of cause. Accident, too, on the grounds that the strong odor of chloroform made this practically impossible. This left only murder.

But, by adroit cross-examination of the medical men who testified, the defense was able to establish that it was most difficult and perhaps impossible to administer chloroform to a sleeping person without waking him. But, if by some miracle, this had been done, then it was a further remote possibility that the liquid could be swallowed without burning the throat.

The jury retired, and returned to announce: "Although we think grave suspicion is attached to the prisoner, we do not find sufficient evidence to show how or by whom the chloroform was administered. We therefore find the prisoner not guilty."

The courtroom burst into cheers and applause. Mrs. Bartlett, in a fainting condition, was assisted down the stairs, a free woman.

Had justice truly been done? Popular opinion of the day seemed to be with the verdict of the court. But there were many who agreed with Sir James Paget, surgeon and pathologist, who remarked: "Now that it is all over, I believe that Mrs. Bartlett should tell us, in the interests of medical science, just how she did it."

"IT'S THE MANNER OF TELLING"

An Interview with Alfred Hitchcock

Anthony Macklin

"'It's the Manner of Telling': An Interview with Alfred Hitchcock," by F. Anthony Macklin, was originally published in *Film Heritage* 11 (1976): 15–22. Bracketed comments and ellipses are in the original.

INTERVIEWER: *In the ten years we've published* Film Heritage *we've gotten more quality articles on your work than anybody else's. What is the tone of your latest film* The Family Plot?

HITCHCOCK: Well, I think the general tone is colorful and, in certain respects, amusing—although it's about kidnapping and the innocent people who get involved in it. As a matter of fact, it's really two stories: it's a story of a fake medium and her taxi driver–cum–actor partner who is her research man so that if she goes into a rich old lady for a seance she's got all the material provided for her by him. That's how the fakery is accomplished. You see, she comes out with certain facts about her client, and the client is astonished that she knows so much. Now they're charged with the job of tracing a missing heir, hopefully through psychic means. So you get the innocents setting out to trace a missing heir. Meanwhile, a number of kidnappings have taken place by a rather sophisticated couple, and they hide their victims for ransom in a house right in the middle of the city—not on a lonely moor, as they would have it in the movies. And the two stories gradually meet. They kidnap a bishop from a cathedral in front of the whole congregation, based on the theory that if anything happens in a cathedral, you don't exactly get up and start screaming and yelling. People just wonder what's going on. And he's whisked out in no time. They put the bishop in the house. They're just going in to administer the sodium pentothal, and at that moment the front door bell rings and it's the medium who tracked down, innocently they think, the missing heir just as they're about to deliver the bishop for ransom. So that's the apex of the two stories. But it's all done, I would say, in a fairly light, amusing manner—sophisticated, but not at all heavily melodramatic.

INTERVIEWER: *Would you agree that* Frenzy *is a pessimistic picture?*

HITCHCOCK: Yes, because *Frenzy,* you see, dealt with a sex maniac. That was more serious.

INTERVIEWER: *This writer [in the article on* Frenzy *in this issue] argues that one can't find solace in marriage anymore in that film.*

HITCHCOCK: That's true. In this film *[Family Plot]* we don't even indicate whether the people are married or not. Everybody's just living together in this film. A sign of the times.

INTERVIEWER: *I was listening to the dialogue at one point. Then I moved up when you reshot it and looked at the faces. The dialogue is really menacing. But Devane's smile, it's kind of wry.*

HITCHCOCK: After all, a kidnapping is a menacing thing. And not only that, but this man who is the kidnapper—he really runs a jewelry store in the city—has a past. He, as a boy of sixteen with the help of another boy, set fire to the house while he locked his foster parents in a room. One went on, went abroad, and did well; the other stayed behind in the village and now runs the garage. So they both have guilt. And this man uses his boyfriend of years ago to actually try and kill these two innocent people. It's the dramatizing of coincidence. For example, one of the clues for the seekers is that the original parson who baptized the foster child has now become a bishop. So when the kidnapping takes place, the taxi driver partner is observed to be at the end of the church. Innocently he's saying, "I'd like to see the bishop to ask him some questions." At that moment the kidnapping takes place, and our kidnappers have already observed the medium and her boyfriend through the garage man. So they drive away with the bishop in the back of the car wondering, "How the hell did this man get here? Do you believe in ESP?" They know she's a spiritualist. They're bewildered. The kidnappers themselves are completely bewildered as to why this man is present in the cathedral. Therefore you get an attempt to kill them by tampering with the brakes of their car in the mountains. So you get a wild ride of a car with no brakes. And even that is treated comically although they're in danger of going over the side any minute—which I've shot up in the mountains here [California]. So there's quite a lot of color, but wherever I can, I turn it to amusement rather than heavy-handed melodrama.

INTERVIEWER: *What film does it remind you of that you've done?*

HITCHCOCK: Well, you could go back as far as, let's say, a film like *The Lady Vanishes*. There you had the kidnapping of an old lady, but the whole thing was treated with comedy. And that's the essence of this film: it's treated in a very sophisticated way.

INTERVIEWER: *In* North by Northwest *when the intelligence agents created this person who didn't really exist, one of them says about Cary Grant's being pursued by killers, "It's so horribly sad—how is it I feel like laughing?" It seems to epitomize much of your tone. Do you remember that line?*

HITCHCOCK: Vaguely, yes. Well now, he's really saying, "If the risk of life weren't so awful, I would laugh at the situation that the man finds himself in." Cary Grant is mistaken for a man who is nonexistent.

INTERVIEWER: *Do you feel that way?*

HITCHCOCK: Well, it's a comic situation.

INTERVIEWER: *But there is that menace to it.*

HITCHCOCK: Oh, the menace is always underneath. In *Family Plot* the medium goes around to the side door to the garage when they're ready to deliver the bishop. And the medium sees him. "My god, the bishop." She realizes she's face to face with a kidnapper. Well, they grab her, and they try and stab her and put her out because they've got a thirty minute deadline to deliver the bishop and pick up the ransom. So they're fighting against time. That's very dramatic for a moment, but because you have a dramatic story, you don't have to play into it. You play contrapuntal behavior patterns and characters. Like a film I made years ago, *The 39 Steps*. Hell, they had a stabbing of a woman at the beginning. But the sophisticated attitude of the man gave the film a different tone.

INTERVIEWER: *A lot of people have said that the audience for* Frenzy *is supposed to sympathize in a sense with the killer. They want him to get away.*

HITCHCOCK: Audiences are very strange. For example, if you see a burglar in the bedroom of a well-to-do woman and he's stealing her jewelry, and you cut to the front door of her coming in . . .

INTERVIEWER: *They want him to get away.*

HITCHCOCK: They want him to get away. "Quick, you're going to get caught." They don't sympathize with the victim at all. It's like in the murder situation. The victim is the last person they ever think about. They're always thinking about, "Will the murderer get off? Will he get life?" Everything about him is looked into and examined, but the poor victim is just disposed of.

INTERVIEWER: *In* Frenzy *why didn't the cops take the fingerprints off the potato truck?*

HITCHCOCK: I'm not sure.

INTERVIEWER: *He wasn't wearing gloves, I don't think.*

HITCHCOCK: No, but I think by that time the truck had been dealt with. I think the thing they went after was the potato dust on the man. You see, when you take fingerprints, obviously even if they'd have done so, this man being a sex maniac had no prison record. And even if you leave your fingerprints on, well what are you going to compare them with? Now, the kidnapper in *Family Plot* makes a mistake when the bishop says, "Can I keep this book?" The kidnapper replies, "With our fingerprints on it." Well, actually that's an unnecessary statement. He only says it because he's not an established criminal or, shall we turn the phrase, he's an uncaught criminal. Taking fingerprints is only good if you discover in the files the fingerprints which match an already established criminal.

INTERVIEWER: *You work very much on suspension of disbelief in every film, and we in the audience do suspend our disbelief instead of . . . I don't know, what?*

HITCHCOCK: I have a phrase I say to myself: "Logic is dull." And it is. A lot of footage is devoted to making up a logic, but there's no drama going on at the time, at all.

INTERVIEWER: *Now the critics have come and have discovered what they think are some of the things that Alfred Hitchcock represents, but the audience doesn't . . .*

HITCHCOCK: No. They take it on the surface. What was it Sam Goldwyn once said, "Messages are for Western Union."

INTERVIEWER: *But don't your films have a message? Not a big message, not in big lights.*

HITCHCOCK: They usually follow a pattern of the innocent man who gets involved in bizarre situations. Self-plagiarism is style.

INTERVIEWER: *What about the ending to* The Wrong Man? *Now that seems like the tone is absolutely pessimistic, and then there's a grafted-on upbeat ending. We are told that later she was released from the sanitarium, and they lived happily ever after. What happened?*

HITCHCOCK: We were just doing the true story.

INTERVIEWER: *Really?*

HITCHCOCK: Oh absolutely. We followed everything. As a matter of fact, if there was anything wrong with that picture, I would say that the director had imposed himself too much on it.

INTERVIEWER: *How so?*

HITCHCOCK: Because I put in directorial touches which never happened in the real story. You see? In the real story the man was ultimately caught in a delicatessen store. But I didn't do it that way. I showed Henry Fonda's face looking at a picture of Christ on the wall and murmuring a prayer. And slowly I dissolved a street scene over Fonda's face and a man walking toward the camera. As he got nearer the camera his face superimposed itself over the face of Henry Fonda. So I was really cinematically indicating the resemblance between the two. I should never have done that—no matter how clever one may have thought one was being. That never happened in the real story, and that was the error. If you're doing a documentary-type picture, then it's wrong to be fictitious.

INTERVIEWER: *In other words, you think that film would have worked better with basic simplicity. Just stick to the facts.*

HITCHCOCK: In that type of film, definitely. It's the manner of telling. The trouble with a lot of films is that they are what I call photographs of people talking. If I can do it visually, so much the better.

INTERVIEWER: *How about Bruce Dern?*

HITCHCOCK: Dern is a very accomplished actor. He has a great sense of comedy too. I've used him before, in *Marnie*. He was also in some of my television shows.

INTERVIEWER: *Did you find the comedy then? He can be bizarre and he can be . . .*

HITCHCOCK: Sinister.

INTERVIEWER: *Yes, sinister. Exactly.*

HITCHCOCK: Well, I knew him, and I knew that he could play sinister. I know he did a TV show where he really was a horror. I forget the girl in it. It was in a peach field in Georgia.

INTERVIEWER: *Teresa Wright.*

HITCHCOCK: Teresa Wright, was it? That's right, yes. But I knew him personally, and I knew he had a sense of humor. And, of course, thank God he's not the typical leading man. He's a character actor really. Just the same with Barbara Harris. Both our leads are character people. I think that's the trend, away from the Clark Gables and Ronald Colmans that we used to have. In the late twenties or early thirties people would say, "Oh, he's another Ronald Colman." I always remember an actress, who was one of those grande dames with which the English stage is sprinkled, and a man, I don't know whether the name would mean anything to you, Basil Dean. He was a leading stage producer in London; he was one of the biggest London producers in his day. He's in his eighties now. (I'm talking about copying Ronald Colman or Clark Gable.) He married a girl called Victoria Hopper, a little blonde actress. He used to put her in leads like Selznick did Jennifer Jones. A play opened called *The Mask of Virtue,* and it was the first appearance of Vivien Leigh on the stage. And at a party afterwards this girl Hopper, Dean's wife, who wasn't all that much of an actress . . . Somebody made a remark about Vivien Leigh and said, "Oh, she reminds me a lot of Victoria Hopper." And the old dame said, "Do we want another Victoria Hopper?" Very caustic.

INTERVIEWER: *When you were on the Tom Snyder show, I winced when he said to you, "Do you ever crack a joke?"*

HITCHCOCK: All the time.

INTERVIEWER: *Yes, of course.*

HITCHCOCK: What was it Henry Fonda once said of me? I don't know whether he told it to somebody or whether it was in print. He said, "Just before you're going to do a dramatic scene, he cracks a joke."

INTERVIEWER: *You do that intentionally though, don't you?*

HITCHCOCK: It depends. It depends on the circumstances. But you know I can afford, I suppose, to make a joke whenever I like because I'm not all that concentrated because to me the film was already made long ago. When the script was finished, which I worked on with Ernest Lehman, the whole creative element was complete. I wish I could say, "Well that's that. Now let's go on to the next script." But you can't. You've got to go through the whole process of making it.

INTERVIEWER: *A lot of people think that film is essentially an intuitive act. Do you think it is?*

HITCHCOCK: It is intuitive if you've been at it long enough. You see, the great point that I continually make is not enough people have a visual sense. They cannot project. See, I don't even look through the camera; I can visualize it on the screen. And that's the great difference. It's not what the camera sees; it's what you see on the screen. And it's a white rectangle that has to be filled with imagery or a succession of images, one after the other. Got nothing to do with the camera at all. You can make all kinds of statements without the use of words. The only thing wrong with the silent picture was that people opened their mouths and no sound came out. Chaplin was very good in his early days. I remember a film of his, *The Pilgrim*. There you open up with a prison guard pasting a wanted notice on a wall, and it's Chaplin in convict's clothes. The next shot is a man, a tall man, coming out of the river from having had a swim onto the bank and finding he has no clothes, but just convict's clothes left there. The next shot is a railroad depot, people waiting for a train, and there walking along is Chaplin dressed as a person with clothes much too long for him. The legs are long and everything else. Three images—look what they tell. That's the kind of thing that I believe belongs to the camera.

INTERVIEWER: *Some people discover things as they're making a film. Their film is almost accidental; it's fortuitous, a large part of it. Does this ever happen to you?*

HITCHCOCK: No.

INTERVIEWER: *It never happens.*

HITCHCOCK: No. Sometimes there are little slipups that happen in the script that you catch when it becomes live on the stage. Just now I caught one. I had four takes, and I had to take a fifth. I had to go back and do it again.

INTERVIEWER: *What was it?*

HITCHCOCK: The bishop—we saw him kidnapped. We've shown that. He's wearing vestments. You mean to tell me he's been sitting in the room with the toilet there and everything else wearing the vestments all the time? It didn't make sense to me. I suddenly stopped them while I added a line: "Have you got your vestments on?" "Yes."

INTERVIEWER: *Ah, but that's logic, isn't it?*

HITCHCOCK: It's only logic for a special purpose. I don't want the audience to think that he went to the toilet with vestments on, which a lot of them are liable to do. They've got one of those chemical toilets in that room where he's been incarcerated. When they first showed it to me, I said, "That's ridiculous." They said, "It's the sort of thing that this man would go out and buy because they use these on yachts." I said, "I don't care. It's way too low. The audience is going to imagine a tall man sitting with his legs sticking out." I said, "You lift that up about six inches. Make it normal height."

INTERVIEWER: *You've a lot of faith in the audience. You're saying that they would think about that?*

HITCHCOCK: Yes, they do. They pick on the most extraordinary things. You'd be amazed. I'll never forget. There are two occasions that happened to me. I made that film *Trouble with Harry*. We had an opening with it before the governor. Now Montpelier is the capital of Vermont, and Barre is the town next to it. They adjoin each other, rather like twin cities. And we had this opening with the governor there at this moviehouse in Barre, Vermont, and Montpelier next door. And a sheriff in the story on the screen picked up the phone and said, "Montpelier 2000, please." Biggest roar of laughter I've ever heard. It happened to be the correct number for the police. What would you do? You'd use the proper number to be correct. But it tickled them. They roared. How do you account for that? Familiarity of it.

I remember years ago, I was sneaking a picture I made with Cary Grant and Joan Fontaine, *Suspicion*. The whole trend of the story was, is her husband a murderer or not. That's what the film was all about—is he a murderer or is he not a murderer? Toward the end of the film she finds in his coat pocket a letter from an insurance company and opens it. She's been suspecting him. And the letter just says, "Policy number so-and-so and so-and-so is only payable in the event of your wife's death." She reads the letter and just raises her head and stares out. Belly laugh from the audience. Next thing, I took all that stuff out and ended on the letter. No laughter. Now why did they laugh at that? I haven't any idea. Audiences are very peculiar. I think the most amusing audience story, which is a true one, my assistant Mrs. Robertson went to see that film *Sweet Charity* with Shirley MacLaine. Went to the matinee. Behind her were two young married couples. The lights went on, and one woman said to the other, "Oh, I do like her, don't you?" And the other one said, "Well, I've always liked Barbra Streisand." So one of the husbands said, "Barbra Streisand. What are you talking about? She's in *Funny Girl*." The other one said, "Well this is *Funny Girl*, isn't it?"

INTERVIEWER: *I asked you originally about faith in the audience, and you paused and then we went on to something else. Do you have faith in the audience?*

HITCHCOCK: I believe in playing with the audience, definitely, especially with suspense. You have to say when you're doing the script, "What are the audience thinking now?" You'd better make sure they're thinking the way you want them to, not the way they want to think. You're telling the story, and with suspense you're putting them through the wringer.

INTERVIEWER: *What was the incident that taught you the greatest lesson about the audience?*

HITCHCOCK: A film called *The Woman Alone [Sabotage]*. It was based on a Joseph Conrad story called *The Secret Agent* laid around the turn of the century. In it I had a small boy carry a package across London, and he was held up for various reasons. You, the audience, knew a bomb was in that package, and it would go off at one o'clock. Well, he was stopped here, he stopped there. In fact the Lord Mayor's Show was going to go, and he started to run across and the police said, "Get back, get back." So he stood there with his package under his arm and watched this thing go by. Well, at the end of the procession the traffic is renewed, but it takes the tempo of the procession. So he got on a bus. This bus is crawling along, policemen stopping it, customers on and off. And I kept photographing the bomb. The boy was playing with a puppy in a woman's arms. I shot this package all directions. I didn't grind off one hundred feet of package. I'd just keep cutting to it. I shot it this way, that way, to give it this vitality. Then I kept shooting clocks, different kind of clocks. Ten minutes of one, six, five, four, three. One o'clock. Nothing happened. One minute past one. Two minutes past one. Nothing. Relief. Three minutes past one. Off goes the bomb. Bus and everything. Huge explosion. Well, I remember the woman critic on the London *Observer,* I was there at the press show, coming up to me with raised fists. She said, "How dare you do a thing like that!" She said, "I've got a five-year-old son at home." She was absolutely livid. And I've never made that mistake since. If you get the suspense from an audience from a thing like a bomb, it mustn't go off. It's got to be discovered and thrown out of the window. You've got to relieve that suspense in other ways. Otherwise they get angry with you.

INTERVIEWER: *You can't kill children or dogs either. Can you?*

HITCHCOCK: No. But the main thing is suspense must be relieved. In *Family Plot* this brick door, now I got that idea from 21 Club in New York. They had a door down below when it was a speakeasy. There was a brick wall outside. Couldn't tell. And a small wire indicated it, and it swung open. So I copied that idea of a real New York speakeasy. Later on when they get the woman— they do eventually get the woman medium—her boyfriend arrives here, sees her car outside, keys in the car, a trickle of paint that she's kicked over in her struggle. They've given her the needle and put her down in this room and locked her in. Now he gets through a back window and goes right by that wall, and the whole audience knows that she's in there. So there's the suspense. "Don't go by there," they want to call out and tell him. "She's in there, behind that brick wall." And he's searching, calling out all over the place. Meanwhile the other two are on their way back. They've delivered the bishop, and he's going to be caught in their house, he as well. They've already caught the woman; he's going to be caught. So you get your suspense that way. And eventually what they're going to do, they're going to dispose of the woman by putting her in her own car way out in the country and running a hose from the exhaust into the car to make it look like suicide. And they make all preparations to do that because she's lying there, apparently out.

INTERVIEWER: *Do you think the ending of* Frenzy *was too complicated for the audience?*

HITCHCOCK: Not really. It was a twist ending. He thought he was going to have his revenge and kill the red-haired man. Of course, he was aiming his blows at the . . .

INTERVIEWER: *At a corpse.*

HITCHCOCK: At a corpse, yes. But in *Family Plot* the audience will worry when our friend the taxi driver gets into this house. He'll be standing right outside that wall. The audience will say, "She's in there. She's in there." But there's nothing to show it.

INTERVIEWER: *Does the audience remember the ending of* Psycho?

HITCHCOCK: No, they don't remember the explanation. They remember high spots—shower scene.

INTERVIEWER: *How about* The Birds? *Do you think that ended as it should have, because the audience seemed like they needed some explanation.*

HITCHCOCK: There was no explanation, any more than there is for the bats in the Carlsbad Caverns. It's a rabies situation really. The birds have got rabies. But it's a form of rabies that's in the air; it's not done by physical contact. In Carlsbad Caverns all the bats have got rabies there. But it's in the atmosphere rather than one biting the other or anything like that, as in dogs or other animals.

INTERVIEWER: *I got the feeling that the audience would have liked the love bird to be the leader or some explanation.*

HITCHCOCK: Well, you know, how far do you go? Does one go on till you get to the Golden Gate Bridge and show it covered with birds?

INTERVIEWER: *You were going to do that, weren't you?*

HITCHCOCK: Yes. Too much. You've got to stop somewhere. Where do you go beyond that? In Daphne du Maurier's idea the birds are all over the world. They're taking over. That's science fiction!

PURE CINEMA AND
THE HITCHCOCK TOUCH

INTRODUCTION

Hitchcock began to articulate his notion of "pure cinema" even before he became a director, and though he later often proclaimed his wish to avoid intertitles altogether and rely on otherwise unaided visual storytelling, he perhaps thought differently about the subject when one of his main jobs at British Famous Players-Lasky was that of title designer. In an essay written at this time, "Titles—Artistic and Otherwise," which may well be his first published article specifically on film, he never challenges the need for titles. Instead, he methodically outlines the most common practices and concerns in designing and presenting them, and makes thoughtful suggestions about what should and shouldn't be done in order to make them contribute most effectively to the film.

Throughout the first part of the essay he comes across as a very careful craftsman, with clarity as his goal. But he goes on to discuss the "very interesting subject of Art titling" and the idea that titles can do more than convey simple information directly. With "spoken titles," anything on the insert other than the actual dialogue will undoubtedly be a distraction that confuses the "reader." "Subtitles," though, not only allow for pictorial enhancement but almost require it: they "benefit greatly by some kind of illustration, as illustration gives color to the action of the story and helps to space the episodes." Hitchcock bases his recommendation on a precise and insightful analysis of how the spectator processes a title, first reading the words and then "*looking* at the picture until the fade out, thus giving continuity to the story."

What is most intriguing here is that this early effort is such a comparatively mature and thoughtful attempt to make the most of all the resources of film. He followed his own advice, and in the films he started to make only a few years later he often effectively blended words with still life, symbols, landscape, and ornamental letters in some titles to "create a harmonious setting, and help the picture to run smoothly." Hitchcock's plea for and instructions about the careful and creative use of titles may also alert us to the even more far-reaching ways in which textuality is part of his pure cinema: printed and hand-written words are key components of the visual landscape of Hitchcock films throughout his career, even outside his carefully designed and executed title cards.

Hitchcock's brief mention in this article of the film *Dangerous Lies* as a "fair example of the use of symbols" in titles is worth commenting on briefly as something more than an early illustration of his oft-repeated advice to avoid cli-chés. The title designer for this film was in fact none other than Alfred J. Hitch-cock, and this essay was perhaps written as part of the publicity effort for it. And other publicity material for *Dangerous Lies* may well account for the first public mention of his name in connection with film work. A newspaper article unearthed by Christopher Philippo, undoubtedly based on studio publicity material announc-ing the local premiere of *Dangerous Lies,* features Hitchcock prominently, and the anecdote it relates about the way titles are constructed and how "odd things fre-quently happen during the filming of motion pictures" is worth quoting in full:

> One of the titles of the picture describes the influence of a young girl in the house-hold of a man whose interests are entirely centered in musty folios of first editions. For this A. J. Hitchcock, art designer, had evolved as an accompanying design a ray of sunlight resting on a file of dusty books. He made a rough sketch of his idea and sent it to his staff of artists with other material to be put into execution.
>
> When the work was returned he found one illustrated sketch representing a dilapidated boot and a superannuated white slipper amidst an artistic medley of old gloves, handkerchiefs and other symptoms of allegorical disorder. An explanation was demanded.
>
> The artist confessed that he had mislaid one of the sketches and had been obliged to make his design from the memorandum pencilled on the margin of the list of titles, and produced the list by way of vindication.
>
> "Well, here it is all right," said Mr. Hitchcock. "Rays and old books."
>
> "Sorry, sir," the artist apologized. "I found it a bit difficult to read, so I did my best with 'rags and old boots'!"
>
> The sketch was changed. ("'Dangerous Lies' Is Coming to Utica," 9)

Hitchcock was not yet Alfred the Great, but his essay and the above newspaper story indicate that by 1921 he was at least starting to gain attention as Alfred the Title Designer and was taking advantage of new opportunities to develop and express his ideas about pure cinema.

By the end of the decade interest had shifted to another topic, the introduction of sound into films, and the former title designer and now director of what was often billed as Britain's first all-talking picture, *Blackmail,* was asked to "tell all the secrets—if there are any secrets" of this new process. The resulting essay, "How a Talking Film Is Made," is an engaging step-by-step description demystifying this process. We would of course expect that in choosing a story he would gravitate toward tales involving "plenty of action and yet good opportunity for dialogue and sound effects." And it is no surprise to hear that casting now must take into account vocal qualities as well as looks and acting ability: the unequivocal statement that "voice must express the character that the artist is called upon to play" may not at first seem typically Hitchcockian, but a close study would indeed reveal how care-fully he chose and directed the voices in his films. He also, however, recounts many details about "complications which never arose in silent films" that only a special-ist would be aware of: the need to construct sets of different materials in order to eliminate problems caused by sound reflection; the shift to long rehearsals to make everything not only "action perfect but word perfect"; and the introduction of a new technician working in "absolute conjunction" with the cameraman, previ-ously the one in charge of the actual shooting. The introduction of sound also affects a film's structure as well as production: Hitchcock reports that the average shot length (during filming and in the finished film) was far longer in a talkie than in a silent film, a major concern for a filmmaker who grounded pure cinema to a large extent on montage, the artful combining of shots.

Hitchcock is remarkably confident: "New problems are always arising, but it is simply a matter of solving them." The use of multiple microphones, for example, is a quick and promising response to the distressing fact that when sound was intro-duced, motion pictures had a tendency to stop moving. But as important as tech-nological adjustments are, what is really at stake is the overall conceptualization of film, and he is driven by the underlying concern that "too much talk has ruined many a promising talking film." In what on the surface is an unambitious anecdo-tal essay offering a studio tour showing current practices, Hitchcock also takes serious steps toward envisioning how a talking film should be made, and he aims high in his compact manifesto: "We are reaching the point where this new form of entertainment will contain the best of the old silent film and the best of the stage molded into something which is neither one nor the other, but which will be a completely distinct medium of expression." His subsequent writings and inter-views often describe and his films characteristically embody this new form of entertainment and expression in which the full resources of sound are smoothly integrated with and complement and enhance rather than banish the art of silent cinema.

As much as Hitchcock is associated with suspense and the thriller, in one of his essays written during the mid-1930s, the period that established this reputation, he makes what may seem to be a surprising confession about his real interest. In "Why I Make Melodramas," he admits, "I prefer to make films that may be so clas-sified." Defining this term is necessary, he says, in order to understand its appeal and uses, but is very difficult, especially because it turns out to have a protean form and mixed reputation. Melodrama is often caricatured as a "naive type of play or story, in which every situation was overdrawn and every emotion underlined," leading to the common use of *melodramatic* as a pejorative term that "suggests behavior which is hysterical and exaggerated." Hitchcock takes a much different view: insofar as melodrama focuses on emotion and "sensational incidents," ines-capable and engaging aspects of "real life," it is exactly the kind of "meat" that audi-ences demand and therefore "has been and is the backbone and lifeblood of the cinema."

Problems arise, though, because of the contradictory demands of cinema. A critical challenge in making a film is "how to combine color, action, naturalism, the semblance of reality, and situations which will be intriguingly unfamiliar to most of the audience." He relies on melodrama, defined in a strikingly unconventional and counterintuitive way, to help him accomplish all this. First, he says that he uses melodrama because he has "a tremendous desire for understatement," which is necessary to achieve naturalism and realism "while keeping in mind the entertainment demands of the screen." Contrary to popular opinion, melodrama need not be excessive: it energizes but also mediates, ameliorates, and balances. Equally important, and perhaps surprising, it does the same when it comes to satisfying what he calls his "own greatest desire . . . for realism," for which he says he employs "what is called melodrama—but which might as well be called ultra-realism." For Hitchcock, melodrama encompasses the unfamiliar and grotesque but without relinquishing the sense that such incidents are "lifted bodily from real life."

The current resurgence of scholarly interest in melodrama highlights many broad ways in which this genre overlaps with key elements of Hitchcock's films: for example, the emphasis on powerful emotions, represented on-screen and experienced by the audience, often thought of as largely female; the focus on women's vulnerability and relentless victimization; the prominence of an empowered villain and the common theme of crime; and a reliance on image, spectacle, and music, rather than words (in keeping with the etymology of *melodrama* and also the genre's historical evolution, which at times limited its use of spoken words). Hitchcock's own comments on melodrama in this early essay give an even more personal definition of the term and a brief but vivid discussion of how he envisioned it as a vehicle of cinematically powerful "simple statement" and lively and engaging storytelling.

Turning back to technical matters in the next essay, the introduction of color was another significant innovation requiring new adjustments in designing and making films. Hitchcock was not exactly an early adopter—he didn't make his first color film, *Rope,* until 1948—but he was at least an early advocate and a thoughtful commentator on the subject. He begins "Some Thoughts on Color" with an unequivocal declaration, "I am whole-heartedly in favor of color films," and then briefly but persuasively outlines some of the ways that this new element fits into his broad conception of cinema. He begins by allying color with realism, and while there is no reason to question the seriousness or sincerity in his claim that realism is "desirable" or to doubt his implicit or explicit depiction, here and elsewhere, of himself as a realist (much of course depends on the definition of this term), all the advantages of color that he goes on to enumerate in fact have nothing to do with how it may increase accuracy in representation. Instead, he praises color insofar as it enhances the expressive, dramatic, and emotional power of film, noting how it will allow him to create effective contrasts of drabness and glory, give him "much more power to punch home a point" about the "stark horror of a murder," and add "greater potency" and "three times the dramatic quality" of a comparable scene in black and white. His essay is framed by nods to conventionality—to realism at the beginning and unified and focused narrative at the end—but in between Hitchcock is uncharacteristically enthusiastic, noticeably excited about this new cinematic innovation, and the colorful "moments" that he describes here look forward to his remarkable exercises of and experiments with color starting a decade later. He concludes with the proviso that color, presumably like all other cinematic elements, must not overstep its bounds: "It must help the script—never conquer it. After all, the story is still the most important thing." But in saying this Hitchcock is not so much cautiously reining in an unruly power as praising the overall—pure cinema is a carefully coordinated synthesis of integrated parts—to which color can contribute enormously.

The emphasis on the overall continues in "The 'Hitch' Touch," which begins with the dramatic suggestion that the director who cares about his pictures is in as precarious a position as his protagonists, walking on a tightrope over the perilous divide of "art" and "box-office." He acknowledges that "movie-goers require their interest regularly jerked." But as important as the individual effects are, "every scene goes to make up a whole," which not only heightens the effects but also turns what would otherwise be merely a series of jolts into a work of art, "like a piece of music." His effort is to give his "work the changing rhythms and climaxes of a concert or symphony," and each of the techniques he goes on to describe should be not only used to its fullest advantage but also orchestrated.

His recurrent emphasis is on the camera as his primary instrument in composing what he insists must be a visual symphony, and he uses two sequences as illustrations of how he proceeds. The first is from *Spellbound*: Hitchcock's precise description of how he shot Gregory Peck coming down the stairs holding a razor in his hand clinches his case for "making drama out of camera angles." The second is not from a film he had made but is similarly effective in envisioning how the "tremendous shock" felt by a woman who has just been told by her husband that he is leaving her for another woman can—and should—be conveyed by careful camera placement and movement to capture their wordless gestures. Nothing needs to be said. When Hitchcock in fact shot a version of this scenario years later, he added to the drama by having the woman club her husband to death with a leg of lamb, but this was not a betrayal of his basic principle: the key part of the sequence was without dialogue, and there as elsewhere the defining mark of the "Hitchcock touch" is that "the use of the camera," resisting the lure of the microphone, is equivalent to "the use of cinema."

Hitchcock was a capable analyst of and publicist for the "Hitchcock touch" even on his own, but he was often helped greatly in this dual effort by interviewers, who sometimes simply gave him a platform to voice his ideas but other times steered him in directions that he might not otherwise have taken. The latter is much in evidence in his "encounters" with the always provocative *Cahiers du Cinéma* critics, and when Charles Bitsch and François Truffaut introduce their early interview with him by noting, "There is not a trace of mistrust in his answers to our questions," they account at least in part for why what follows is a valuable glimpse of candid, not canned, Hitchcock.

A large part of the interview revolves around Hitchcock sorting out his oscillating thoughts on "documentary," a term that he introduces and then both associates himself with and distinguishes himself from as he runs through its various meanings, connotations, and requirements. He initially uses the term somewhat conventionally, contrasting it with films "with a plot, good comedy, or entertainment value." In proposing that this is the kind of film favored at film festivals, with what I interpret as a bit of edginess in his voice conveyed by the expletives that frame his comments, he no doubt has two things in mind: that at the most recent Cannes Film Festival the major awards went to *The Silent World* (Jacques-Yves Cousteau and Louis Malle) and *The Mystery of Picasso* (Henri-Georges Clouzot) and that, as Bitsch and Truffaut remind him, his films have never won an award at the Cannes or Venice festivals. Prompted by his interviewers and perhaps also eager on his own to confirm that his films had something more than "plot, good comedy, or entertainment value" to recommend them, he focuses extensively on the formal, aesthetic, and technical matters that are his primary concerns: the use of counterpointed colors and characters with "peculiar behavior" in *The Trouble with Harry* to capture the complexities of autumnal beauty and his preference for "the absurdity of logic"; stylized moments in *Dial M for Murder, Rear Window,* and *To Catch a Thief* that, in the words of Bitsch and Truffaut, "seem calculatedly poetical"; and his presiding intention to "play" with the "thousands of images" that compose a film, ever attentive to the "matter of rhythm, or, if you prefer, of orchestration."

Then *The Wrong Man,* his most recent film, enters into discussion and complicates everything, because it both is and is not a documentary. In discussing at length his "particular liking" for this film, he gives many examples of how he wanted to make something far different from documentary-inspired films such as *Boomerang* and *Call Northside 777,* mostly insofar as his "direction is entirely subjective," conveying "the point of view of the guy in prison." But he also repeatedly affirms that the film is based on real events, aimed for authenticity and accuracy, and in fact gained dramatic power by depicting incidents as they happened rather than as he imagined them: he gives a detailed "example of what one can learn in making a film where one reconstitutes all the scenes from life," contrasting a sequence as he scripted it with the ultimately far more exciting and cinematic version that really happened.

Nearly all of Hitchcock's statements here are reprinted intact in Truffaut's *Hitchcock* (see 235–42) but with many additional comments by Truffaut, who presses

Hitchcock to admit that this apparent inconsistency is a major defect of the film and that it would be better if it was one or the other: documentary or fictional art film. What comes across more clearly in the early interview, though, where Hitchcock goes on uninterrupted for an unusually long time, is the intimation that one can—and perhaps should—have it both ways, especially over the course of a fully and richly orchestrated film. Hitchcock recalls that one of the most stunning moments in *The Wrong Man* is highly stylized: when Rose hits Manny with a hairbrush and we see his image in a broken mirror, "you think you're seeing a Picasso." But this is followed immediately by a completely different kind of sequence, a snapshot of a sudden return to calm, ordinary life, and for Hitchcock it is the combination of these two contrasting elements that is artful and effective. The pull toward and away from documentary is thus not a damaging inconsistency but an energizing, creative dialectic. With this interview in mind, we may need to modify one of Hitchcock's most well-known statements and recognize that for him pure cinema was both a slice of cake and a slice of life.

Moving from a high-powered conversation featuring three knowledgeable and committed cineastes to a publicity piece headlined "Alfred Hitchcock Murders a Blonde" may come as a bit of a letdown, but we should not be too quickly dismissive. Such articles often accomplish numerous things: they give good insight into the fashioning of the Hitchcock persona and the insertion of him into our homes and consciousness via TV and print media; continue the acts of provocation that are characteristic of his films and television shows, although on a somewhat lighter level; and more than occasionally contain striking statements of his interests and intentions.

All this is true of "Alfred Hitchcock Murders a Blonde." Much of it is taken up with a dutiful and not entirely engaging roundup of the usual suspects and a rehash of familiar tales. But Hitchcock comes to life here when he exemplifies rather than directly defines one of the fundamental elements of the Hitchcock touch: his penchant for humor. Every time that the interviewer alerts us that Hitchcock is being funny, this is a sure sign that something interesting is coming. When Hitchcock is "waggish," he offers a charmingly concise overview of the enterprise of filmmaking: "What you do is take a given piece of time, add color and pattern and there you have it." After the droning discourse on suspense, his "tongue in cheek" capsule version of his cinematic challenge and responsibility is refreshing: "All you have to do . . . is to make sure you can keep your audience awake. . . . You've got to put something in there to keep them looking." And when he speaks "cheerfully," he memorably summarizes a haunting feeling that he is trapped by success in a fine one-liner that was not yet worn out by repetition: "If I did *Cinderella* . . . people would start looking for the body."

For Hitchcock, humor involves not only verbal wit but also placing the serious and disturbing aspects of life in the frame of a joke, and it is this essential and

defining element of the Hitchcock touch that structures the opening of the interview, where he concentrates on the topics proposed by the title: violence and sex.
("Blondes" are specified in the title, but Hitchcock explains that blonde women are
merely the visual signifier of sex, which is his broader theme here.) In a minidra-
matic monologue modeled on the comically macabre introductions to his TV
show, Hitchcock talks dispassionately about a gruesome subject, in this case giving
instructions about how to murder a blonde: "with peroxide," he first jokes, and
then with poisoned champagne. It's only an interview, of course, about what is
only a movie, but it is creepy, to say the least, to watch as the artist who vividly
imagines, stages, and narrates the event becomes virtually indistinguishable from
a murderer and to hear one of the truly horrifying experiences of life being
described in terms of enjoyment—one of many reminders that Hitchcock is the
archetype and creator of guilty pleasure in its most iconic and problematic forms.
Ironically, his "chuckle of triumph" as he envisions a successful murder is not as
troublesome as the following "chortle" when he speculates that, rather than murdering a blonde, he should let her live and "keep her . . . as a pet." This is said jokingly, but we might recall that the most recent Hitchcock blonde at this time, Judy
Barton in *Vertigo,* was circumscribed by these two options: horrifying death or a
grim life in male captivity. She, like Marnie some years later, is a striking illustration of Hitchcock's very revealing comment here that not violent murder but "only
the softer destruction of the human being appeals" to him. As with so many of the
key moments in this interview, the seriousness and significance of this statement
is cued by comedy—"A grin was starting to spread over his face" as he prepares to
make this point—and it stands out as simultaneously the most disturbing and penetrating comment in the entire interview, shedding light on his psyche, his films,
and our interest in his films.

We need to be careful in drawing conclusions about Hitchcock's psyche, but his
writings and interviews are filled with teasing invitations to do just that as they
repeatedly suggest his pure cinema is also in some ways very much a personal
cinema. He admits as much in "My Favorite Film Character Is—ME!," which
begins as a discussion of his cameo appearances in his films, one of the more well-
known elements of the Hitchcock touch that "has become, in a manner of speaking, my film signature." He uses this subject initially as an opportunity to make
some self-deprecating comments, noting his recurrent role in his films as "a fussy,
flustered, bewildered man; short and obese." But it is also a chance for him to fan-
tasize about making an entire film with this character as not an incidental
bystander, uninvolved with and oblivious to the plot, but playing the "leading
role." Following up on a recurrent theme in his cameos, he casts this man as a
musician, an oboist, with a "wife who is a shrew," a son with a frustrated ambition
to be a baseball player, and a job that literally involves "blowing his brains out daily
for a pittance."

Hitchcock regularly described scenarios of films that he would like to make, usually generated out of a vividly imagined, highly visual and dramatic moment or sequence. But ironically his extended outline of a screen story based on himself is not at all like these quintessentially Hitchcockian moments. If he or someone like him is to be the main character, the story will resemble not *North by Northwest* but *Marty,* and the suspense will be not that of a crime or spy thriller but that of a melodrama, in which Fate (in the form of the man's young son) busts the lip on which his livelihood depends. At the end, we are left wondering if the "poor devil 'gets his lip back'" and perhaps even moreso whether he is an accurate representation of how Hitchcock thought about himself, whether he speaks for the director, especially in this final dramatic monologue: "I am important, he says to himself; without people like me no symphonies would be performed—or even written. What happens to me, therefore, is of consequence to the world." Hitchcock surely knew that he himself was hardly laboring in "obscurity among four-score other anonymous musicians," but when he says "amen" to the final words of his stand-in, it may be a nervous cry from a deep well of insecurity, worry, vulnerability, and frustration that fame and worldly success can never seal.

Hitchcock's comments on cinema usually revolve around what he does to fill the film frame, but a large part of "A Lesson in PSYCHO-logy" concentrates on strategies that help fill the theaters. The artist is also the showman, and while in numerous other places he talks about the creation of *Psycho,* this publicity piece published in a trade journal is quite literally a manual about "the care and handling of *Psycho,*" which serves as the title of a training film sent to exhibitioners. Hitchcock's instructions are clear and emphatic: a "see the picture from the beginning" policy is to be strictly enforced—a policy that has since this time become commonly and mistakenly identified as one of Hitchcock's innovations in cinematic showmanship. He comments at length about the success of his manner of exhibiting *Psycho:* the audience is presold by seeing an intriguing trailer (a "Hitchcock special" that addresses them not "like captives but like grownups being spoken to in a grownup manner"), gathered in an anxiously expectant line awaiting showtime, ushered in en masse to watch a film that is a masterpiece of artful manipulation, and then ushered out, making way for the next audience. This memorably named "spill-and-fill-and-chill schedule" not only maximizes the efficient use of theater time but is also a particularly effective way to reinforce "the patrons' complete enjoyment of the show—and to start them talking as soon as they leave the theater."

Ultimately, though, the scrupulous care and handling of *Psycho* is mandated primarily because it is a serious work of art by a serious artist. Maintaining "a policy of top secrecy about the story" is not only a shrewd marketing strategy but also "a vital step in creating the aura of mysterious importance this unusual motion picture so richly deserves." Watching *Psycho* from beginning to end, without any spoilers, is necessary to preserve the integrity of the film: "This was the way the picture was conceived—and this was how it had to be seen." Hitchcock was a shrewd and dedicated showman, but his primary concern is for the artist.

The final essay in this section returns our attention from the marketing to the making of pure cinema, and not surprisingly the focus is on, as the title indicates, *Rear Window,* because, as Hitchcock notes, "Of all the films I have made, this to me is the most cinematic." There is nothing in this compilation of postscreening comments that an experienced Hitchcockian has not heard before—except perhaps for a final off-handed remark about Truffaut's *The Bride Wore Black,* where Hitchcock momentarily impersonates one of the "plausibles" that he normally decried—but if it is, to some, by far the most familiar of all the essays in this collection, it is also useful and illuminating. Many of the chestnuts—or golden nuggets—are here, including the succinct definition of pure cinema as visual storytelling via montage, "pieces of film put together to make up an idea," illustrated by a brief summary of the Kuleshov experiment confirming that the meaning of a shot depends on the shots around it; anecdotes conveying his emphasis on preplanning, composing in advance rather than improvising on the spot; illustrations from *Rear Window* and *Psycho* showing his careful attention to rhythm in editing, artfully creating tension and the impression of violence; and detailed discussions of the MacGuffin, the paradoxical enjoyment of fear, and the mechanism of suspense. While the "news" value of this essay might be low for some, the information value is high: it serves as a compact introduction to what we need to know about what Hitchcock wanted us to know about his approach to filmmaking.

TITLES—ARTISTIC AND OTHERWISE

"Titles—Artistic and Otherwise" was originally published in the *Motion Picture Studio*, July 23, 1921, 6.

There are many elements that go to the making of picture titles—both good and bad.

Apart from their actual phraseology—upon which subject more than enough has already been written—there is much to consider in the matter of their design.

The first and most important aim is to make the title readable. This may seem a fairly obvious statement, but so many cases exist to-day of titles that present difficulty in reading. If an audience have to read a title that is not legible, they immediately conclude that it was not on the screen long enough for them to decipher, whereas, allowing exactly the same footage, if that title had been clearly written, the result would have been entirely satisfactory.

In the choice of a type, the essential consideration is to select a style of lettering or type face that can be easily read. There are a number of type faces that make easy reading; the best is always a "bold" face, the type of all one strength, that is without any variation in thickness, because a letter that has thick and thin portions will present difficulties for photography, inasmuch as the thin portion will not reproduce.

Type presents one or two minor difficulties in spacing. Letters, for instance, have to be spread out to justify a uniform length of line, causing the title to look a little weak in parts. There is also a difficulty at the present time to obtain good quality white foil, with the result that under the present circumstances an even white is not always attainable.

Hand-lettered titles have an advantage over printed ones. In the first place, an even strength of white will always be assured, the letters can be spaced and balanced without upsetting the appearance of the title, and, again, they are much better looking, as they do not have the hard appearance of a type face. Much of the success of a hand-lettered title depends upon the style of lettering. There have been cases of letters running riot in the use of ornament, such as enormous tails on g's and y's, etc., the result being a mass of "curly queues."

We now come down to that very interesting subject of Art titling. One or two of the leading directors in the States have made a practice of illustrating all sub and spoken titles. The result of illustrating a spoken title can only confuse the reader, for the essential point in a spoken title is that it is read quickly, and does not hold up the action. Subtitles, however, benefit greatly by some kind of illustration, as illustration gives color to the action of the story and helps to space the episodes. The quick reader derives some benefit also from an Art title, for he reads the title, and then his mind is occupied in *looking* at the picture until the fade out, thus giving continuity to the story.

There is much to be said about the type of illustration used in the title. Cooperation with the director will always be productive of the best results, because a situation may exist in the picture, and can be improved by the use of an appropriate symbol in the accompanying subtitles. Experience in this studio in the matter of subjects has found that still life is the most effective, as it can be most easily interpreted by the audience. If figures are used, they often clash with the actual photography, for the mind has been reading photographs all the time, and comes up against a change which is too sudden to grasp at a glance.

Symbols are the most effective subjects, provided they are not too subtle, for we must always remember that we are catering for all grades of intelligence, and it is only safe to aim at the understanding of the greater portion of them. But beware of repetition. The hour glass and scales of justice, their day is ended. A fair example of the use of symbols can be seen in Paul Powell's production, *Dangerous Lies,* by E. Phillips Oppenheim.

Another fairly effective type of illustration is the landscape background, which often suggests the *locale* of the current action. This requires careful treatment so as to avoid any "whites" behind the letters. The usual way to overcome this difficulty is to show the silhouette of a large tree in the foreground, and thus provide a black ground for the title itself.

In regard to the actual treatment, we have found that the most effective surface for art work is a black canvas, for it gives a richness and depth to the illustration, at the same time combining softness, which is essential where the titles are shot on positive stock, the latter having a tendency to harden the drawing.

A large ornamental index letter for each sub-title—*not* spoken titles—has been found to be very effective, as it stands out, and a part from ornamenting the titles, focusses the eye, as it were, and acts as a guide to where the lettering commences, thus avoiding any attempt for the eye to stray to the illustration first.

Bad titles can harm a picture; they create an indifferent atmosphere, and look shady.

Good titles will create a harmonious setting, and help the picture to run smoothly.

HOW A TALKING FILM IS MADE

"How a Talking Film Is Made" was originally published in *Film Weekly*, November 18, 1929, 16–17.

I don't think it has ever been fully explained just how a talkie is made, and also how talkie production differs from that of silent film-making. The Editor has set me rather a difficult task, because when he asked me to write the article he insisted that, while I should not be too technical, I should tell all the secrets—if there are any secrets—of talkie-making in simple language.

Of course, the production of talkies is, so far as I am concerned, a mass of technicalities, but I am going to endeavor to keep these in the background as much as possible.

IMPORTANCE OF SILENCE

Although it may seem odd at first glance, the most important factor in the making of a talkie is silence. I am no longer able to give instructions to my artists while the camera is turning; no longer can the cameraman call instructions to the electricians; and no longer can the noise of the crank be heard. Carpenters on adjoining sets who, in spite of the studio whistle to cease hammering, still managed to break noisily into a dramatic scene by the banging of nails, are dumb, and all the myriad noises of the old "silent" studio have been stilled.

THROUGH THE TALKIE STAGES

In their respective order I will explain all the stages through which the talkie goes before you see and hear it in the cinema.

First we have the consideration of the story, and here we have to select a tale in which there is plenty of action and yet good opportunity for dialogue and sound effects. In my opinion, too much talk has ruined many a promising talking film. This was probably unavoidable in the first rush, when producers took stage plays and photographed them merely because it was the simplest and quickest thing to do; but we are beyond that stage now. We are reaching the point where this new form of entertainment will contain the best of the old silent film and the best of the stage molded into something which is neither one nor the other, but which will be a completely distinct medium of expression.

Following the selection of the story comes the treatment. Treatment of the story is naturally of importance, and the scenario now contains all the dialogue which is to be spoken by the artists.

CASTING DIFFICULTIES

Casting is the next point, and here we are faced with greater difficulties than ever before. A pretty face and a shapely figure are no longer sufficient, even if they are allied with acting ability, for the exacting needs of the talkie. The voice must express the character that the artist is called upon to play, and if the voice is wrong, the whole characterization is false and unreal. The choosing of the artists, therefore, is one of the most important jobs entailed in preparation. I don't think that it is necessary any longer, save in exceptional cases, to test artists by the microphone. With each talking picture he makes, the director is able to judge better and better the reproduced voice of an artist by his or her ordinary speaking voice, and as his experience grows he should seldom make a mistake. This, of course, means a considerable saving of time and expense for the producing company.

POROUS WALLS AND DOORS

The building of sets and their arrangement is the next item on the program, and here complications which never arose in silent films are at once apparent. For example, it has been found that when an actress has to be photographed standing with her back to a door or wall the voice is picked up twice by the microphone, first when she speaks and secondly when it is thrown back by the door or wall behind her. This, of course, has to be overcome by the building of the set. That portion of the wall against which the artist will stand, according to the action, has to be built of porous material which will absorb and not throw back the sound.

REHEARSING

In rehearsing, to which we come next, we have one of the biggest differences between talkie and silent production. In silent films, as you no doubt know, the rehearsing for a scene is done in small sections on the floor itself immediately prior to shooting. This is impossible, principally because of the great cost, in talkies, and the whole action of the film has, therefore, to be rehearsed long before actual shooting is begun. Artists must not only be action perfect but word perfect; and this entails no small difficulty in certain cases, because in talkies longer sequences than ever before are photographed at one time. Thirty seconds or one minute was quite an average period in silent films for the length of a scene. Now very frequently scenes extending to four or five minutes are done without a break.

Rehearsing for talkies is equivalent to rehearsing for a play. No detail is omitted in rehearsals and, when the director and cast go on the floor to shoot, they have full knowledge of every incident in the story which they are to transfer to the screen. Although preparation for talkies is so much greater than that necessary for silent films, shooting time is considerably lessened, and the risk of costly error is practically eliminated.

SHOOTING AND RECORDING

The mechanical part of shooting and recording is now the joint work of two men, and not that of the cameraman only, as in silent films. The recorder, or "mixer," as he is called in America, is equally entitled to praise or blame as the cameraman, with whom he works in absolute conjunction. The cameraman no longer turns the handle of his camera, which is now set and kept in perfect synchronization with the sound-recording apparatus.

It must be remembered that all voices do not record in the same way, and that various sounds and effects which appear to be perfect in the studio would be far from perfect if recorded exactly as they take place.

That very essential man, the recorder, has a difficult and very important job to perform. It is he who is responsible for the quality of sound and speech recorded on the film.

He sits in a soundproof room (portable boxes similar to that in which the camera is housed are now being used on small sets), where he controls the reception of the sounds picked up by the microphone on the set, with the object of obtaining the most natural result when the record is reproduced in the cinema.

When the recorder has heard an action and voice rehearsal, and is satisfied that everything is in order from the recording point of view, he gives the signal to start. The camera and the sound record film start simultaneously, and the recorder marks the film in the camera and the sound film by setting up a violent vibration. This is necessary in order to synchronize the film and the sound track exactly afterwards. Following this the action proceeds and the talkie is under way.

It is a common belief that sound and action are photographed on the same strip of film during production. As will be seen by the foregoing this is not the case. Although the action and the sound are recorded simultaneously, they are recorded separately and synchronized at a later stage.

MORE WORK ON TALKIES

So far as the director is concerned, I think I can say definitely that talkies are considerably more difficult to make than silent films. The director, in addition to all the qualifications necessary for efficient silent film-making, must now possess knowledge of elocution and diction.

In the early days of talkie-making it was considered impossible to move the microphone too far away from the artists, and this was particularly noticeable in the earliest examples of this type of film, when an actor could almost be seen to stop whatever action he was making in order to speak. This difficulty has now been largely overcome by a system of multiple microphones and moveable micro-phones, so that it is possible to record the voice of an actor who may be either walking or running across the set. New problems are always arising, but it is simply a matter of solving them.

I do not think that talkie production will ever present a difficulty which thought, knowledge and enthusiasm will not overcome.

WHY I MAKE MELODRAMAS

"Why I Make Melodramas" was originally published in *Film and Stars,* Daily Express Publications, 1937, n.p.

WHAT IS MELODRAMA?

If I admit I prefer to make films that may be so classified I must first define it. Try to define it for yourself and see how difficult it is.

One man's drama is another man's melodrama.

In the Victorian theater there were only two divisions of entertainment—the melodrama and the comedy. Then snobbery asserted itself. What you saw at Drury Lane was drama. At the Lyceum it was melodrama. The only difference was the price of the seat.

"Melodrama" came to be applied by sophisticates to the more naive type of play or story, in which every situation was overdrawn and every emotion under-lined.

But still the definition is not universal. The "melodrama" of the West-end may be taken as drama in the Provinces. To some extent "melodrama" seems to be in the eye—and mind—of the beholder.

In real life, to be called "melodramatic" is to be criticized. The term suggests behavior which is hysterical and exaggerated.

A woman may receive the news of her husband's death by throwing up her arms and screaming, or she may sit quite still and say nothing. The first is melodramatic. But it may well happen in real life. In the cinema a melodramatic film is one based on a series of sensational incidents. So melodrama, you must admit, has been and is the backbone and lifeblood of the cinema.

I use melodrama because I have a tremendous desire for understatement in film-making. Understatement in a dramatic situation powerful enough to be called melodramatic is, I think, the way to achieve naturalism and realism, while keeping in mind the entertainment demands of the screen, the first of these being for colorful action.

Examine what was popular in the provincial theater before films and you will see that the first essential was that the play had plenty of "meat." It is to that audience, multiplied many times, we must cater in films.

But—and it is a difficult "but"—the same audience has been taught to expect the modern, naturalistic treatment of their "meat" dramas. The screen has created the expectation of a degree of realism which was never asked of the theater.

Now realism on the screen would be impossible. Actual life would be dull, in all but its more exceptional aspects, such as crime. Realism, faithfully represented, would be unreal, because there is in the minds of the cinema or theater audience what I would call the "habit of drama." This habit causes the audience to prefer on the screen things that are outside their own, real-life experience.

So there is the problem—how to combine color, action, naturalism, the semblance of reality, and situations which will be intriguingly unfamiliar to most of the audience. All these must be blended.

My own greatest desire is for realism. Therefore I employ what is called melodrama—but which might as well be called ultra-realism—for all my thinking has led me to the conclusion that there is the only road to screen realism that will still be entertainment.

Perhaps the strangest criticism I encounter is that I sometimes put wildly improbable things, grotesque unrealities, on the screen when actually the incident criticized is lifted bodily from real life. The reason is that the strange anomalies of real life, the inconsequences of human nature, appear unreal.

On the other hand, if they *are* real they may be too near the onlooker's experience and he does not go to the cinema to see his own troubles at closer range.

The man who understands the psychology of the public better than anybody else to-day is the editor of the successful, popular modern newspaper. He deals to a great extent in melodrama. The modern treatment of news, with its simple statement, which makes the reader "live" the story, is brilliant in its analysis of the public mind.

If the film-makers understood the public as newspapers do they might hit the mark more often.

SOME THOUGHTS ON COLOR

"Some Thoughts on Color" was originally published in the *Advertiser,* September 4, 1937, 13.

"I am whole-heartedly in favor of color films," said Alfred Hitchcock, British director, who is now making *Young and Innocent* (Nova Pilbeam), in Pinewood Studios, England.

Truly reproduced, Hitchcock says, color is a step towards greater realism in photography, and as such is desirable; but films must be color films, not colored films, he emphasizes.

"Color will give me the chance to portray what I want to portray most—lack of color," he said. "I know that sounds paradoxical, but think it over. How can I show the drabness of a slum street compared with the glory of a lovely landscape when I must photograph them both in tones of grey?

"Color too gives the director much more power to punch home a point— imagine the red drops of blood dripping on to a bunch of white daisies—just that would bring out the stark horror of a murder much more strongly than any gun or knife scene in monochrome.

(Hitchcock, it will be remembered, has produced some famous British screen "thrillers," including *The 39 Steps.*)

"Even the conventional scenes take on a greater potency. For instance, a convict sitting in his grey cell with a shaft of golden sunlight shearing its way through the gloom; imagine that for a moment. In color, that shaft of sunlight would be really rich gold, not merely a lighter tone of grey.

"Take again a real London pea-soup fog in color. Such shots as those coming slowly up to a red traffic light through a volume of swirling yellow, have three times the dramatic quality of their black and white counterparts.

"How well we could show rain. Not just torrents of studio rain pouring down from pipes, but puddles, gleaming pavements, with the reflection of a pale blue sky and the occasional glisten of a wet mackintosh.

"But although I'm all for color, it must help the script—never conquer it. After all, the story is still the most important thing."

THE "HITCH" TOUCH

"The 'Hitch' Touch" was originally published in *Band Wagon,* July 1946, 27–28.

If you have ideals about pictures *and* you direct them it's like walking on a tightrope with an umbrella in one hand and a script in the other. For however artistically inclined a director may be he can't afford to turn an entirely blind eye to "box-office."

Anyway, all this talk about cinema "art" never did cut much ice with me. Art and money were married a long time ago and perhaps, after all, it wasn't such a bad thing. They're not divorced yet, and I can't see it coming. In any case, pictures that are a balanced mixture of commercialism and "art" are almost always the most successful.

What makes a picture successful? In my films, the "touch" is suspense and for this good reason. The action of a film is non-stop and you can't ask an audience to sit through ninety minutes of film without dramatic relief of some kind. In the theater you have curtains and intervals—an audience doesn't require "holding" for the same length of time as in a cinema. Movie-goers require their interest regularly jerked—either by movement, dialogue or atmosphere.

One of the director's most obvious difficulties is getting "outside" the film—seeing it as a whole and as the audience will see it. Every scene goes to make up the whole, and film is like a piece of music—one phrase out of place and the sweep of the melody is lost. I "feel" a film like a piece of music and try to give my work the changing rhythms and climaxes of a concerto or symphony.

Only when I have my theme firmly set in my mind do I really feel ready to start filming. That's why I never study the shooting script closely until a day or two before the film is scheduled to go on the floor. I let story and theme grow on me—then I study the script.

On the set I always sketch the layout of a scene on paper so that my cameraman knows exactly what angles I want and how I wish my characters placed on the screen.

Here is one way of making drama out of camera angles. In *Spellbound* you'll remember the scene where Gregory Peck comes down a curving flight of stairs with an open razor in his hand. The audience knows that he has murder on his mind; his would-be victim, the doctor, is waiting at the bottom of the stairs. Now, in that scene I hardly move the camera at all. It is placed facing the stairs and Gregory walks right into the camera—right into the audience. As he gets closer his face and shoulders fade from the lens until all you can see is the razor in his hand. *Then* the camera moves.

But there's no dialogue and really very little movement. The whole scene depends on suspense and the use of camera. We pan to the doctor and hold him while he talks to Gregory. Then, back to Gregory—but not to the hand with the razor, but to his face. You get a close-up of his eyes. The doctor moves off to get him a glass of milk—which, incidentally, he dopes—and the camera stays with Gregory. Back comes the doctor and hands him the glass of milk.

The camera moves to a back shot, so that the audience is behind his eyes as he drinks. You get the impression of the white liquid obscuring his sight as he tilts the glass. This is doubly effective because in the film white is the color which affects his mind.

Before I shoot a scene I know what I want and generally I know just how to get it. Of course, here you do come up against the actors—perhaps I'd better say actors' opinions. What I generally do is to get them to play the scene my way and then say, "Now we'll do it the way you want it." Whichever way turns out better—that's the one we use.

The secret of good directing is to remember that you are telling a story *visually.* Your medium is that of sound and sight. The screen should tell this story as much as possible—not the dialogue. For example, take a simple scene. A woman has just been told by her husband that he is going to leave her. This is a tremendous shock to her. She always believed that he loved her. He tells her he's in love with another woman.

She's sitting there stunned. She asks him for a cigarette. Now here's the point. There's no need for him to say anything. Any answer he could give would only be trite. Just pan the camera with him over to the mantelpiece. He picks up the box, hands her a cigarette, lights it. She inhales. Nothing more has been said.

In that way you heighten the dramatic moment. Dialogue is out of place at such a time. Of course, your story might need some very significant remark at that point. But this example does emphasize the use of the camera. Or, if you like, the use of cinema.

ENCOUNTER WITH ALFRED HITCHCOCK

Interview with Charles Bitsch and François Truffaut

"Encounter with Alfred Hitchcock" was originally published in *Cahiers du Cinéma* 11, no. 62 (August-September 1956): 1–5. It was translated from the French text for the present volume by James M. Vest. I have slightly reformatted the interview, adding "*Cahiers*" and "Hitchcock" to identify the speakers and inserting a footnote in the original into the text (in brackets). Note that some of the details in the description of *The Wrong Man* are inaccurate. *D'Entre les morts* (From among the Dead), mentioned at the end of the interview, is the novel on which *Vertigo* was based.

Whenever he stops over in Paris, Alfred Hitchcock never fails to grant us an interview and to chat with us. The French language is gradually becoming familiar to him and there is not a trace of mistrust in his answers to our questions. He knows that it won't be we who reproach him for being too serious in making *I Confess* or not earnest enough in *The Man Who Knew Too Much*.

Although they have been shown at the Cannes and Venice Film Festivals, *Notorious, I Confess, Rear Window, To Catch a Thief,* and *The Man Who Knew Too Much* have never received any awards there. Hence our first question:

CAHIERS: *Mister Hitchcock, what do you think of the Festivals?*

HITCHCOCK: I think that in the festivals a documentary makes more of an impression than a film with a plot, good comedy, or entertainment value. Right?

CAHIERS: *Quite so. Why is it that, just before the opening credits for* The Man Who Knew Too Much, *you can read over the image of the cymbals these words:* "A crash of cymbals can rock the life of an ordinary family"?

HITCHCOCK: That statement is there because I needed it. When the point of a film is suspense, it's important that everything should be very clear in the mind of the viewer. The public must not have any doubt as to the element on which the mental tension of the suspense will hinge. Since people are generally not at all familiar with musical instruments—do they even know what cymbals are?—I had to direct their attention to these two metal disks from the beginning of the film, even before the credits. Then I added the written commentary because it's better to be safe than sorry. I must apologize for that somewhat shameless but necessary procedure.

CAHIERS: *It's not shameless.*

HITCHCOCK: Yes, yes, shameless but necessary.

CAHIERS: *Why are the autumnal colors in* The Trouble with Harry *so deliberately attractive? Was it to make fun of the poetry of nature, or of VistaVision, or to establish a counterpoint with the macabre subject, or did you think of fall as the cadaverish season* par excellence *in that it reflects nature decomposing?*

HITCHCOCK: All of that, to an extent. Although the action unfolds in the course of a single day, the film begins green and ends red. It was essentially a counterpoint. Nothing ugly should enter the picture. The autumn colors are magnificent, and you may have noticed that I never show the corpse in a way that could be disagreeable. Rather than show the face, I show the drawing that represents it. To my way of thinking, the characters in *The Trouble with Harry* have reactions which are absolutely normal and logical. It's their peculiar behavior, free from affectation, from dissimulation, from worldly concerns, from conformity, that makes us believe they cannot be real. In other words, instead of the logic of the absurd, I preferred the absurdity of logic.

CAHIERS: *What is the film from your American period that you like the most? [Note: We have purposely adapted in the course of this interview the method pursued by Karl Malden to conduct a successful police investigation in* I Confess: *jumping from one point to another. Voluntary lack of logical progression. We limited ourselves to sticking to the same subject no more than two minutes and there were no obvious connections among our questions.]*

HITCHCOCK: *Shadow of a Doubt.* I was fortunate to find in Thornton Wilder an ideal collaborator, thanks to whom the characters in this film are successfully conceived. Suspense, psychology, character traits, setting, everything pleases me in *Shadow of a Doubt.* It's an exceptionally solid film, very solid.

CAHIERS: *We have finally been able to see* Lifeboat *in Paris, which seems to prefigure, reference, and explain all your other films, particularly* The Trouble with Harry. *Do you agree with André Gide that the whole of one's oeuvre may be summarized by the phrase: "Don't judge"?*

HITCHCOCK: Yes, one cannot judge because, according to the circumstances, the situation, each one has a good reason to act in a certain way. In my films I show sympathetic and intelligent criminals, attractive murderers, because people are like that in real life. Don't you think so? Ordinary-seeming people are often more than ordinary; they have appearances against them. And not just appearances. On the other hand evil-doers are often rather striking people.

CAHIERS: *But one must free oneself from evil-doers, and the just, even if they are stupid and boring, must come out on top. Is that it?*

HITCHCOCK: Yes. Exactly.

CAHIERS: *The moral of* Shadow of a Doubt *is, then, that it is better for a family to bring a cop under its roof than harbor a criminal?*

HITCHCOCK: Yes, yes, and yet I don't like policemen. When I was five my father, as a joke, had me locked up for several hours at a police station. Afterward I was told it was a joke, but from that episode I retained an intense fear of the police. You can sense that in my films, right?

CAHIERS: *Yes, certainly. In your recent films there are several scenes that seem calculatedly poetical: mirrored images, slow motion, speeded-up action. We are thinking especially of the trial in* Dial M for Murder, *of the final chase scenes in* Rear Window, *of the kiss in* To Catch a Thief. *Why these tricks? Would you like to go further in this direction?*

HITCHCOCK: It's because when you use a technique you have to refine it thoroughly, down to its essential form. A film is made up of thousands of images. You have to play with that in every way possible. It's a matter of rhythm, or, if you prefer, of orchestration. So, for example, Stravinsky will abruptly follow an arresting musical phrase with a contrasting, very soft one. In *The Wrong Man* there is a scene in which the wife strikes her husband with a hairbrush. Here's how I made it: flash of the brush; flash of hair that the brush has just hit; then a shot of the woman who, pulling back her arm after the blow, breaks a mirror in which you see the head of her husband. Now the mirror cracks from top to bottom and the two parts shift in such a way that for a second you think you're seeing a Picasso. Then I cut and the story proceeds calmly. The woman goes over to the bed, sits on it and says: "You see. I don't know what came over me. Forgive me."

CAHIERS: *Do you have a particular liking for* The Wrong Man?

HITCHCOCK: Yes, because it's a film that taught me a lot as a director. I understood how much, when filming in a studio, one forgets how things are in real life. I wanted to do the opposite of films like *Boomerang* or *Call Northside 777*, where you follow the investigator who works to free an innocent man in prison. My film is made from the point of view of the guy in prison. So at the beginning, when they come to arrest him, he is in a car between two police officers. Closeup of his face. He looks to the left and you see, from his point of view, the massive profile of the first policeman. He looks right: his second guard lights a cigar. He looks straight ahead and in the rear view mirror sees the eyes of the driver who is looking at him. As the car starts up he has time for a final glance toward his house: at the corner is the coffee shop he frequented, in front of which some little girls are playing. In a parked car a pretty girl turns on the radio. In the outside world, life continues as if nothing were happening: everything is normal, but he is in the car, a prisoner.

My direction is entirely subjective. For example, he is handcuffed to the person accompanying him. In the course of his journey from the police station to the jail, he changes guards several times but, since he is ashamed, he looks at his shoes and keeps his head down the whole time, so you don't see his guards. From time to time a handcuff opens and a new arm comes into view and directs him. Throughout this journey you see only the policemen's feet, lower legs, floors, bottoms of doors.

The story is based on an article I read in *Life* magazine. Everything about the hero of the story was carefully documented, and as much as possible the film was made with unknown actors and sometimes even, for certain roles, with people who lived the events. All that on the actual site. At the prison we observed how prisoners handled their bedding, their clothes, and then we chose an empty cell for Fonda and had him do what we had seen the other prisoners doing.

In the course of this film I learned how people's memory can be unreliable. Our hero went to a bank to borrow $300 on his wife's insurance policy. That bank had been held up and three of the young employees identified him as the robber. Now when we did the trial scenes the judge in the real trial served as my technical advisor. One day he came into our court room—you must understand that in American courts there is a big table in front of the judge—and said: "This table should not be turned this way; rotate it 90 degrees. I'll be back." As soon as he left, his two assistants came over to me and said, "You know, the judge is mistaken. We remember very well that the table was in this position." When he came back the judge found the table unmoved: "Why the devil haven't you put this table the right way?" In order to appease this fine fellow, I told him that the cameraman's job would be greatly simplified for lighting if the table stayed where it was.

There's an example of what one can learn in making a film where one reconstitutes all the scenes from life. At the end the true criminal is arrested when he commits another holdup in a delicatessen, thanks to the courage of the owner. I imagined doing that scene this way: the man enters the store, takes out his revolver and demands the contents of the cash register; the merchant manages somehow to give the alarm, there is a fight of some sort, and the robber is subdued. Now here's how it really happened and what I put in the film. The man comes into the shop and asks the woman for two sausages and some slices of ham. When she moves behind the counter, he points his revolver at her through the pocket of his coat. The woman is holding the big knife to cut the ham and, without missing a beat, she pushes the knifepoint to the man's stomach, who is bewildered. The woman seizes the opportunity and stomps twice on the floor. The man becomes disturbed: "Temper, lady. Calm down! Take it easy!" The woman remains amazingly calm, not budging an inch, not saying a word. The man is so confused by this attitude that he doesn't even dream of trying anything. Suddenly the grocer comes up from the basement in response to his wife's stomping. He grasps the situation immediately and, taking the intruder by the shoulders, he pushes him into a corner of the store, up against shelves of canned goods, while his wife calls the police. The guy has no reaction other than to implore in a whiny voice, "Let me go. I've got a wife and kids to take care of!" This response pleased me enormously. You would never think of writing it into a script, and if you thought of it you wouldn't dare do it.

CAHIERS: *So we'll eagerly await* The Wrong Man. *We understand that you are going to South Africa?*

HITCHCOCK: Yes, I'm going Kenya to check out the exteriors for *Flamingo Feather,* based on a novel by Laurens van der Post. In the colonies a man finds a dead man in his garden and beside the corpse a flamingo feather associated with a tribe in revolt. The story takes place in Johannesburg, around the Cape, and in Nairobi. I've got to find a way to introduce a woman's role into this story because without a heroine there's no movie. When you're dealing with a Hitchcock film, *cherchez la femme!* If I don't succeed, I won't make this picture. I'm told that it's better to spend two or three million on advance work for a film that may be bad than to discover after the fact that it's no good. In this way, you ultimately save money.

CAHIERS: *And will* D'Entre les morts *be made after that?*

HITCHCOCK: No, *From among the Dead* will be made first. The action of the Boileau-Narcejac book is set in Paris and Marseilles, but I will make the film entirely in San Francisco. Jimmy Stewart will be the star. I'm still unsure of the female lead.

CAHIERS: *And after that?*

HITCHCOCK: Several films, including three with my friend Cary Grant.

ALFRED HITCHCOCK MURDERS A BLONDE

"Alfred Hitchcock Murders a Blonde" was a syndicated article, published in numerous places; it is transcribed here from the *Ottawa Citizen,* Weekend Magazine, 8, no. 22 (May 31, 1958): 6, 7, 33, 44.

"How," I asked Alfred Hitchcock, "would you murder a blonde?"

The master of murder, mayhem and the macabre blinked his heavy eyelids and murmured:

"Did you say how or why?"

"How."

"It seems to me," mused the maestro, "that if you were going to murder a blonde, to conform to pattern, you should poison her."

He gazed reflectively up at the ceiling, waited for the right pause and then added:

". . . with peroxide."

Again the long pause.

"That should give you the requisite counterpoint," he said.

A grin was starting to spread over his face.

"But no violence," he shuddered. "Only the softer destruction of the human being appeals to me."

He turned to his secretary (he has several).

"Get me a blonde," he ordered briskly. Then he swung back to me: "Come up to the house next week and I'll show you how it's done."

When I arrived at his beautiful Bel-Air home, blonde starlet Nan Leslie was already there. We were introduced.

"Where are the props?" Hitchcock barked at me.

I said I thought one of his staff was providing them. At that he grunted, trotted down to his cellar and came back with two bottles of champagne. In a few minutes Hitchcock the director-producer was clearing the decks for action. The orders came fast and direct. Hitchcock the actor would sit there. Nan the blonde would sit here, the photographer would shoot from here and the first scene would open this way, the second that way, the third another way and so on.

"How does that look to you?" he snapped at me.

"Fine," I said meekly.

"Now," he went on, "I have wangled my way into her apartment by telling her that it's my birthday and I want to take her out to celebrate. But I have brought some champagne to have a drink before we leave. First, then, the preliminaries, then 'Would you like some champagne?' After this the plot thickens and I go into the bar to open the champagne and put in the poison. At last, the birthday toast, then the death scene and, finally, my chuckle of triumph. O.K.?"

"O.K.," I replied, a little dubiously.

After the pictures were taken, Hitchcock looked across the room at me.

"Come to think of it," he said thoughtfully, "if you have a blonde, why murder her? Why not keep her?"

He chortled.

". . . as a pet."

The gag, though purely academic, intrigued me.

"Y'know," he said, "we should really work on how to get rid of the body."

He gave this some thought, then shrugged.

"If we don't watch out," he said, "we'll have a full-length feature on our hands, instead of a short."

Nan Leslie had left and we sat chatting.

"As a matter of fact," he said, "talking about blondes, I recall a movie I once made called *The Lodger*. It was in 1926 and was based on Jack the Ripper. Nasty fellow. Only murdered blondes. Part of the introduction, I remember, took 10 minutes. It was a late winter afternoon in London when the news came out of the first blonde murder and it had a terrible effect on blondes. They were all terrified. Of course, the brunettes did not care. I remember reading that the girls working in hairdressing parlors took to wearing little brunette curls under their hats. Why

Jack the Ripper only went for blondes I never could find out. It involves a question of psychology, I suppose. The blonde to me has always been a little nearer to sex in its visual aspects than a brunette. I don't know why."

Why does he always get sex into his movies?

"You might call it a regretful look at my past," he said slyly.

In any event, murder as a fine art, said Hitchcock sorrowfully, has declined in recent years.

"Of course," he said, "all murderers regard their work as a fine art. The better ones, I mean. But there is always a slip-up somewhere. Take the celebrated Dr. Crippen who murdered his wife and buried her in the cellar of her London home in 1910. Then he moved off for Canada. But he didn't have enough sense to keep his wife's jewels off his mistress. Too bad. And that business on the ship with his mistress dressed as a boy. Terrible."

Too many people think of Hitchcock as only a funny little man introducing his TV shows. What they fail to realize is that he has been responsible for some of the finest suspense movies ever made and is world-famous as a director-producer. The deft Hitchcock touch can be seen on every movie he makes, such as *Rope, Lifeboat, Dial M for Murder, Rear Window, The Man Who Knew Too Much,* and *To Catch a Thief.*

"I prefer suspense to the conventional-type story," he told me, "even though there is naturally plenty of mystery in a suspense story. But mystery is withholding information. Suspense is the opposite. It is setting up a situation whereby the audience is given the privilege of knowing all the facts which the characters in the movie do not know. For instance, we are sitting here as characters in a movie with a bomb timed to go off at 11 o'clock. We don't know it. But the audience does. The first requisite is that the audience shall like us and be fond of us all and want to scream out and tell us. If it were three strangers or someone they have not grown not to like, they couldn't care less. So you develop a sympathy for your people.

And the anxiety develops. You give your audience all the information you can. Meanwhile, the unsuspecting characters are indulging in small talk. Take away knowledge of the bomb and the talk is dull. But you know the bomb is to go off, and as the talk goes on and the seconds tick away, the suspense is unbearable. And the small talk by its very triviality becomes added suspense. Now, without the suspense, all you have is surprise. That is, the bomb goes off at 11 o'clock, surprising the audience and the characters. And so what? Surprise is much inferior to suspense but the really important factor is that if you have the suspense of the bomb, it is important to have no surprise at all. The bomb must not go off. Your audience would be furious if you built up an agony of suspense and got no relief. So you must at the last split second have someone dash in and whisk the bomb away."

Hitchcock chuckled.

"I remember," he said, "in one of my very early pictures I had the suspense built up for 12 o'clock and then the seconds ticked past 12 with the bomb still unexploded and ticked on and on and then suddenly the bomb blew up. Well, it was at a screening and one woman came over to me and said she'd like to tear my eyes out. She said it took away all the built-up emotion and left her flat. And that's the last time I did that."

A couple of days later I spent some time with him at the TV studios where he makes his introductions and sign-offs for his series, *Alfred Hitchcock Presents.* He was working in German and French films and had been working all day wearing various gag outfits—an ancient golfer, jockey, bull fighter. After one sequence, he came over, heaved a sigh and said:

"What you have to do for a living!"

Earlier I asked the script girl what language Hitchcock was working with and she replied with a straight face:

"German, French, English and American."

When I repeated this to Hitchcock, he smiled and explained.

"There's no difference between the English and American versions insofar as use of English is concerned. We do have to make a separate run for England because TV there is government-controlled and we must not run our commercial into the introduction."

On the set that day was a huge cake to celebrate the 100th TV show of his series. Grouped around the cake were all the instruments of death which have been used in his pictures. As Hitchcock stood there looking over the cake before the photographers took over, his gimlet eyes suddenly gleamed and be turned to his publicity man.

"You ought to be ashamed of yourself," he mocked, "you've left out the weapon which has appeared in more pictures than any other—the poker."

In a few seconds it was found and lovingly laid beside the poison, the axes, nooses, revolvers, daggers, etc.

Hitchcock is undoubtedly one of the most charming personalities in Hollywood. Exacting where his work is concerned, he will drive himself as he drives others, to achieve perfection. But he is never unreasonable and never raises his voice. He knows precisely what he wants and will painstakingly work until be gets the effect he is seeking. I watched him trying to get one TV sequence right and he went through one speech 15 times before he finally gave it his O.K. He loves storytelling and is a good listener. His work has had the result of making him "typed."

"If I did *Cinderella*," he said cheerfully, "people would start looking for the body."

But unlike some of his confreres, this does not bother him. He does not want to do *Hamlet.* He says it is better to be recognized as an expert in one field than just passable in all. And he finds it rewarding that his TV work has made him a household word in many parts of the world.

"But," he said, "it's kind of awkward when a woman will stop me on the street to say I come into her living room every Sunday night."

How did he get into this business in the first place? "Because I was a God-fearing little boy minding my own business and needed an outlet for my repressions," he says glibly, obviously not believing a word of it. He is not interested in the creaking door, slick private eye or the gangster type of story.

"My hero," he says, "is the average man to whom strange and bizarre things happen. The innocent who gets involved in something be cannot control. The audience is terribly worried because it can happen to them. My villains are always charming, suave and polite. It is a matter of record that some of the most vicious criminals in history were utterly charming. You might even say, about my criminal, that it was his charm which enabled him to get close to his victim and commit murder. And that is to some extent true about real-life murderers."

He will travel (along with an entourage) to the far ends of the earth to get the genuine backgrounds he wants in his movies. Once he was shooting on location in the notorious casbah in Marrakech, Morocco. He was working with a mob when he noticed one of the extras, a local Arab, waving wildly at the camera. Hitchcock stopped the action.

"What in the world are you doing?" he growled loudly.

"I have a brother in England and I want to make sure he sees me in this movie," said the Arab.

Said Hitchcock to me, in relating the tale. "You can't blame him. After all, it's cheaper than sending a snapshot."

Another time he was working on a film in Cannes, France, and wanted to shoot a sequence in the center of town. Everything was O.K., except that a car was parked along the street and impeded the action. The owner was located and asked to move the car. He refused. Several aides were dispatched to argue with him but he was firm. Finally, Hitchcock himself ambled over.

"Why don't you want to move your car?" he inquired politely.

"It makes shade for my little dog," replied the Frenchman.

Hitchcock gave up.

"You can't argue against that kind of logic," he said. For years he did not drive a car, preferring his wife to act as chauffeur. Now he drives.

"But I still think it was a mistake." he says. "Driving is pure torture. I'm fully aware that I am no criminal and have no police record but at the sound of a police siren I die a thousand deaths."

This from a man who has ordered more than 1,000 deaths.

Hitchcock, incidentally, has his "trade mark" which appears in every picture he directs. He turns up once in a walk-on part which takes only a second or two. "This grew," he told me, "from the old days when we had no unions and when I was short of actors I just stepped in myself."

The old days, for Hitchcock, go back quite a bit because he is now nearing 60 and has been in the business some 40 years. He was born in London in 1900, and by the time he was eight he had ridden to the end of almost every bus line in town. When he was asked why he did this he said that it was the best way to see the city. It has served him in good stead and his love of big cities and what makes them tick has not diminished over the years. He was educated at a Jesuit seminary and at the University of London, where he studied art and engineering. Because of this, he never peers into a camera as other directors do while making a movie. He sketches his scenes in advance and knows precisely what he wants before he comes on the set.

"Movies are delightfully simple," he says waggishly. "What you do is take a given piece of time, add color and pattern and there you have it."

Hitchcock's first job was as an assistant layout man in the advertising department of a large London store. From there he went to the London offices of Famous Players-Lasky (now Paramount) as title writer. By 1923 he received his first film credit as art director of *Woman to Woman*. Two years later he wrote the script, was art director and production manager of his first movie, which was then described as "the best American picture ever made in London." This may have been scant praise because not very many American films were being produced there. But soon he was producing and directing many more pictures, both in England and on the Continent.

By the time he came to the U.S. to stay in the late thirties, he was one of the best-known directors in movies on either side of the Atlantic. Some legends had meanwhile grown up about him, particularly his ability to demolish a man-sized meal. In those days be weighed about 290 pounds, which have been whittled down in recent years by 100 pounds or so.

Said Hitchcock: "I'm not really a heavy eater unless you mean that I am heavy and that I eat."

The Hitchcock family today includes his wife Alma, a married daughter Patricia, and two Sealyhams. Their home is unpretentious yet luxuriously modern. The book-lined living room has some fine modern paintings including a Picasso and a Utrillo. Of all this, Hitchcock has been quoted as saying: "We all just pig here together."

Hitchcock views his craft with his usual tongue-in-cheek aloofness. "All you have to do," he told me, "is to make sure you can keep your audience awake. You ask them to look at a square frame for an hour and a half at a time. You've got to put something in there to keep them looking."

To keep them looking at his next movie, *Vertigo,* Hitchcock has James Stewart and Kim Novak. Both are good to look at. When I asked him about Kim Novak, who is good to look at but no Sarah Bernhardt, Hitchcock winced and said smoothly:

"After I got through with her, she could act."

For that alone be should get some kind of an award.

MY FAVORITE FILM CHARACTER IS—ME!

"My Favorite Film Character Is—ME!" was a syndicated article, published in numerous places; it is transcribed here from the *Sunday Herald Magazine* (Bridgeport, Connecticut), August 23, 1959, 14.

Neither Hollywood nor TV has shown any interest in my favorite character, although he has appeared in every one of my films.

You are probably familiar with him—a fussy, flustered, bewildered man; short and obese. He used to be fatter. He is always played by myself, and has become, in a manner of speaking, my film signature.

He appears so briefly on the screen as almost to be subliminal—which means you are not always sure you have seen him. He has nothing whatsoever to do with the plot. At most, he is a face in the crowd, a passer-by, a bystander around whom action swirls in which he is not in the least involved.

He is never even aware that, at the moment of his intrusion, foul murder is being plotted, that the gentleman he passes on the street is on his way to strangle his wife, that the house he stares at contains a corpse.

. . .

Often I am tempted to build a screen story around him, to give him the leading role. I shall never do it, of course. However, in the story I have in mind, he is a musician, a second rate performer in a third rate symphony.

He has been cast as a musician before. In *Strangers on a Train* he was seen clutching a base viol shaped remarkably like himself.

In *Vertigo,* he carried an instrument case containing a horn of some sort—in actuality (secrets of the prop department) the case is made of solid wood.

In my newest film, *North by Northwest* he is boarding a bus, instrumentless. You see, he is a tympanist, and can hardly carry his kettle drums around with him.

As I have cast him in my never-to-be-produced story, he plays an oboe. He has a wife who is a shrew, soured by long years of shabby-genteel existence. He also has a small boy who hates music and wants to be a baseball player when he grows up.

. . .

My man is marked throughout for frustration. He is a bitter man—observe his petulant underlip, the scowl. Who can blame him? Consider the years and the labor involved in the shaping of an average symphony player. And what has been his reward for a lifetime of training, hard work, cruel discipline? Obscurity among four-score other anonymous musicians.

His yearly income would be scorned by a bus driver. His wife berates him daily for not taking a job offered by a relative who owns a shoe store. Our hero is glumly silent in the face of her scolding, obdurate for reasons that he, himself, cannot understand.

Once, when he was younger, in the days of the silent film, he touched glamour, played accompaniment on a clarinet in a small orchestra to the emotional bosom-heaving of a famous movie star. I think it was on such an occasion that I first met him—I was then an art director for a British studio—and was struck by his role: in the scene, but not of it.

Do you know what?—in real life I cannot stand suspense, and, as I said, my character is real to me. At this point I call a halt. I turn with relief to my *North by Northwest* script, in which Cary Grant and Eva Marie Saint are clambering over the face of Mt. Rushmore Memorial, with the villain, James Mason, in close pursuit.

Cary Grant slips, clings by his fingers. A hand appears on the screen. To rescue him? No. A cruel boot is raised, stomps down on the clinging hand.

I say, this is jolly!

How, meanwhile, is our real character faring? Let us hope and pray that the operation succeeds, so that he may return to his job in the orchestra, blowing his brains out daily for a pittance. His wife will resume her scolding. His son's bat will be taken away, and the boy in his bitterness will join the Holy Hitlers, or some such juvenile mob, and get into trouble with the police.

· · ·

I am aware that up to this point my story lacks the Hitchcock touch. Where is the suspense? We are coming to that.

One day he enters the living room of his home just when his son is swinging a baseball bat. Fate is not satisfied with what it has done to our man; has worse in store for him. Fate's timing is perfect; the bat comes in contact with our hero's mouth. His upper teeth are knocked out, his lip split so as to require six stitches.

I can imagine that this scene would draw a laugh on the screen. It used to be funny in Keystone Comedies when the cop got clunked on the head or fell into a manhole. In real life, serious injury might be involved. And my man is real to me.

· · ·

There is nothing a wind instrument player dreads more than injury to his mouth. He might lose his "lip"—the curious conformation of mouth and face muscles that enables him to achieve sounds impossible to others. Without his "lip" his career, his livelihood, is threatened.

Our wretched victim's house is mortgaged, his meager savings thrown into the breach. Money is borrowed from grumbling relatives—all towards a plastic operation that is his only hope. For once his wife, awed by the extent of the tragedy, is acquiescent.

And there is your suspense. Will the operation, upon which a whole life hinges, work? Will our hero ever play again? The day will come when he will raise the instrument tremblingly to his mouth. He will blow with bated breath—if such a thing is possible musically. There will emerge—what?

. . .

I doubt that Hollywood will be interested in this plot. Lately, the movies have taken to voicing the aspirations and needs of the little man, have shown a willingness to make him the hero, as witness *Marty*. But Marty, for all of his ordinariness, represented the triumph of the little man. I can see him now, sided by his perfect helpmeet, owning a chain of meat markets, shining in society. Not my man.

My hero isn't ever a likable fellow like Marty. He is bitter, stingy, and the only thing that keeps him going is his pride. I am important, he says to himself; without people like me no symphonies would be performed—or even written. What happens to me, therefore, is of consequence to the world.

I say amen. I hope the poor devil "gets his lip back." I worry. I have my fingers crossed.

A LESSON IN PSYCHO-LOGY

"A Lesson in PSYCHO-logy" was originally published in the *Motion Picture Herald,* August 6, 1960, 17–18.

Having lived with *Psycho* since it was merely a gleam in my camera's eye, I have exercised my parental rights in urging showmen to adopt a policy of top secrecy about the story, from their very first encounters with opinion-makers. I believe this is a vital step in creating the aura of mysterious importance this unusual motion picture so richly deserves.

The idea of insisting on and carrying out a policy that no one—but no one—can be allowed to enter a theater playing *Psycho* after the start of each performance came to me one busy afternoon in the cutting room. In this confined cubicle, I suddenly startled my fellow-workers with a noisy vow that my frontwards-backwards-sidewards-and-inside-out labors on *Psycho* would not be in vain—that everyone else in the world would have to enjoy the fruits of my labor to the full by seeing the picture from beginning to end. This was the way the picture was conceived—and this was how it had to be seen.

OPENING DATES PROVE SUCCESS

Our opening playdates have proved, beyond the shadow of a showman's doubt, the success of this required policy. If the word "required" startles you, please try to think of a box office besieged by patrons anxious to purchase tickets. Feel better? Yes, my friends, while nothing in this world is fully guaranteed, you will most probably be happily startled all the way to the bank. Every presentation of *Psycho* thus far has had this result, on a fantastic scale.

We cannot over-emphasize the proved efficiency of our policy in selling tickets and enhancing the importance of *Psycho*. Even the reviewers, a hard-bitten clan, were intrigued by such quasi-humorous messages as "please don't give away the ending, it's the only one we have" to quote them here and there in their glowing praises of the picture and the policy.

According to my friends at Paramount, all policy and directory ads for *Psycho* should contain time schedules big and bold! Times listed are those of complete programs, each starting with newsreel and short subjects. This gives you ample time to fill your theater. Times listed in ads must, of course, be duplicated exactly in radio spots, TV trailers, flyers and lobby posters.

MESSAGE MUST BE BROADCAST

Nothing will make it easier for me to separate the showmen from the sheep than an appraisal of the various local uses of available radio and TV commercials. Experience has taught us that our policy message must be broadcast along with the theater playdate. A sample "live" announcement at the end of a commercial would be—*Psycho* starts at the Eupheria theater Friday. You must see *Psycho* from the beginning! See your newspaper for performance times!"

No one but no one (not even I) has to tell you how vital trailers are in pre-selling *Psycho*. We've put together a trailer package that has brought forth mountains of praise, most of it deserved. This package consists of a long (six-minute) Hitchcock special and two teaser trailers, one on policy, the other urging top secrecy. You will discover with delight, as have so many showmen before you, that your audiences watching these trailers do not feel like captives but like grownups being spoken to in a grownup manner.

Even an old dog like myself will learn new and even intelligent tricks, if the incentive is there. I had more than sufficient incentive to learn the fascinating theater phrase, "spill and fill," as we worked out the most rewarding method of spilling all patrons out of a theater after each performance of *Psycho*, and filling the theater up again before the start of the next performance. Much as I would like to be rigid in this advice, because of an inherently dictatorial nature, I cannot. At any rate, the following spill-and-fill-and-chill schedule was about the average for theaters playing the early dates of *Psycho:* end of performance; house dark for 30 seconds; lights up long enough for complete emptying of theater (9½ minutes average); 15 minutes of short-and-newsreel on screen; doors shut as new performance begins; start sale for next performance.

The art of "linesmanship" was, I believe, carried to the pinnacle of good sense in early dates of *Psycho*. While there can be no set rules in the handling of lines because of the variable factors of size of lobby, location of theater, and so forth, there is a certain procedure that we discovered to be basic and beneficial. This is the form line, which will help to keep the box office clear for sale of tickets. Have traffic move from the box office to the end of the ticket-holders'-line. Stationing of a uniformed guard or theater employee near the box office will help your cashier to explain our policy when the doors are closed. Our experience has taught us that such explanations bring refund requests down to a bare minimum.

Paramount and I have set up these minimum showmanship standards for your patrons' complete enjoyment of the show—and to start them talking as soon as they leave the theater. Please do not attempt to alter, change, transform, mutate, modulate, vary or qualify these requirements without prior consultation with the highest authority—and I leave you to guess who that might be.

REAR WINDOW

"*Rear Window*" was originally published in *Take One* 2, no. 2 (November-December 1968): 18–20.

I chose this picture because of all the films I have made, this to me is the most cinematic. I'm a purist so far as the cinema is concerned. You see many films that are what I call photographs of people talking. This film has as its basic structure the purely visual. The story is told only in visual terms. Only a novelist could do the same thing. It's composed largely of Mr. Stewart as a character in one position in one room looking out onto his courtyard. So what he sees is a mental process blown up in his mind from the purely visual. It represents for me the purest form of cinema which is called montage: that is, pieces of film put together to make up an idea.

When the film was originally invented, when cutting was invented, it was the juxtaposition of pieces of film that went through a machine that displayed ideas on the screen. Unfortunately today a lot of that is lost: it's not being used sufficiently, or sometimes not at all. I think it was Pudovkin, the famous Russian director many years ago, who took a close-up and he put various objects in front of a woman's face and it was the combination of her face—she never changed her expression—and what she looked at (whether it was food or a child or what have you) that seemed to give an expression to her face. I made up the whole of the film production section of the *Encyclopedia Britannica* and I took the idea of this film as a prime example of the power of montage. For example, if Mr. Stewart is looking out into this courtyard and—let's say—he sees a woman with a child in her arms. Well, the first cut is Mr. Stewart, then what he sees, and then his reaction. We'll see him smile. Now if you took away the center piece of film and substituted—we'll say—a shot of the girl Miss Torso in a bikini, instead of being a benevolent gentleman he's now a dirty old man. And you've only changed one piece of film, you haven't changed his look or his reaction. This is one of the reasons why I chose this film. You see, many people think that a little dialogue scene in a movie is motion pictures. It's not. It's only part of it. Galloping horses in Westerns are only photographs of action, photographs of content. But it's the piecing together of the montage which makes what I call a pure film.

In *Vertigo* and other of my pictures a lot of the visual "pure cinema" techniques are used, but the subject matter is the thing that lends itself to certain treatments. I use the cinematic technique as often as I can, but sometimes there isn't the opportunity. Certainly I think that this film of all of them presented the greatest opportunity.

I have made films based on stage plays (back in the very early days of talking pictures) where I found that when filming a stage play, it's best not to, what they call in our business "open it up," because a stage play is designed for a limited area of presentation, that is, the proscenium arch. Some years ago I tried to get around this problem when I made a film called *Rope*. It was a stage play and it played continuously in its own time. And I tried to give it a flowing camera movement and I didn't put any cuts in at all. I tried to do it as if I were giving the audience all opera glasses to follow the action on the stage, but basically it was on stage. I think people make a dreadful error when they "open up" stage plays. What do they do when they say "open it up?" Well they open it up with a shot of Fifth Avenue and a Yellow Cab pulls up, the characters come out of the cab, they cross the sidewalk, they go into the building, they press the button for the elevator, they go up, they get out of the elevator, they go around along a corridor, they press another button, and when the door opens, where are we? Back on the stage.

For *Rear Window* each cut was written ahead of time. It's like scoring music—I prefer to make a film on paper. People ask me, "Don't you ever improvise on the set?" and I say, "No, I prefer to improvise in the office while we're writing. That's where the ideas come from." So I prefer to design this kind of film well ahead of time, with each cut in its proper place. It's like composing. A lot of films are made where they have a first draft script and make it up as they go along. To me that's like a composer trying to compose music with an orchestra in front of him. He has a blank sheet and he says, "Flute, give me a note will you." So I work strictly on paper.

There's no score in *Rear Window*. I was a little disappointed at the lack of a structure in the title song. I had a motion-picture songwriter when I should have chosen a popular songwriter. I was rather hoping to use the genesis, just the idea of a song which would then gradually grow and grow until it was used by a full orchestra. But I don't think that came out as strongly as I would have liked it to have done.

Rear Window has a happy ending, but I don't think you have to drag in a happy ending. I think that an audience will accept any ending as long as it's reasonable. Years ago I made a film of Sean O'Casey's *Juno and the Paycock*. It has a tragic ending, a very grim ending, but there was no other way around it. *Vertigo* ended with a girl falling from a tower in the same manner that she had helped a murderer with previously. The ending depends really on the nature of the content of what has gone before. Sometimes if you've created a lot of suspense in an audience it's very essential that you relieve that tension at the very end.

The rhythm of the cutting in *Rear Window* speeds up as the film goes on. This is because of the nature of the structure of the film. At the beginning, life is going on quite normally. The tempo is leisurely. There's a bit of a conflict between the man and the girl. And then gradually the first suspicion grows and it increases. And naturally as you reach the last third of your picture the events have to pile on top of each other. If you didn't, and if you slowed the tempo down, it would slow up considerably. In the film *Psycho,* you start off with just a sack of money and a girl who is suddenly murdered in a shower. The shower scene was made very violent because of what was to follow. The pattern there was that events again increased, but I'd decreased the violence because I'd transferred the violence from the screen to the mind of the audience. So I didn't have to be violent later on because I'd built up the apprehension—having given them a sample, shall we say, and so it was a matter of going on and on increasing your tempo of events but keeping the violence down and letting the audience carry that for you, you see.

When you come down to the question of color, again it's the same as the orchestration with cutting. If you noticed in *Rear Window*, Miss Lonely Hearts always dressed in emerald green. To make sure that that came off, there was no other green in the picture, because we had to follow her very closely when she went across the street into the café. So I reserved that color for her. In *Dial M for Murder* I had the woman dressed in red to begin with and as the tragedy overtook her she went to brick, then to grey, then to black.

Since my scripts are worked out beforehand, there is no opportunity for creative work on the part of the film editor. I don't mind the film editor being in . . . well, in fact, even with the writer I let him be part of the direction of the picture. Working closely with the writer I can tell him how we're going to shoot it, what size image, and so forth. So I'm willing to share the creative end of it with the writer and the same would apply with the editor. But, you see, where the work of the average editor comes in is when he's given a lot of film to sort out. This is when directors use many angles of the same scene. But I never do that. As a matter of fact when this film, *Rear Window*, was finished somebody went into the cutting room and said. "Where are the out-takes? Where is the unused film?" And there was a small roll of a hundred feet. That was all that was left over.

If you want to be really mean towards the character in this film you could call him a Peeping Tom. I don't think it's necessarily a statement of morality because it's a statement of fact. You don't hide from it, there's no point in my leaving it out. When Grace Kelly says that they're a couple of fiendish ghouls because they're disappointed that a murder hasn't been committed she's speaking the truth. They were a couple of ghouls.

The MacGuffin in this story is really the wedding ring, which is the clue. The MacGuffin is really a nickname for what happens in spy stories. Or it's the papers that are stolen. It's something that the characters in the film care a lot about, but the audience doesn't worry about it too much. It's the plan for the fort or what have you. In Rudyard Kipling it could always be the Khyber Pass and the forts around it. Years ago I made a film called *39 Steps* and someone said, well what were the spies after, and it turned out to be a lot of gibberish which nobody . . . it was an airplane engine or bomb-bay door or something. As a matter of fact I refuse to use the kind of thing which most people think is very important. In the picture *North by Northwest*, Cary Grant speaking of the heavy or the spy says to the CIA, "Well, what is the fellow after?" and they answer, "Well, let's say he's an importer-exporter." And Grant says, "But what of?" and they answer "Government secrets." And that's all that was needed. The word MacGuffin comes from a story about two men in an English train, and one says to the other "What's that package on the baggage rack over your head?" "Oh," he says, "that's a MacGuffin." The first one says, "Well, what's a MacGuffin?" "It's an apparatus for trapping lions in the Scottish highlands." So the other says, "But there are no lions in the Scottish highlands." And he answers, "Then that's no MacGuffin." To show you how people do make a big mistake about this kind of thing, I once designed a picture with Ben Hecht. It was called *Notorious*. And it dealt with the sending of a woman, Ingrid Bergman, and an agent down to Rio to see what some Nazis were up to. They were up to something. So the producer said, "Well, what are you going to have the Nazis doing down in Rio?" And I said, "Well, I thought that we were going to have them searching for samples of uranium 235." And he said, "What's that?" And I said—this is 1944—"Well, that's the stuff they're going to make the atom bomb out of." And he said, "What atom bomb? I've never heard of it." And I said, "No, it isn't out yet." As a result of me making this mistake, the producer didn't believe a word I said and finally sold the project to another studio, for only 50 percent of the property. He could have made 100 percent had he not made that cardinal error. Then I did meet some producers years after who said, "You know, we were offered a story of yours, *Notorious,* and we thought that was the Goddamndest thing on which to base a picture. How did you know years before it happened?" I said, "Well, there were all kinds of rumors. The Germans were dealing with heavy water in Norway." And so those producers lost all kinds of money for the wrong kind of thinking. But they still think that way. They still think that if the film's a spy film that it's all about . . . well, the MacGuffin.

On the question of violence, you see, you've got to go right back to the three-month-old baby. He's held in his mother's arms and the mother says to him, "Boo!" And the mother is being violent. And the child gets the hiccups and then the child smiles and the mother is very pleased with what she's done. It starts as early as that. In other words she scares the hell out of the baby. And that's how fear is born. And later the child grows up and goes on a swing and becomes violent itself. It goes higher, and higher, and higher, and then it goes over the top. And next it tries a new kind of violence by going to the midway and going on the roller coaster, and then it goes shooting at rifle ranges, and knocking down objects. And the child is forced to read Hans Anderson or Grimm—you'll notice the word "grim." They take the child to see Hansel and Gretel and how they push an old woman into the oven. So there's nothing new in it. We've always had violence—it's communication. We've always had violence. We didn't have television, we didn't have radio years ago, but the violence was always there. Little boys point at each other and say, "Bang, you're dead." And the other boy rolls over. They don't believe it. People are fearful that children who are brought up to look at movies and television are violent. It isn't true. A little boy once came up to me and said "Oh, Mr. Hitchcock, in that scene in *Psycho,* what did you use for blood, chickens' blood?" And I said, "No, Chocolate sauce." But he said, "What did you use?" So I'm not sure that all the hullabaloo about violence is really correct. So far as the average individual child seeing movies, seeing Westerns with horses rolling over and bodies falling . . . It reminds me also, going back to *Psycho,* I had a call from the Los Angeles *Times.* One of the reporters said, "A man has just been arrested for the murder of three women. And he confessed to murdering the third woman after seeing *Psycho.*" What did I have to say about it? I said, "What film did he see before he murdered the second woman? And am I to assume that the first woman was murdered after he had just finished drinking a glass of milk?"

The delineation of suspense covers a very, very wide field. Basically it is providing the audience with information that the characters do not have. The most simple example, the elementary example, is if four men are seated around a table and they're having a discussion about baseball, anything you like. Suddenly a bomb goes off and blows everyone to smithereens. Now, the audience get from that fifteen seconds of shock. But up to that time you've spent five minutes on a conversation about baseball. And the audience are without any knowledge that the bomb is under the table. Now let's take it the other way around. We show the bomb under the table, and let the audience know it's going to go off in five minutes. Now you go on with your conversation. Now the conversation becomes very potent, with the audience saying, "Stop talking about baseball, there's a bomb under there." Just as in *Rear Window* people were anxious about Grace Kelly being in the room and the man coming along the corridor. You're giving them information that neither of the characters have. So now you know there's a bomb under there and at the end of five minutes it's about to go off. You've driven the audience to the point of anxiety. Now a foot must touch the bomb and someone must look under, discover there's a bomb, pick it up, and throw it out the window. But it mustn't go off under the table.

Because if you create suspense in the audience, it needs to be relieved of that suspense. Now, I made a film years ago from a Joseph Conrad story called *Secret Agent*. And I had a scene where a small boy carries a package across London. And he didn't know, but the audience knew, that a bomb was inside. And it had to be left at a certain place at a certain time. Well. I showed every form of holdup. He was even held up by the Lord Mayor's procession. Then he got onto a slow-moving bus, stop signs, go signs, policemen. And it drove the audience crazy. And I'd told them one o-clock and then I let it go on one minute past one, two minutes past one. And at four minutes past one the bomb went off and blew up the bus, the boy into little pieces. I'd committed a cardinal sin. I had let that bomb go off. People were furious, angry. I remember at the press show the leading London press woman critic came up and nearly hit me. "How dare you do a thing like that!" I hadn't relieved the suspense.

Yes, I saw Truffaut's *The Bride Wore Black*. I thought it was quite well done. Well, people said that it was a tribute to me. The only thing that bothered me was I didn't know how the woman got to know that there were five men up in that room. But maybe he was getting mixed up with the MacGuffin.

ON DIRECTORS AND DIRECTING

INTRODUCTION

Some of Hitchcock's most interesting and important comments on directing come from an early watershed period in his career, late 1927 and early 1928, after the delayed release but then stunning success of his first three films, a time of a remarkable burst of creative activity (he made four films in 1927 alone), critical acclaim, and financial reward. He and Alma were also expecting their first child, reason enough for him to think deeply about his responsibilities as a father in his home and a father figure in his studio. This latter image is prominent in "An Autocrat of the Film Studio," Hitchcock's fullest statement, at this or any other time, of his idea of what in another essay published a few months earlier ("Films We Could Make") he called "One-Man Pictures." His follow-up essay clarifies what kind of films these are, what skills are required to make them, and how he is uniquely qualified for the task.

His emphasis throughout is on various "freedoms" for the medium and the director: from literature and the stage, audiences, actors, and writers. Beset by distractions on all sides, filmmaking requires an autocrat in the studio who is dedicated, knowledgeable, and commanding. Although he may occasionally appear to be brusque and imperious, he is ultimately "a kind of father figure providing for his family," and when it comes to what he calls "the making of their feast," Hitchcock has no doubt at all that father knows best.

This role calls for him to educate an audience that he is justifiably impatient with because of their "flippant indifference" and overall belief that one goes to the cinema "merely for the sake of exciting entertainment." Hitchcock attempts to combat and remedy all that by insisting that film is a serious, strenuous, and complex art and industry "worthy of intelligent support." His hope is that if audiences look in a properly informed way at how films are really made, they may then look at cinema in general and individual films in particular in a new way. A key point to remember in furthering the development of a medium fully "capable of telling a story in its own way" is "Don't forget the camera in film work." This dictum requires abandoning words and static, fixed-perspective visual images, the legacy of "the book and stage," in order to rely instead on "the substitution of a series of moving images which tell a story without the aid of titles and captions." One of the secrets of cinema that he reveals is that the studio is an "emotion factory," a joking but respectful metaphor underscoring the difficulty and complexity of the production work involved and the need for a strong supervising presence in the value-adding process that turns the raw materials into "the finished product, the completely *manufactured article.*"

Hitchcock shrewdly plays on what he assumes is his audience's fascination for behind-the-scenes and on-the-set stories about actors in order to correct the misconception that actors make films. A large part of the article revolves around specific examples of how he handles actors, relying on his ability as a "student of psychology" to determine how to "adapt his methods to the nature of the temperament of the individual." Sometimes this is relatively straightforward, but he often had to "resort to tricks and catch them unawares to get the result I aimed at," which he illustrates by a teasingly mysterious description of how he told Isabel Jeans an unspecified "childhood legend" to get "the sort of smile I wanted." Ironically, these beguiling stories of actors are meant to deflect attention from them and to reinforce the underlying message of Hitchcock's careful and creative ingenuity, as well as to disarm any criticism of his "brusqueness."

Hitchcock acknowledges that writers are also important component parts of a film but wants to be sure that the author is not mistaken for the auteur. The demands of cinema are far different from those of literature, and a writer who fails to realize that fact and who does not have a deep knowledge of the medium of film "cannot turn out an acceptable story." Cinematic professionalism is far more important than "inspiration"; as a result, a "gifted hack" is preferable to "famous writers" and the "good and kind literary people who bombard me with scenarios," who are "worse than a hindrance."

Scenarios also fail when the story they tell is deficient. The two overlooked stories that Hitchcock wants to turn to are ones that he is prepared to write himself, and we might be surprised by what he outlines: "One will be about railways and the other about our mercantile marine." What is especially important is that his proposed subjects open up a "wealth of possibilities in romance." He defines this element broadly and identifies it with a particular theme that accounts for so much of the appeal of American films: "the life of incentive, of big endeavor and handsome reward." Filmgoers "want stories throbbing with life," and Hitchcock carefully points out that this throbbing takes place in the audience as well as on the screen. As young men and women watch heroes and heroines and share in a "wonderful journey" that "takes them out of themselves," they experience something quite remarkable and perhaps lasting: "They hug themselves and each other in ecstatic joy under cover of the darkened cinema, and then—?" This essay ostensibly about the autocratic power of a director is thus also centrally about the power of film, and long before Susan Sontag used the phrase, Hitchcock describes and dedicates himself to an "erotics of cinema." Even when he turned to suspense thrillers, he held true to his fundamental principle that pure cinema is always "rich in romance."

In an article published the year after "An Autocrat of the Film Studio," Roger Burford adds an interesting angle to Hitchcock's consideration of the tremendous responsibilities and strains of a film director. A brief outline of some of the details that confirm his premise that "no profession is quite as exacting as making films" leads very quickly to an intentionally provocative statement: "Hardly a woman's job, one would think." Hitchcock's comments on whether or not directing is "a new 'chair' which a woman might fill," in an essay of that title, are brief but fascinating, as much for his direct statements of the qualities he thinks are necessary for "making a good film director" as for his analysis of why women are unlikely to possess or develop these qualities. He initially emphasizes that a "director is called upon to portray life in *all* its aspects" and that "no one should undertake a subject of which he has not first hand knowledge." This criterion doesn't automatically qualify all men as directors. (Hitchcock himself couldn't pass such a test and didn't feel that he had too: in later writings and interviews he frequently highlighted his own naïveté and inexperience in life without ever letting this challenge his mastery of cinema.) But it does apparently automatically disqualify women, because Hitchcock assumes that they are "less versatile in observation than men," and a woman is inevitably restricted to a "smaller scope of the life she may be expected to have experienced."

Even though women make up "the larger proportion of the cinema public," the cinematic edifice is still best built by men. The most that Hitchcock will admit is that women's special experiences and talents may qualify them as advisers or contributors, albeit on what he considers to be lesser matters, such as "domestic subjects," or on constituent parts of films. He praises his wife's screenwriting and assistance on his own films, for example, but even her "utmost value so far as the story, and even the action," doesn't compensate for her inability to handle "the more unwieldy departments of film productions," such as art design. Film requires "generalship, a masculine strain," the ability to "command," and the "capacity for decision." All these qualities are necessary for control on the set and the achievement of the director's individual and independent vision of "exactly what effect he wants." Linking a large part of what he defines as the required comprehensive mastery of all aspects of film production to gender means that his concluding statement—"there is nothing to keep the best man, or woman, from the top"—while perhaps meant to be generous and accommodating, is, alas, only half true.

The image of a director as a manly man and then some is developed even further in Hitchcock's early tribute to and critical appraisal of D. W. Griffith, "A Columbus of the Screen." Such a masterful figure is needed to discover, explore, and perennially remake the cinema and do battle with powerful anti-cinematic forces outside and inside the industry. Hitchcock makes an impassioned case for Griffith as a "romantic figure," "incomparably the greatest" director, fully deserving of his reputation as "the Old Master," and still a vital force in filmmaking. The essay is filled with hyperbolic praise, and many of the details seem to be little more than gleanings from a studio pressbook, repeating "facts" (some of which are incorrect) about Griffith's life and works and rehashing familiar cinematic legends. But behind all this is a serious and thoughtful effort by Hitchcock to reveal the essence of Griffith's ability and achievement; to use him as an illustration of the challenges, responsibilities, and characteristics of a cinematic auteur; and not only to directly acknowledge his great personal debt to Griffith but also to fashion Griffith's life as an inspirational fable useful to him at this time in his career, when he was, as Spoto notes, "confused and professionally adrift" (149). This essay confirms that for Hitchcock, Griffith was the master's master, his ally, and in many ways his double.

Griffith's strengths are almost mythological, and he seems to be as much Ulysses as Columbus, especially the Tennysonian Ulysses, tinged with pathos as well as heroism in his perennial effort "to strive, to seek, to find, and not to yield." As Hitchcock tells it, cinema had stalled in 1907, held in place by the "mass of regulated opinion," and desperately needed a push from someone with "not only the perception of greater things in the future of the screen, but the driving force and independence with which to insist upon experiments and to carry them out successfully." Griffith's innovations take on increasing value as Hitchcock describes them. They first appear to be technical matters, but ultimately they stand for something more far-reaching: our pathway into modernity and the fulfillment of what we are, at our best, as human beings—creative, forward-looking, and courageous. Just as Columbus was more than a sailor, Griffith is more than a filmmaker.

Hitchcock credits Griffith with a variety of specific improvements in filmmaking, including the reaction shot, soft-focus, and the development of not only the war picture but also the large-budget film. His "discoveries" include numerous actors who went on to become great stars, and there is perhaps some intimation here that Griffith played an active role in the transformation of a Gladys Smith into a Mary Pickford. One of Hitchcock's most intriguing claims is that Griffith's *The Avenging Conscience* was "the forerunner and inspiration of most of the modern German films," a statement that may prompt a useful reconsideration and modification of what we normally think of as the German influence on Hitchcock. But the innovation he spends the most time on is the close-up, and the tale he tells is very revealing, whether or not it is historically accurate. When Griffith proposed that "shots should be taken close enough to show expression on the human face," his cameraman, Billy Bitzer, not only "threatened to walk out" but "*did* walk out" when Griffith persisted with his plan. At stake in this battle is not only film form but also who controls the making of a film. At that time, "the all-important personage in the studio was the cameraman," so the drama surrounding the development of the close-up is very much about the birth of the director as the presiding force in filmmaking. (Hitchcock's own ambivalence about cinematographers surfaces memorably later in his career when he famously and not entirely jokingly says, "I wish I didn't have to shoot the picture.")

Hitchcock describes the innovation of the close-up as "revolutionary," and especially when combined with Griffith's other innovations, the revolution is far-reaching. One of Griffith's major accomplishments was that he not only forged but also "obtained popular recognition of the new art-form." Fighting the public's tendency to infantilize and trivialize cinema, Griffith brought maturity and respect to the latest of the lively arts, and through his efforts its "legitimacy . . . was publicly acknowledged." Beneath Hitchcock's simple comment—"that was a great step forward"—is the awareness that something truly momentous had happened, akin to the discovery of a new land of enormous promise, opportunity, and profit.

Griffith's personal drama becomes particularly prominent and significant as the essay builds to its conclusion. After languishing for some time, written off as a "man whose career the world thought finished," Griffith came back to life: dreaming again of "great new voyages." Hitchcock had every reason not only to admire but also to identify with Griffith at this time. He too was languishing, several years past the great success of *Blackmail* and several years before his breakthrough spy thrillers, and in general "running for cover." In "A Columbus of the Screen" the story told of the birth and also the rebirth of the director may have been exactly what Hitchcock needed for consolation and inspiration, as he too faced the same daunting challenge as his mentor: "a man who has built up for himself such a giant reputation has an uphill task to keep that reputation intact." Hitchcock's stirring homage to Griffith indicates that he carries not only Griffith's torch but his burdens as well.

"Running for cover" in the years just preceding *The Man Who Knew Too Much*, a time not only of self-doubt and worry but also of some public concern about whether Hitchcock's career was "finished," led him in several directions. He continued to direct films of scattered kinds, with mixed results: four of the six he made between 1930 and 1934 are on just about everyone's list of his least interesting or accomplished works. But he also turned to a new role in filmmaking, and his brief article "Britain Must Be Great" announces his "appointment as a production supervisor at the B.I.P. Studios at Elstree" and expresses some of his ideas on the responsibilities of his position and the relationship between a director and a producer. These two terms were often used interchangeably in the early days of film but had increasingly come to be distinguished and, at least in some circles, defined as adversarial. Hitchcock outlines what characterizes an ideal producer, indicates why he is particularly well-suited for such a job, and stresses the overall importance of this position.

He notes that he is uniquely prepared for his new job because of his long experience doing just about everything related to filmmaking, including art design, editing, writing, operating a camera, and directing. In other writings and interviews, this comprehensive expertise defines him as a director, but here it is required of a "good producer," who "must have every thread of the film in his hands and be entirely answerable for the success of every department." The creation of a film rests on auteurial activities on the part of both the director and the producer, but the former's tasks are somewhat circumscribed: "The director, as I see it, is answerable solely for the handling of the human material—for getting the most out of the actors on the set." The producer takes care of everything else: "All the rest should carry the producer's stamp—script, sets, treatment, choice of staff, and cast." Hitchcock acknowledges the partnership required for great films: there may not have been a Murnau without a Pommer at work in the studio, doing substantive creative work and upholding "high standards" without his directors "losing their own individuality."

Hitchcock's underlying argument is that for Britain's cinema to "be great," as the title implores, echoing one of the perennial pleas in film circles of the time, it must have a great producer, and he is up to the challenge of, in effect, becoming Britain's Eric Pommer. In the 1920s Hitchcock was heralded as the great hope for British cinema as a director, and now in the 1930s he attempts to position himself as the great hope for British cinema as a producer. He ends the article by stressing how dedicated he is to the task of renovating the film industry, already casting his eyes on several people as part of his plan to "train a new generation of directors and players."

But Hitchcock was surely at least beginning to envision a future for himself as far more than Britain's Pommer. The awareness that he has the experience and talents that qualify him as both the ideal director and the ideal producer and that both roles are essential creative forces in filmmaking leads logically and perhaps inevitably to the conclusion that the true auteur is the producer-director. His immediate goal at this time may have been to "produce a group of Elstree pictures that will win a place on their own merit on the screens of the world," but his ultimate goal was to set himself in a position where he could make a group of Hitchcock pictures, bearing his "stamp" in all ways, that would win such a place.

The next article in this section jumps ahead more than twenty years, and while it doesn't rebut his common insistence that the auteur, as defined above, is ultimately the one who must preside over the making of a film, he acknowledges other elements that have a palpable effect as something other than distractions, obstacles, and intractable material. In a brief essay discussing his then-current film, *The Man Who Knew Too Much,* the experience of remaking a film that he had made some twenty years earlier prompts what he realizes is a dangerous "look backwards," awakening nostalgia for "the good old days" and sharpening his awareness of how the conditions of filmmaking have become quite a bit more difficult. As it turns out, though, this is not all bad. He gives a detailed and in some respects surprising explanation of why the remake is a better film than the original: because he had to respond creatively to the fact that "now *audiences know too much.*"

In contrast with what he said in "An Autocrat of the Studio," Hitchcock now points out that audiences have "become so deucedly sophisticated." Those who watch his films are no longer children, and "life would be a lot easier for me if they hadn't grown up." His effort here, though, is not so much to complain as to highlight how he responds to a new challenge, one that he captures in a scenario that he would describe repeatedly in later writings and interviews: he envisions filmgoers returning home and gathering around a refrigerator to cut up both a "cold chicken" and the film that they have just watched, analyzing and criticizing "a perfectly passable bit of entertainment . . . to the point that by the following morning the picture involved has become an intolerable bore." Hitchcock's very revealing fantasy—which bears a striking resemblance to the "Hate Parties" that he and his colleagues often indulged in after they went to film screenings (McGilligan, 76)—is that films he elsewhere describes as intended to "put the audience through it" routinely suffer the same fate at the hands of the audience.

His new responsibility is clear: "Today the director must anticipate this dissection" and take great pains to make films that stand up to the close inspection and high expectations of the audience. In particular, "the movie-goer actually expects a story to make sense," so scripts need to be carefully prepared, "with an eye to clarifying every detail," explaining and unifying everything. The visual details of a film also need close attention to ensure freshness, consistency, and accuracy: audiences now "demand authenticity and realism." Hitchcock bemoans the loss of some freedoms that he had during an era "when you could make a movie casually and informally." But ultimately his approach to filmmaking is, of course, neither casual nor informal, and it makes sense for him to recognize "the movie-goer and his refrigerator" as essential parts of the apparatus of pure cinema and to pay tribute to a new audience whose "capacity for chicken and criticism certainly is responsible for the improvement of motion picture entertainment through the years."

One of the purposes of this present volume is to supplement the most comprehensive source of Hitchcock's comments on his own films and filmmaking in general, Truffaut's *Hitchcock,* assembled primarily out of material generated from a week-long series of conversations between them in August 1962. But much valuable material in their epic conversations was not included in the published volume. Truffaut's editing of the raw material was masterful but involves substantial omissions and reshaping. The unedited recordings reveal even more about Hitchcock than we might otherwise know, by allowing us to hear him directly, speaking in his own words.

Toward that end, in this section I include a sequence in the conversations not carried over into Truffaut's book. It captures a moment when there is a sudden shift from the usual focus on either "Hitchcock on Hitchcock" or "Truffaut on Hitchcock" to "Hitchcock on Truffaut," as I have titled this excerpt in which they

discuss theoretical notions of Hitchcockian pure cinema applied to practical problems in shooting and editing *The 400 Blows*. Even though the ostensible subject is
a film by Truffaut, their comments provide a case study of how Hitchcock would
approach a sequence, and the exchanges outline a remarkable compendium of
Hitchcock's techniques, motifs, and concerns.

The excerpt I include begins at a point when Truffaut turns the discussion again
to *North by Northwest*. Truffaut's question about whether Hitchcock was "pleased
with Eva Marie Saint" prompts a detailed description of his extraordinary effort to
"groom" not just her in particular but each of his featured actresses. He wants it
known that "every look was directed," in a process that is not only strenuous but
also distressing for him: he confesses "the heartaches I've had, and the pain, and
the emotion I've poured into the thing." Given that he is speaking specifically
about working both with Eva Marie Saint and with Tippi Hedren, at a time when
he was making *The Birds,* these comments provide an ironic counterpoint to
Hedren's now widely known stories of what she portrays as her victimization and
abuse by Hitchcock. In any event, vulnerability and betrayal are very much on
Hitchcock's mind at this point in his conversation with Truffaut, moments before
an extended discussion of a pivotal scene in *The 400 Blows* that focuses on these
specific themes.

Truffaut brings up his own film after Hitchcock comments on editing in terms
of tempo and the careful control of subjective and objective points of view, and
Truffaut's description of how he constructed one particular sequence—where
Antoine sees his mother in the street kissing her lover—provides an opportunity
for Hitchcock to tell how he would have shot and edited it. Not surprisingly, the
alternating accounts of Truffaut and Hitchcock at work are very much in synch.
Hitchcock immediately slips into the interrogative mode characteristic of his
method of planning a sequence: raising questions to ensure that all details relevant
to the sequence are well thought out in advance and properly addressed. He
focuses on the fundamental question from which others radiate—"from a story
point of view, what was the intention?"—followed by a direct statement of one of
the guiding principles of pure cinema: "I would have hoped that there was nothing
spoken." He then gives a quick version of how he would shoot and edit the scene,
revealing, as we might expect, that his main building block is the gaze. Both he and
Truffaut envision a sequence that revolves around a complex visualization of characters looking at but also away from each other, with the latter motif of the averted
gaze particularly critical in conveying the shame, inwardness, hurt, and anger that
is at the emotional core of this and, as it turns out, other sequences as well.

Truffaut dominates the remainder of the discussion by offering a detailed
description of a later sequence—Antoine at school, punished in front of his class-
mates for lying and playing hooky—structured around a variety of gazes, including Antoine's downward look of isolation, humiliation, and vulnerability in the

midst of a sea of varied looks at him. Truffaut's technical analysis is clearly framed as an homage, intended primarily to illustrate his debt to Hitchcock, relating one instance presumably of many "where I really got out of difficulties by thinking of you, what you would have done." And this is an orientation that turns out to be doubly Hitchcockian, because it not only leads him to carefully preplan his sequences, a key element of Hitchcock's method, but also defines this preplanning as basically an effort "to try to think of how you would handle that scene."

What makes this part of their conversation particularly valuable is that it not only recounts the specific lessons of the master but also enacts "what would Hitchcock do?" The comments of these two directors—each on himself—are informative and instructive about the essence of Hitchcockian pure cinema and, at the risk of hyperbole, magically overlaid with an uncanny time-shifting aura as Hitchcock and Truffaut are shown at work, "collaborating" on a film that Truffaut had already made.

One of Hitchcock's most extended and focused discussions about the preeminence of the director comes not in an interview, a publicity piece, or an article in a film journal or magazine, but in a legal deposition reminding us that the debate over auteurism also involves professional credit, property rights, power, and profit. The "Declaration of Alfred Hitchcock," filed in May 1967, was an important part of the response of the Directors Guild of America (DGA) to an attempt by the Writers Guild of America (WGA) to substantially broaden the ability of writers to gain "possessory credit."

Hitchcock's role in this group action was critical, and his "Declaration" is, unique among his writings, a detailed biographical statement, theoretical manifesto, and practical (and remarkably successful) intervention. His first concern is to establish his credibility as a spokesperson for directors' rights, and he does so by giving a detailed résumé of his long experience in Great Britain and the United States, his Academy Awards and nominations, and the enormous number of television shows that he has produced. But his underlying emphasis is on how all of this has been accompanied by possessory credit: the television shows (all 363 of them) bear his name and "a caricature of his likeness," and throughout the declaration when he refers to his films made over the last two decades, he does so by giving the full titles as they appear on-screen, on the marquee, and in advertising (in increasingly large letters): Alfred Hitchcock's *Stage Fright,* Alfred Hitchcock's *Rear Window,* Alfred Hitchcock's *The Birds,* and so on. The intimation is that the director is as important as the film and in fact over time more important than any individual film.

Possessory credit for the director is a long-standing tradition, but Hitchcock also makes an effort to clarify its ongoing rationale. It is an essential part of creating a recognizable, distinctive, and desirable brand that links, calls attention to, and predisposes audiences to seek out and respond positively to the films that he

makes. He identifies his particular brand and stakes out his territory very succinctly: "In fact, I believe my name has become known to motion picture audiences throughout the world as a trade-mark for the startling, out-of-the-ordinary
psychological suspense mystery film." Essential to his success is the repetition and
reconfirmation of his possessory credit in "the hundreds of thousands of newspaper clippings, articles and paid advertising which have been utilized to exploit my
name." Failure to recognize and identify him as the auteur of his films would
undermine his "box office value." For all that Hitchcock is usually the custodian of
pure cinema, here he speaks up for other equally important practical matters: "I
have always considered my name and reputation to be the most valuable property
right owned by me . . . and if I am prevented from using this trade-mark identification in the future, I shall be deprived of my most valuable asset." The Shakespear-
ean echo, whether intended or not, is apt: in Hollywood in particular, he who
steals my good name makes me poor indeed (*Othello* 3.3.159–61).

The introduction to the interview that concludes this section mentions that the
questions Hitchcock responds to were asked by a group of Columbia University
film students as they all sat around a centerpiece composed of two of the key elements of his latest film, *Frenzy,* which they had just watched. Using the title "Of
Potatoes and Neckties" would be a witty Hitchcockian variant of Lewis Carroll's
call to talk "of cabbages and kings" and would convey the delightful and far-
ranging character of the interview, touching on assorted topics low and high, from
concrete production details (including a discussion of what went into the potato
truck sequence in *Frenzy* besides potatoes) to more sophisticated observations
about film theory and history.

The students steer him to many interesting and often interrelated topics, and
his comments are often fresh and occasionally surprising. For example, he reiter-
ates some of his favorite points in defining the essence of pure cinema, complain-
ing about films that are "photographs of people talking" and correcting the
common notion that "galloping horses are cinema." But when he describes the
Kuleshov experiment yet one more time, it is not primarily to illustrate how montage creates meaning, manipulates an audience, or demonstrates the power of the
director to shape the film by the choice and order of the images, but rather to
underscore the way film can "create a thought process."

What comes through particularly clearly throughout this interview is how an
emphasis on montage is tied to his more far-reaching conception of a film as a
carefully planned, unified, integrated, sequential whole. When the students ask
him about shots, he responds by talking about the overriding importance of coor-
dinating and combining shots. When the students ask him if he admires "exquisitely framed films," he acknowledges that there are "very good pictorial directors,"
like Joseph Sternberg and the Mexican cinematographer Gabriel Figueroa,
but then he caricatures their art as an unambitious lesser achievement: merely

photographing beautiful images for which, in effect, "God is the art director" is an abdication of the real challenges and responsibilities of a filmmaker. Pure cinema is not contained in one frame or a mere accumulation of individual frames, no matter how pictorially beautiful they may be.

The lively anecdotes he tells have a common theme: his ongoing struggle to rein in the anti-cinematic centrifugal forces he confronts. These include actors, who often resist the primary requirement "to do as they're told" and are unaware that this commandment makes their need to rehearse of secondary importance and their suggestions "of very little help"; composers, over whom the director has "absolutely no control" and whose music that is often unchangeably "already orchestrated" may not suit the more important orchestration of the entire film; and producers, whose pressure to radically modify the ending of such films as *Rebecca, Suspicion,* and *Topaz* typifies their ignorance of how disruptive such interference is to the carefully unified and integrated design that is Hitchcock's primary goal.

There are numerous brief but important miscellaneous comments throughout this interview on such topics as his "experiments with sound" in *Frenzy,* orchestration of color not so much for representational accuracy as for expression and effect, and concern for "pulling an emotion out of an audience," which keeps him from becoming "a self-indulgent director." A film may be made by a director, but he says very clearly that "the whole power of film is that it belongs to so many people on a given night." The culmination of a carefully constructed film is a powerful shared experience.

Finally, Hitchcock doesn't often mention directors by name, so his few particular references here are worth close attention. Several are qualified: he brings up Lois Weber and Ida Lupino as exceptions that prove the rule that women directors are an anomaly because of the "root problem" that he states categorically: "I don't think men will take orders from women"; and as noted above, he admits that Sternberg and Figueroa are good directors but of a lesser kind of picture. (Whether consciously or not, this echoes John Grierson's stinging description of Hitchcock as the "best director of unimportant pictures.") But his tone changes markedly when someone brings up Lubitsch, and his unqualified admission, "Yes, I think that Lubitsch was one of the principal men that I admire," is not the least of the many provocative moments in this important interview and may perhaps inspire a long overdue examination of the numerous ways that the Hitchcock touch is grounded in the Lubitsch touch.

AN AUTOCRAT OF THE FILM STUDIO

"An Autocrat of the Film Studio" was originally published in *Cassell's Magazine,* January 1928, 28–34.

The most important development of the film will be its entire severance from both the stage and the novel, and the command of a medium of its own. It should be a medium of itself, and cannot reach what I should call absolute perfection until it can function irrespective of the book and the stage. That is to say, it must be capable of telling a story in its own way, which will be in a way different from both the stage and the novel. Today it takes something from both.

A NEW DEVELOPMENT

How is this change to be brought about? As near as I can describe it I should say by the substitution of a series of moving tableaux which tell a story without the aid of titles and captions. Experiments in this direction have not so far been remarkable for their success, but that does not disprove the desirability of the development. And for my part I shall do what I can to develop the film along these lines. It is a practical proposition and an achievement worth striving after.

So far as I can see at present the only other developments possible are on the mechanical side. The ideal film will be the colored stereoscopic film. This perfect film may come in fifty or thirty years. I do not hold out much hope of it coming sooner. But when it has arrived, and we have also the film which tells its own story without the aid of titles or captions, we shall have an entertainment with an identity all its own and capable of commanding equal attention with the theater and the novel.

So much for the film. Now for a word or two about personalities. First and foremost I should like it to be more widely known that a film director does not select casts for his pictures. At least, not in the way a vast congregation of film aspirants seem to think. They bombard me mercilessly with letters setting out their remarkable qualifications for making a name on the films.

An ideal film face is not necessarily superbly beautiful without artificial aids. It must be a strong face. That is, one with the features so clearly cut that the lights and shadows of photography get a real chance. The mouth, chin and forehead must be well formed and the eyes fairly deeply set. Each feature must be definite and firm, yet there must be a mobility of expression covering the whole range of human feelings or emotions, from mild surprise to a tornado of rage, from lukewarm interest to devouring passion.

Next to the face the legs are the most important part of the anatomy. The film aspirant of the fair sex must have a shapely pair of legs, or legs which match the character to be played. This is not to satisfy a special interest of any section of the community, as might—I am not going to be dogmatic about it—as might be the case with revue choruses. Don't forget the camera in film work. In this matter of personal appearance it is more a question of correct focus and lights and shades than a pleasing general appearance.

This would be plain to all if only cinema audiences would pay films the compliment of a more critical observation. If only the public would give the photoplay the same serious attention they give to stage plays, they would see these things for themselves. Unfortunately they will not—not yet, at all events. They are so careless and unobservant that it is only a case of "going to the pictures." Many do not even trouble to discover the titles of the films before taking their seats.

EARLY MEMORIES

My own mother has been to cinema shows in this casual way and vaguely felt a grudge against somebody or other because she found she had already seen the films. This is a flippant indifference which makes me very angry at times, more especially because it seems as if the public, my own mother among them, cannot take the film seriously. It is a grave fault and an injustice to a work of art and an industry worthy of intelligent support.

Perhaps I feel so keenly about it because films have always been important to me. Even as a boy I never went to a cinema merely for the sake of exciting entertainment. I studied films while taking my pleasure out of them. I formed the habit of thinking in the terms of the film wherever I went. I never saw a play in a theater without automatically visualizing the play as a film. With the arrogant bombast of youth—that is, inexperienced youth—I could settle the point immediately as to whether the play would make a good film or not. Similarly I decided which film had and which had not been worth the trouble and expense of creating.

I remember seeing Mrs. Belloc Lowndes's *Who Is He?* at the Haymarket and making up my mind there and then that there was a good film in it. That was my view years ago, and although experience taught me to modify that view, I was right in the main. Experience taught me that the stage presentation of the story would need to be drastically altered for the film, but the idea remained perfectly sound as a film proposition. Around this idea I evolved *The Lodger*, familiar by now to millions of cinema-goers. As a boy I saw possibilities in the play for the screen. As a man in my twenties I directed it—which was something the boy certainly did not dream of.

I tell this story only to illustrate my point, that when you take the trouble to study the film—a mental exercise which will not diminish your enjoyment by a fraction, but rather tend to increase it—you will really learn something about it. You will see in it more than you dream of at present.

The astonishing thing to me is that with all their indifference to the points which make or mar a film the public remain susceptible to their influence. By some miracle of sub-conscious understanding they know when a film is good and when another is bad. It is the director's business to know how to produce the film which embodies all those points likely to meet with the approval of his critical yet untaught public. He is a kind of film father providing for his family. The family know what they like, but are sublimely ignorant of all that has gone to the making of their feast.

Let me disillusion them about one detail. All the romance is in the story, not in the film making. The average applicant for a film test has no idea at all of the workaday, unromantic atmosphere of a studio. It is nothing more than an "emotion factory." Emotions of many varying sorts, shades, degrees and colors have to be *manufactured,* and all must be photographically clear. There are innocent people abroad who sincerely believe they can portray a vast range of emotions with little or no experience before the camera. They see only the finished product, the completely *manufactured article* on the screen; they are swayed by the emotions photographed for their benefit and on the way home earnestly tell themselves and each other "they are sure they could act for the film."

They are entirely oblivious to the fact that the emotions from which they are suffering—I say "suffering" because they are temporarily abnormal—have been created for them by the camera, that before they came under the influence of the combined attack of the director, the artistes and the camera, their emotional nature lay dormant. If they really think they can become so emotional at will and draw sympathetic response from people who have paid away good money to see the show, let them give a dumb play before their friends. When they can do this in the presence of a multitude of distractions, say in the midst of a cabinet making factory with determinedly indifferent people moving about them, and can make their friends love as they love, hate as they hate, laugh as they laugh, cry as they cry, feel with them their every mood and fancy, then will they be justified in saying to themselves, "I am sure I can act for the film." All I say is, let them try. Until they have tried they cannot realize how difficult is this business of "emotion manufacture."

Not only is tremendous patience required to achieve perfection but in the studio the novice must be prepared for the assaults of a very commercially-minded critic in the person of the director. Remember, the director is a business man as well as an artist. He must produce something he can sell; something he has got to sell. And he is not making something which costs only a few thousand pounds, as is the theatrical producer. He has to spend anything from £100,000 to £1,000,000 on one production and he has got to get that money back with a legitimate percentage of profit.

It is no wonder that he appears autocratic. He *is* the autocrat of the studio, and he has *got* to be. His brusqueness, which may make it hard for the lovers before the camera to act as if they really "meant it," is a natural consequence of his determination to have the thing done properly in view of the enormous loss which follows if it is not done properly. He is not a bully at heart, but the novice might be forgiven for thinking he is. The star, always a person with experience, knows differently, but the star is no less than the novice subject to some pretty rough handling at times. All come under the omnipotent autocrat of the studio.

Not that cave-man methods are the only sort employed. It depends upon the temperament of the artiste, whether he is brusque or persuasive. It certainly does not depend upon the status of the artiste. Once the director has made up his mind how to get the best from the artiste—whether world-famous star or unknown novice—he adapts his methods to the nature of temperament of the individual. With some the gentle, persuasive method is best. With others only a raging, tearing temper will bring them into his line. The director must therefore be a student of psychology as well as an artist and a business man.

Virginia Valli was a type to be cajoled. Not because she was a great star, but because her temperament was such that rough treatment upset her and she could not give of her best. On the screen she was a lively vivacious character and played the part splendidly. Actually hers was a quiet, subdued nature which called for delicate handling.

Nita Naldi, whom I have always regarded as the world's greatest "vampire," was entirely opposite to Virginia Valli. Off the screen site she was as vivacious as Miss Valli was subdued. On the screen she was a cold, calculating, measuring vamp. Indeed, she was what we call the complete vamp. That is, she could play all kinds of "vampire" parts brilliantly—the baby vamp, meaning a girl in her teens; the youthful vamp; one a few years older and less obvious in her methods; and the vamp which Americans call "the gold digger," the sophisticated woman who can disguise her vamping or indulge in an orgy of it according to the character of the victim.

I never had to mind my "p's" and "q's" with Nita Naldi. Brusqueness did not matter a pin to her. She was temperamentally fitted to withstand any onslaught. She was, too, a wonderful artiste, and now that she has gone to live in retirement in France the cinema world has lost one of its real jewels.

My impression is that the age of the "vampire" has passed. It was a vogue which belonged to the early days of the film and nowadays people do not care for obvious vamping. They do not object to being made fully aware of the intentions of the love-thief, but sheer, blatant vamping is no longer interesting. The subtle, cajoling woman who is fighting for her love with no mercenary motive at all is preferred to the obvious vamp. She has in a sense replaced the vamp.

Whether it is a reflection of the times I am not prepared to say, but if the popularity of film stories implies anything at all, it is that love counts more today with women than sheer pelf. Women will sympathize with a woman struggling to get possession of the man she loves, even though she has no moral right to him. On the other hand, they have little patience with the type who merely want the men who can give them an abundance of this world's goods.

MAKING HER SMILE!

Ivor Novello and Isabel Jeans are two other artistes with whom I have found it delightfully easy to work. It has been unnecessary for me to watch for foibles which must be avoided to get the best from these two artistes. Sometimes I have had to resort to tricks and catch them unawares to get the result I aimed at, but I have never had to lose my temper to get them into the right pose and really tell a story in action and expression.

The most I have had to do with Isabel Jeans has been to recite a childhood legend to make her smile in her sleep. That happened when I had her tucked up in bed in a scene in *Easy Virtue*. She had to smile through her dreams. She smiled several times, but it was not the sort of smile I wanted. I cannot explain in cold print the infinite varieties of the smile, but this time I wanted one belonging rightfully to innocent slumber and peaceful dreaming.

To repeat the legend would spoil the story and might interfere with the effect when you see the film—that is, for those of you who have not already seen it. Besides, one cannot reproduce here the atmosphere of the setting when the scene was "shot." I tell the story only to illustrate my remark that a simple device of this sort was all I needed to aid me in getting from Miss Jeans just the exact expression I wanted.

THE AWKWARD AUTHOR

I might tell some stories of dealings with authors who have to be convinced that they are all wrong in their ideas when their stories are being filmed. As a rule they are all wrong, but it would be better to be tactfully silent as to individuals. I would certainly never employ a famous writer to turn out a film story for me. For this reason, famous writers are artistes who write by inspiration. When they write to order they are so far below their best that it is ten chances to one they will turn out poorer stuff than the gifted hack. But then I do not favor writing to order by anyone. If there is a story in a man's brain he will tell it, and it is almost bound to be worth the telling. And if he is writing for the film with a knowledge of his medium it will be well worth filming.

Scenario writers, or rather a multitude of people who send me scenarios, fail to appreciate the fact that without a knowledge of their chosen medium they cannot hope to turn out an acceptable story. All you good and kind literary people who bombard me with scenarios can place me everlastingly in your debt by holding on to your scripts until you have mastered more technical details. And, incidentally, you will save yourself a mountain of wasted labor.

Naturally, I want the co-operation of all who know anything about film stories and their making, but those who know nothing are worse than a hindrance to themselves and to me. Now I will tell you a secret. I want two good stories. But I am sorry to disappoint you. I am going to write them myself.

One will be about railways and the other about our mercantile marine. Both are magnificent services with a wealth of possibilities in romance. Neither has been exploited in English films. For obvious reasons I cannot say more at present. Perhaps I have said too much as it is.

So far as the English film is concerned, I am convinced that it lacks the incentive theme and, therefore, lags behind the American. Artistically, the English film is as good as anything turned out in America. But in how many American films do you see the village youth leaving home, fighting adversity, winning his way through and finally returning to live near his native cottage, but in marble halls and with the girl of his youth adorning the magnificence in beautiful bridal array!

It may be all banal and highly sentimental, exaggerated even to flunkeys, but there is something incentive about it all. The young man and the young woman, ardent lovers, see themselves in the places of the hero and heroine and they enjoy a wonderful journey through the flowering, perfumed land of make-believe. They hug themselves and each other in ecstatic joy under cover of the darkened cinema, and then———?

What happens? They resume their ordinary daily English round, coming to earth with a bump and realize that in their lives there is no real incentive. Politics apart—and they are the last thing I would discuss anywhere—where is the incentive in British industry? Perhaps characteristic English home-life is the wrong kind of soil for the incentive plant to flourish in, being too home-spun.

The life of incentive, of big endeavor and handsome reward, runs through the American film, and because it is something different from the run of things in England, English youths flock to see the American film. It takes them out of themselves and gives them something to look at which is utterly different from what they can themselves experience.

There is a marvelous field of opportunities for the English producer who will try to understand the characteristics of his own people and work from the clues they give him. Million and two-million pound spectacular productions are not needed. Our people want stories throbbing with life, magnificent in effort, clean in humor and rich in romance. And that I believe I shall continue to put into practice as a director.

Let me close with a word about my own routine. Both at home and at the studio there is always a large post to be gone through. The more persistent among the ambitious ferret out my home address, with the result that letters pour in upon my inoffensive head even before I can sit down to breakfast.

As a hint to those concerned, I may add that the invasion of what little privacy I get over my eggs and bacon does not help their cause.

By nine-thirty every morning I am at the studio, and there I delve once again into a prodigious mail. But the subsequent sorting out of letters I have to leave to my secretary. Those dealing with scenarios go to the story department, and applications for employment on the screen go to the casting department—if they go anywhere at all.

DEALING WITH TEMPERAMENT

Then I go to the projection theater where I inspect all the sets photographed the previous day. I think it is common knowledge that each set has to be photographed several times, which, incidentally, adds a respectable lump to the total mountain of expense in making a film. The several sets are run off before me and I then select the best. If none come up to scratch, the set has to be acted over again several more times.

This is not necessarily caused by inefficiency of the artistes. Sometimes they are not in the mood for the particular work in hand. As a rule I can detect temperamental defects during a setting, and when I do, the filming is abandoned. Neither "bullying" nor coaxing will avail in such circumstances. If the artistes are, as it were, out of gear, it is better to send them home. I do.

The previous day's work reviewed, I pass them to the "floor," or the stage where the acting is done, and inspect the make-up of artistes detailed for the day's filming. My production secretary will have already decided upon the section of the story to be photographed and ordered the attendance of artistes.

A DAY'S WORK

Stars do not attend this inspection, for they can generally be trusted to make-up properly. Sometimes they fail, and when they do they also have to retire and re-makeup. It is essential that all taking part in the day's work before the camera must be perfectly made-up, otherwise the lights and shades would be out of joint.

Next I go through the day's work mapped out by my production secretary—sometimes called "floor" secretary. She keeps a complete diary of the details of the production, of the artistes who have to be called and the possible order of filming the story.

These tasks usually fill in the morning and there is an hour's break for lunch. At two o'clock I deal with interviewers, and it would surprise some people how many interviews I can get through in the allotted half-hour. The afternoon is given up to "shooting" scenes or sets until six or seven p.m., after which I spend an hour going over "takes" and selecting the best for connected exhibition the next morning. Nine o'clock, dinner at home and then "house" interviews. That is, if anybody has been lucky enough to force me to break a rule.

I object to working more than twelve hours a day, but sometimes it can't be avoided. Holidays! I never take them like other people. Since January 1st I have had three days off. All the others, including Sundays, I have been compelled to keep my nose to the grindstone. But I am not grumbling. The film is my baby, and who can tire of his baby?

A NEW "CHAIR" WHICH A WOMAN MIGHT FILL

Roger Burford

"A New 'Chair' Which a Woman Might Fill," by Roger Burford, was originally published in the *Gateway for Women at Work* 1, no. 3 (July 1929): 100–103.

No profession is quite as exciting as making films: every talent is called for in the film director, and a very severe physical, mental and psychic strain is imposed. Thousands or tens of thousands of pounds are at stake, and the effort is highly concentrated for three or four months, during which there can be no other preoccupation of any sort. Hardly a woman's job, one would think. Yet there are a few woman film directors, of whom Dorothy Arzner is the only one to be widely known. She has made about half a dozen effective comedies with a feminine viewpoint. Among these are *Ten Modern Commandments* and *Manhattan Cocktail,* which have been commercial successes, though not in the highest rank of films.

The prizes in the film industry are glittering, and there is scarcely any prejudice against woman, as woman, in any branch of the cinema, where capacity is the only criterion: it seemed to me that the opinions of two of the best known English film directors would be of the greatest interest, even though there are all the chances against a woman's name reaching the back of one of the canvas chairs of the studio, except in the capacity of actress.

MR. ALFRED HITCHCOCK'S VIEWS

Alfred Hitchcock made his name with *The Ring,* the first English film to compete with the artistic experiments of the German cinema. It was a success everywhere, and he was invited to join British International Pictures, at Elstree, at a salary which was a newspaper sensation. Since then he has made *The Farmer's Wife, Champagne,* with Betty Balfour, and *The Manxman.* He is now making a talking picture, *Blackmail.* He is a man of ideas, with a real grasp of the visual medium of the cinema, and a great fertility of invention.

"It is not so much the lack of the necessary physique that would prevent a woman from making a good film director," he told me, "but rather the smaller scope of the life she may be expected to have experienced."

"I think women are less versatile in observation than men, who have more 'angles on life.' And scope of observation is fundamental in creating an impression of reality. The film director is called upon to portray life in *all* its aspects. The most versatile man can only have a certain amount of experience, and no one should undertake a subject of which he has not first hand knowledge. Of course," he added, "I am thinking of a woman *as* a woman, and not of the type who should have been a man."

DOMESTIC SPACES

I suggested that women were specially qualified to treat domestic subjects. "That is so," he admitted, "but I believe my argument still holds good. Diverse experience in other branches of life will still qualify the man to make a truer picture: the more he knows and feels about other things the more complicated, and therefore complete, will be his reactions."

When I reminded him that the larger proportion of the cinema public was feminine and that the first thought of the theater manager was "Will it appeal to the ladies?" his answer was ready and incisive.

"Would you expect a girls' school to be built by girls?" he asked, with a twinkle. I suggested that it might be profitable to take the opinions of the girls.

"I agree," he hastened to put in. "A woman could very likely produce some scenes even better than a man. I should call her in as an expert to advise, say, on a fashion parade, or on babies. My wife, who, as Alma Reville, writes scenarios and was responsible for the script of *The Constant Nymph,* has assisted me in certain films. I found that although she was of the utmost value so far as the story, and even the action went, some of the more unwieldy departments of film producing were difficult for her to control: the art department, for instance."

SHE MUST COMMAND!

"Novel writing, the easiest form of self-expression, is a more suitable medium for a woman. But supposing that an exceptionally gifted woman had set her mind on becoming a film producer, the qualities she would need are generalship, a masculine strain—for she would have to command men—and the capacity for decision. A film director must know exactly what effect he wants before he goes on the set, and never relax until he has achieved it. Indecision is fatal. A director would lose his grip at once if he had to rely on anyone else's brains for *anything*. He must have knowledge and experience of all the departments of film production, and he must know his tools so well that he is quite unconscious of them while he is working. A woman would find it difficult not to be self-conscious in the atmosphere of the studio.

"How could she gain the necessary experience and knowledge? Only by several years in a studio. She could begin at the bottom as a typist, and rise, through a position as floor secretary, to be assistant director or scenario writer, or she could begin half way by entering films with an established reputation as an artist, writer or theater producer. There is no regular method of breaking into films, it is always something of a fluke: but at the same time there is nothing to keep the best man, or woman, from the top."

WHAT CAPTAIN SUMMERS SAYS

Captain Walter Summers directs for British Instructional Films, a firm which also sponsors Anthony Asquith and Frank Wells. He produced many of the war films, but his finest work is *The Lost Patrol,* exceptional in its treatment and sincerity. He recently made a little fantasia, after the German fashion, on the Chamber of Horrors.

His attitude to women is less stern than Mr. Hitchcock's. He believes that a woman, if she had the flair and the talent, could make films, not technically better, but with more penetration, more *élan,* than men. "Her thoughts have more freedom—guided by instinct instead of convention she is more likely to search for, and find, truth, the cornerstone of art.

"There may be something in the idea that a woman *not* being a man, might therefore be a piquant critic of his behavior, and thus amuse men, and delight other women. But though she has intuition, her critical faculty, sharp as it is, is often distorted by her instinctive feelings, her likes and dislikes. One could imagine a class of film where this was not without its effect. Again, although a woman would seem to be specially qualified to treat of love, her view of it is likely to be too colored by the personal.

"It is hard for a woman to achieve directorship: woman is a commercial asset in films only as an actress. Wardour Street would laugh at the idea of a woman making commercially successful films. I think that if you find a woman capable of film direction, she would be more likely to turn out a masterpiece than a money-maker, but I for one would welcome her into our ranks with open arms."

A REALISTIC "ACCIDENT"

Mrs. Summers once played a plucky part in filming a street accident—a fall under a lorry.

Balks of woods were arranged to prevent the wheels of the lorry from actually touching her, but she still ran a considerable risk. The first two "takes" were no good, and finally she threw herself so violently against the radiator of the oncoming lorry, advancing far out of the safety zone for this purpose, that she was thrown to the ground several yards away. Her acting was so realistic that the ambulance men, who were to appear later, rushed in thinking that she was seriously hurt, and spoiled the take. But Mrs. Summers was ready to repeat it till it was perfect.

A COLUMBUS OF THE SCREEN

"A Columbus of the Screen" was originally published in *Film Weekly,* February 21, 1931, 9.

The Film Public—that Public which is the final judge of our efforts, the arbiter of our destiny, and the be-all and end-all of our professional existence—rarely lifts aside the thick veil before which the players perform, to catch a glimpse of the personality behind. It imagines a shadowy figure with a megaphone bawling confused orders, and leaves it at that—and it is just as well that it should be so, for the director is not usually a romantic figure, ready to capture the imagination.

INCOMPARABLY THE GREATEST

However, there are exceptions; and incomparably the greatest of these is David Wark Griffith, who has just completed his twenty-third year in connection with moving pictures, and who, in spite of his comparative youth—he is not yet fifty-one—is known affectionately and even reverently throughout the film world as "The Old Master."

A giant, this man Griffith, as successful pioneers must be. It is not only, or even chiefly, the hard work and the thought, the creative ability and the almost uncanny foresight for which we are indebted to him, but the fighting spirit which prompted him to force his way against opposition, to overcome prejudice, and to bore his persistent path through the mass of regulated opinion which held, in 1907, that moving pictures had attained their final level and their ultimate, perpetual form.

DRIVING FORCE AND INDEPENDENCE

As to his qualifications, he certainly touched life at many points, as newspaper reporter, dramatic critic, actor, book salesman, free-lance journalist, "puddler" in an ironworks, rust-scraper, hop picker, dramatist, film actor, scenario writer, and, finally, director—albeit this last in the days when the all-important personage in a studio was the cameraman, and a director was rather less than the dust beneath his tripod-foot. However, Griffith has the distinction of having been the first of his line who really mattered, for he had not only the perception of greater things in the future of the screen, but the driving force and independence with which to insist upon experiments and carry them out successfully.

In these days of hundreds of thousands of pounds being lavished on a single film it is almost incredible that there should have been a serious split, amounting to a major crisis, in the old Biograph Company because Griffith kept his unit on location for half the night and ran the total cost of a production up to ten pounds! Yet that was considered mad extravagance in those groping days.

And this was nothing to the upheaval caused by his revolutionary suggestion that shots should be taken close enough to show expression on the human face. This was so wild, so fantastic, so utterly impossible an idea that Billy Bitzer, the all-powerful cameraman, threatened to walk out if it were proceeded with. It *was* proceeded with, and Bitzer *did* walk out—and the first close-up was recorded by his successor!

Bitzer's judgment seemed vindicated when the audience, thinking there was something wrong with the picture, hooted and yelled, "Where are their feet?" but the close-up has survived their disfavor, and even, though with greater difficulty, surmounted the obstacle of the talkies.

HIS DISCOVERIES

During his association with Biograph, D. W. Griffith tried out quite a number of players whom he considered promising, among them being a pretty girl named

Gladys Smith, who afterwards adopted the screen name of Mary Pickford; two sisters named Gish; Blanche Sweet, Owen Moore (who afterwards married Mary Pickford), Alice Joyce, Lionel Barrymore, Mabel Normand, Mack Sennett, Henry B. Walthall, Richard Barthelmess, and Constance Talmadge.

A formidable array—but even more vitally important than these were his discoveries in the realms of cinematography. In a film called *The Barrel,* long forgotten except as pure history, Griffith first cut away from a scene to show the reaction of bystanders. This, together with the close-up, gave the film its first mobility and thus its first advantage over stage plays.

Then, after he left the Biograph Company and found himself, in association with Mutual Reliance, actually in command of a sizeable sum of money, he "splashed" twenty-thousand pounds on *The Birth of a Nation.*

A GREAT STEP FORWARD

With this picture, at one stroke, the director obtained popular recognition of the new art-form. "The cinema," the world persisted, "is in its infancy"—oblivious of the fact that it was then twelve or fourteen years old. But the legitimacy of the child was publicly acknowledged, and that was a great step forward.

In *Hearts of the World* we had our first war picture. In *Broken Blossoms* (his first film with United Artists) we made the acquaintance of soft focus.

Hardly any filmgoer of today has ever heard of *The Avenging Conscience,* but that picture, made in the first year of the War, was the forerunner and inspiration of most of the modern German films, to which we owe so much artistically.

A long series of arduous voyages into uncharted seas, and explorations of unknown territories . . . and at last the traveller, weary but full of honors, put his slippered feet on the fender and began to dream. And in his dream he saw possibilities of great new voyages; gradually the old power came into his brain, the old joy of conquest into his heart, and the Old Master, the man whose career the world thought finished, set sail again and made *Abraham Lincoln,* one of the most moving and essentially true works of art ever accomplished.

THE OLD FIGHTING SPIRIT

It was not an easy voyage. A hundred new problems had arisen; and a man who has built up for himself such a giant reputation has an uphill task to keep that reputation intact. But he tackled the job with his old fighting spirit and his old thoroughness (he is said to have read 182 accounts of the life of Lincoln before beginning to outline the story)—with such result as the world will acclaim.

Remember David Wark Griffith; every time you go to the cinema you enjoy, in some indirect but plainly traceable form, the fruits of his labors; to the vast multitude of filmgoers he is the man who has contributed more than any other to the perfection of their entertainment; and to us who are endeavoring to explore new territories and to carry on his torch he is the honored Head of our profession.

BRITAIN MUST BE GREAT

"Britain Must Be Great" was originally published in *Film Pictorial,* April 30, 1932, 15.

This is not the first time there has been a producer in a British studio, although the producer here does not occupy the public eye to anything like the same degree as Samuel Goldwyn, Irving Thalberg or Howard Hughes in America, or Eric Pommer in Germany. But it is the first time, I think, that the job has ever been given to an ordinary working director on the studio staff.

I know about it from the bottom right enough. I suppose during the last ten years I have been everything that a man can be in a studio. I broke into the movies at the old Paramount studio at Islington, as a designer of art titles. I used to draw a sun rising out of a calm sea behind the caption, "Came the Dawn," and a nicely-bent candle, burning at both ends, beneath the words "The Life of the Gay City"! Since then I have been art director, cutter, scenario-writer, camera-man, assistant director, director, pretty well everything you can think of in film-making except the star and the performing dog.

The good producer must have every thread of the film in his hands and be entirely answerable for the success of every department. When you watch a man like Pommer at work in the studio, sitting in conference on the script of his films, supervising the sets, the camera-work, the sound, the choice of cast, and training directors all the while to adopt his high standards without ever losing their own individuality, you begin to realize what production means to an industry.

There are few of us who can hope to be a second Pommer, for that great little German who produced *Vaudeville* and *Siegfried,* and the talkies *The Road to Paradise* and *Congress Dances,* is one of the giants of the movies. But no one who has ever been lucky enough to watch him at work has any excuse for underrating the task of the producer. The director, as I see it, is answerable solely for the handling of the human material—for getting the most out of the actors on the set. If he does that well, he has fulfilled his job. All the rest should carry the producer's stamp—script, sets, treatment, choice of staff, and cast.

If I am to do my work at Elstree as I know it should be done, I have a busy year in front of me. I have, for a start, six stories to choose, directors, stars, six individual casts. I hope in the end to be able to bring in raw material from outside the industry, and train a new generation of directors and players. I have my eye on several people at the moment, who, I expect, have never heard of my existence and would be horrified to learn that I planned to make them into the talkie directors of the future! But that will take time. All worthwhile developments must come slowly and all worthwhile material must go through the mill. In the meantime I have my work cut out to select from existing material and to justify my appointment and John Maxwell's courage by producing a group of Elstree pictures that will win a place on their own merit on the screens of the world.

THE MAN WHO KNEW TOO MUCH

"*The Man Who Knew Too Much*" was originally published in *Films of the Year 1955–56*, ed. Peter Noble (London: Express Books, 1956), 33–35.

One shouldn't look backwards, I know, but there are times when even the most modern of us sigh and yearn for what are popularly called "the good old days." I seem to have been reminded of this more frequently in the last few weeks than ever before—during the filming in Marrakesh and in London of *The Man Who Knew Too Much*.

Because *The Man Who Knew Too Much* is frankly a remake of a picture I made in 1934, and because there has been no attempt to conceal the fact, the question asked of me most often is what is the difference between making a picture today and two decades ago. I can only answer that it is considerably more difficult. And if I doubted the fact before the present time, the expansive VistaVision version of the thriller has convinced me.

Making *The Man Who Knew Too Much* in 1934 with Leslie Banks, Edna Best, Nova Pilbeam, Pierre Fresnay and Peter Lorre (in his first English-speaking role) was a comparatively simple affair. We simply padded around London, made one location trip to the Riviera and the picture was in the bag. By the standards of the time, it was a success—a fanciful pursuit drama about a projected assassination in the Albert Hall, foiled by a husband and wife whose child has been held hostage by the assassins. It was a simple, direct and rather exciting script. And no one, it seemed, questioned the holes in the plot.

Today I couldn't possibly make *The Man Who Knew Too Much* as it was originally conceived for the very practical reason that now *audiences know too much.*

Mind you, I like audiences, and it is my business to please them. But life would be a lot easier for me if they hadn't grown up, and become so deucedly sophisticated. Moreover, I wish they would leave their refrigerators alone.

Where a few years ago people would go to a movie, take it for what it was, wander home quietly and pass on an endorsement to their friends the following morning, they now speed home in their streamlined cars and head directly for the refrigerator. Out of the deep freeze comes the cold chicken—in a matter of minutes a perfectly passable bit of entertainment has been dissected, analyzed and criticized to the point that by the following morning the picture involved has become an intolerable bore.

Today the director must anticipate this dissection. The movie-goer actually expects a story to make sense. A character cannot wander casually into the action as he used to. Now he must be explained. All the plot threads have to be coordinated. Scripts must be written with an eye to clarifying every detail. What this has done to *The Man Who Knew Too Much* is to improve the picture immeasurably. But it certainly has added to the labor involved.

As a location the Riviera would not be acceptable to the story, particularly since I had utilized the Blue Coast last year for *To Catch a Thief.*

So we chose Marrakesh, a place I had never seen although I had long pondered the possibilities of developing a chase through the Souks. I visited Marrakesh early in January, made a few photographs and by June our company was there ready to shoot. It would have been much easier to have to reproduce the Souks on a Hollywood or London stage, and twenty years ago one could have. Today audiences wouldn't accept a substitute. They demand authenticity and realism.

Similarly, we had to come to London to photograph parts of our story at the Albert Hall and at the Garrard Brothers' Taxidermist Shop. No one would have considered reproducing the Albert Hall in a film studio but conceivably a taxidermist establishment could be duplicated. Yet the moment I saw the photographs taken by Paramount in London of the hundred-year-old building with its priceless collection of stuffed gorillas, birds, zebras, cats and dogs, I knew I could not match the atmosphere anywhere else but on the spot. Again, I was thinking of the movie-goer and his refrigerator.

His capacity for chicken and criticism certainly is responsible for the improvement of motion picture entertainment through the years. And I am certainly agreeable to the idea of keeping up with him. But there are times when you wish you could travel a less prescribed road—when you could make a movie casually and informally—bringing in a character without explaining him and, maybe, even losing a principal player along the road.

This is how films used to be made, and I'm candid enough to admit it was a lot easier on the director!

HITCHCOCK ON TRUFFAUT

The transcription that I have titled "Hitchcock on Truffaut" is based on part 22 of the French radio broadcasts of selections from the original tapes in the Hitchcock Collection at the Margaret Herrick Library of the Hitchcock-Truffaut conversations (August 1962). I transcribe just the English, that is to say, Hitchcock's comments and Helen Scott's translations of Truffaut's French. (The only exceptions are several interjections by Truffaut worth preserving because they seem to me to be useful indications of his assent and even enthusiasm at key moments in the discussion.) I preface a statement with Helen Scott's name on a few occasions when she is not directly translating a comment by Truffaut but elaborating further on something that he already said. I have not corrected the occasional grammatical errors or incomplete sentences. Spaced periods in a sentence indicate a brief pause and, at the end of a sentence, indicate that the statement was interrupted by what follows.

TRUFFAUT: North by Northwest, *which we've already discussed considerably, on a number of occasions. I don't know what we might have forgotten about it. Were you pleased with Eva Marie Saint?*

HITCHCOCK: Well, I did my best to make her attractive. I, you know, watched every look and every, I did almost the same job with her that I did with Hedren in *The Birds*. Um, you know, she'd always played a kind of waif sort of part.

TRUFFAUT: *It's true, that changed her. She's good.*

HITCHCOCK: Yes, and as a result, here's one of the big problems in grooming girls: What happens when they get away from you? Eva Marie Saint then went into *Exodus*.

TRUFFAUT: *Ah, oui, oui.*

HITCHCOCK: And looked terrible, I'm told. Did you see *Exodus*?

TRUFFAUT: *I saw the picture and I like the picture, but throughout the whole picture, I kept on thinking that I was looking at Joanne Woodward, and afterwards I was told that this was Eva Marie Saint. I didn't realize it.*

HITCHCOCK: So you see what can happen. You take a girl, you groom her, you give her sophistication, you give her the technique of acting for the camera, and apparently, depending upon the girl, it doesn't always stick.

TRUFFAUT: *Preminger doesn't like the actors, I think.*

HITCHCOCK: Well, he chose her as a result of the scene in the dining car in *North by Northwest*. He made some remark about what wonderful direction that was of the girl. They were all retakes in that dining car scene, because I couldn't get the right understatement and all the sex.

TRUFFAUT: *Ah, oui.*

HITCHCOCK: You know, little details like when she's given a light from a lighter, to lean with her cigarette, and look into the man's eyes, and not with the cigarette. I mean her eyes were, every look was directed.

TRUFFAUT: *In the restaurant?*

HITCHCOCK: Yes, that's right.

TRUFFAUT: *Yes, that was very nice.*

HITCHCOCK: Yes, but this becomes a big problem. When you go to work on these girls and teach them how to use their face to convey thought, to convey sex, everything, in an unstated subtle way. Apparently one film isn't enough for them to learn it. It's like the problem I have with the Hedren girl, who does everything perfectly for me in this film. That's why I'm almost forced to put her into the *Marnie* part. If I were to loan her out now, what could happen? I mean, all the work I've done and all the heartaches I've had, and the pain, and the emotion I've poured into the thing, ends up nothing. Eva Marie Saint, you see, the effort: completely wasted. I know it's another consideration: the money alone that you spend on this is enormous. So many retakes, for example.

TRUFFAUT: *It would have interested me to discuss with you the scene with the wheat field. It's a very Hitchcockian scene, with the domination, with the mastery over the timing, which was very great. I think this scene lasted seven minutes.*

HITCHCOCK: Yes.

TRUFFAUT: *And there's something which we didn't discuss, for this type of scene, the style of editing. That is, in many pictures, in this case, there's an old tradition which is to accelerate the editing, where the shots . . .*

HITCHCOCK: Increasing the tempo, you mean?

TRUFFAUT: *Increasing the tempo. And it's something that you do almost the opposite. The shots are not longer and longer, but they remain very equal in their length.*

HITCHCOCK: Um hm. You were dealing with space. The length of the shots were to indicate the various distances that a man had to run for cover, but it went to show there was no cover he could go to. And the necessity for showing the full approach of the airplane, because it goes fast and if the shots are too fast, the airplane's in and out of the picture so quickly that you don't get an awareness, you aren't conscious enough. For example, in the, in some of the gull attacks at the children's party in *The Birds,* we still need shots showing gulls coming down. In other words, in theory, you shouldn't show that, because it should attack a person before they're aware of it. The girl in the boat, when the gull attacks her, it's in and out of the picture so quick that the audience might think it's a piece of paper coming in. Therefore, I had to, while the scene is subjective, the girl is watching the car or watching the dockside, suddenly something hits her. You see, you have to break a rule there, and show that gull just before it hits her. You must leave your subjective and deliberately go to the objective so the audience are aware of what is happening, which tends to lengthen the shots, you see. Now in the case of the airplane in *North by Northwest,* you had to prepare the audience for the threat of each dive. Prepare the audience for each dive of the plane. And that perhaps would account for the reason that the shots are long or they're the same way all the way through.

TRUFFAUT: *But I think, as a matter of fact, that the accelerated tempo in many pictures is a sort of, is an evasion of when they have problems, because in the editing the director has not been aware of the phenomenon of the swiftness of the events. Therefore he doesn't have enough material, so he cuts all the little pieces, like when someone is run over in the street, for instance. It's rarely satisfactory, satisfying, because . . .*

HITCHCOCK: You mean it happens too quickly?

TRUFFAUT: *In pictures as a rule, yes.*

HITCHCOCK: Well, I had the street accident in the hour show of television. It's the basis of the whole trial. So what I did was to show five scenes of people seeing the accident before I showed it, and hearing it. Five times. Then go to it, the end of it, afterwards, just when the man hits the ground and the motorcycle turns over and the offending car drives away. These are moments when you have to stop time.

TRUFFAUT: *In my first picture, The 400 Blows, I had the experience of this. When the kids were skipping school, the kid in the street met his mother with another man who wasn't his father, and I filmed very little material, particularly because when in the middle of the crowd, I did an exterior. But in the cutting room it was absurd. There was a look of the child towards its mother, and then when you see his back already, a look of the mother, and it was decidedly insufficient. And the way I got out of it is that I used all of the takes twice, the doubles.*

HITCHCOCK: Intercut, you mean.

TRUFFAUT: *Intercut, I mean.*

HITCHCOCK: Intercut?

TRUFFAUT: *But it was less good than if I had thought it out beforehand, because I would have had a variety.*

HITCHCOCK: Now describe to me in detail what the action was.

TRUFFAUT: *With the children, who instead of being in school were walking in the streets. And then they go across the street.*

HITCHCOCK: Yes.

TRUFFAUT: *The kids look towards the camera, a little bit towards the camera. I cut.*

HITCHCOCK: Are they walking toward the camera? Are you dollying across the street? Are you in a fixed shot?

TRUFFAUT: *No, the camera was held by, in the hand, and it was only made in panoramics.*

HITCHCOCK: I see, panning them across the street.

TRUFFAUT: *Panning them across the street. And then I cut over to the mother, and I showed . . .*

HITCHCOCK: You cut to the mother before the boy saw her?

TRUFFAUT: *No, the child saw her. You passed over her with the man, but she didn't see yet, she was not looking at the child yet. And you saw the children, who turned their faces away and kept on going, and then you show the mother who saw them walking away.*

HITCHCOCK: I mean that was the action. I'm not asking how it was shot. I'm asking from a story point of view, what was the intention?

TRUFFAUT: *It was to show that both of them had seen each other.*

HITCHCOCK: I see. In other words, in other words . . .

TRUFFAUT: *Both of them were in an abnormal situation because the child was seeing his mother with another man in the street and the mother didn't want to be seen on the street with another man by a child, because neither one nor the other could speak about it afterwards.*

HITCHCOCK: I realize that. But in other words, the boy saw his mother, and the mother was aware that the boy had discovered her with another man. Is that the scene? Did the boy have to know that his mother had seen him? In other words . . .

TRUFFAUT: *No, he, no, it's not certain, it's not definite.*

HITCHCOCK: Ah, well that's what I wondered. You see, I'm wondering whether the extra shouldn't have been the mother is aware that the boy has seen her with another man.

TRUFFAUT: *Yes, she says to the man, I'm sure he saw me.*

HITCHCOCK: Why does, I mean I would have hoped that there was nothing spoken.

TRUFFAUT: *Ah, oui, oui.*

HITCHCOCK: You see, that the boy, the cutting is this: Boy is coming along. He looks and he sees the mother going along there. The mother turns her head and sees the boy looking in her direction. The boy turns his head, embarrassed, and the mother turns her head, embarrassed. Now when they meet, with that, that in the background, they don't like to look at each other, they don't look at each other, they avoid each other's looks when they first meet again.

TRUFFAUT: *Yes, that's true. And I had another scene that was very difficult, where I really got out of difficulties by thinking of you, what you would have done. After having skipped school for a number of days, since he has no apology to give to the teacher for having played hooky, he does an idiotic thing. He tells the teacher that his mother died, that's why he was away. So one guesses that there was naturally a lot of excitement at home, and the professor doesn't ask him for an apology, an excuse. But that very morning there's a little friend who, since he hadn't been to school for a few days, had gone to his home and asked his parents was anything wrong. Therefore we know that the parents know that he hasn't been to school, and that they will go to school to find out about it. So now we find ourselves in the schoolroom, and the lesson starts. So the teacher feels very guilty towards the child because at first he's hard, because before the kid told him that his mother was dead, he was sort of rough on him. Give me your apologies and I'm not going to tell and all that. And when the kid burst out and said my mother's dead, the teacher feels guilty, ashamed. So in class he questions the children as usual. He calls a child, as he would normally do, and then all of a sudden he realizes no, no, excuse me, and he asks another one to get up to question him. And at that moment, at the end of the class there's a window, a window-door, and you hear a knock at the door. The professor looks and at the door you see the director of the school, who's beckoning him over. And the teacher goes there and he goes to the other side of the panel, the glass door with the director. At that moment all the children turn back to look at the door, and one is worried about the hero of the picture, the young boy. And gradually all the other boys start to look at him, because the teacher and the director are looking in his direction. And after a while they call over the kid . . .*

HITCHCOCK: Why do the other boys look at the other little boy?

HELEN SCOTT: *Because the director and the teacher are looking in his direction while they're talking. See, the kids are looking behind, and they see that they are looking in his direction.*

TRUFFAUT: *Because there's always that, see, there's that window.*

HITCHCOCK: I know that. What I meant was, isn't the boy in the class?

HELEN SCOTT: *Yes, he's in the classroom.*

HITCHCOCK: How can they tell that they're looking at one particular boy?

HELEN SCOTT: *Because they look back. When the teacher goes out, they follow him, they keep on looking back to see what's happening in the back.*

HITCHCOCK: I know that, yeah.

HELEN SCOTT: *And so that they can see the director and the teacher looking in the direction of the boy.*

HITCHCOCK: I see.

HELEN SCOTT: *And they're talking about him. It's obvious.*

TRUFFAUT: *All of this is silent. And when they beckon him over, the kid makes a question gesture: "Me?" And before he gets up, you see his mother coming in just behind the two others in the window-door. So I had the small, the window, the bottom part of the window painted in white, so that from the level of her eyes it would be clear only 'til here, so you could see her arriving and without looking into the classroom, as if she knew where her son's usual seat were, she looks, she looks at him. And so the child gets up and goes towards the door, and behind the mother is the father, who grabs the boy like that, smacks him, and the kid goes back to sit down in his seat. It was very cut out, and I didn't have any, I hadn't written the whole thing out, I had done it the day before, the scene, because I didn't think I could get out of it unless I prepared it a bit, and I tried to put myself, to try to think of how you would handle that scene. And it's the only scene in the picture in which the people in the audience were almost shouting.*

DECLARATION OF ALFRED HITCHCOCK

"Declaration of Alfred Hitchcock" is printed from *In Their Own Words: The Battle over the Possessory Credit, 1966–1968,* Directors Guild of America, typescript, May 2, 1967.

Alfred Hitchcock declares and says:

I have been employed in the motion picture industry since 1925, during which period of time I have directed more than fifty photoplays, many of which I have produced as well as directed, both in the United States and in Great Britain. I have been employed by most of the major motion picture producing and distributing companies, including Gaumont-British Pictures, Ltd., United Artists Corporation, RKO Pictures, Inc., Paramount Pictures Corporation, Metro-Goldwyn-Mayer, Warner Bros. and Universal Pictures Company.

In 1940, I directed the motion picture *Rebecca,* which won the Academy Award for the Best Picture of the year and which was also nominated for Best Direction. I have since that date received several other Academy Award nominations for Best Direction, including *Lifeboat* (1994), *Spellbound* (1945), and *Psycho* (1960).

During the last ten years, I have been executive producer on 273 half-hour and 90 one-hour television films broadcast from coast to coast over the facilities of Columbia Broadcasting System and National Broadcasting Company; each of which television films has not only borne my name preceding the title but also a caricature of my likeness which has become a personal trade-mark.

Since 1948, I have been accorded the following possessory presentation and production credit in both motion picture and television films:

"ALFRED HITCHCOCK'S

_____ "

(name of film)

In virtually every film produced or directed by me, I have striven to create unusual suspense and I have many times utilized unusual psychological developments. In fact, I believe my name has become known to motion picture audiences throughout the world as a trade-mark for the startling, out-of-the-ordinary psychological suspense mystery film.

In all of my contracts commencing with my five-picture deal with Warner Bros. on October 13, 1948, I was granted the right to have my name as a possessory credit above the title of the picture, and the pictures produced under such contract were respectively entitled: "Alfred Hitchcock's *Stage Fright,*" "Alfred Hitchcock's *Dial M for Murder,*" "Alfred Hitchcock's *The Wrong Man,*" "Alfred Hitchcock's *Strangers on a Train.*"

While at Warner Bros., I made another picture entitled *Rope,* under a contract dated March 21, 1949, which expressly provided for credit in the same form as in the contract dated October 13, 1948, in which my contractual credit above the title was required to be "displayed in size type at least fifty per cent (50%) of the size type used to display the title of each motion picture hereunder."

I entered into six contracts with Paramount Pictures Corporation during the years 1953–1959, during which period of time I produced the following motion pictures for which I have received credit on the film, in paid advertising and in publicity as follows: "Alfred Hitchcock's *Rear Window*" (1953), "Alfred Hitchcock's *To Catch a Thief*" (1954), "Alfred Hitchcock's *The Man Who Knew Too Much*" (1955), "Alfred Hitchcock's *Vertigo*" (1957), "Alfred Hitchcock's *Psycho*" (1959).

I have entered into three separate contracts with Universal Pictures Corporation in which I have likewise been given contractual credit that my name be displayed in size type one hundred per cent (100%) of the size type used to display the title of such motion pictures, such pictures being as follows: "Alfred Hitchcock's *The Birds*" (1963), "Alfred Hitchcock's *Marnie*" (1963), "Alfred Hitchcock's *Torn Curtain*" (1965).

In 1965, a book was published in several countries throughout the world, entitled Hitchcock's Films (published by A. Zwemmer Limited, London; A. S. Barnes & Co. Inc., New York; Beaux Livres S. A., Switzerland, and Drukkerijen vh Ellerman Harms nv, Amsterdam, Holland).

Likewise, in 1965, a second book was published in several countries, entitled *The Films of Alfred Hitchcock* (published by E. P. Dutton & Co., Inc., New York; The Chaucer Press, England).

Similarly, in 1965, Random House, Inc. published a book entitled *Alfred Hitchcock's Monster Museum*, containing twelve stories, none of which was written by me but all of which were selected by me, and my name was used in a possessory title in order to identify my personal selection.

In Germany, the magazine entitled *Film Woche*, issue of September 14, 1963, reproduced my picture on the cover, together with the German title of the picture as "Alfred Hitchcock's *Die Vogel*" *(The Birds)*. Attached hereto, marked Exhibit A is photocopy thereof. In connection with the same picture, a huge billboard appeared in Paris, duplicating my figure and likeness, and was placed on top of the billboard, which contained in huge letters "*Les Oiseaux* d'Alfred Hitchcock" (*The Birds* of Alfred Hitchcock). A photocopy of that picture is attached hereto, marked Exhibit B.

In the *London Evening News* for August 29, 1963, appeared huge advertisements for "Alfred Hitchcock's *The Birds*," copy of which is attached hereto, marked Exhibit C. Also attached hereto, marked Exhibit D, is a photocopy of a London billboard advertising the same picture. Similar exploitation appeared throughout the United States and elsewhere throughout the world.

I direct the attention of the Court to the fact that my current Universal contracts require my name to be used in a size type 100% the size of the title. However, as far back as 1946, I was still given possessory credit upon the prints of the film and in publicity and advertising, wherein my name was less than 100% the size type of the title but was clearly used in a possessory sense: "Alfred Hitchcock's *Spellbound*." Attached hereto, marked Exhibit E, is copy of advertisement which appeared in the magazine *Fame*, published in 1946.

In connection with exhibition of theatrical motion picture films, it is customary and usual in the trade to prepare so-called "press books" which contain many pages of publicity, advertising, lobby stills, advertising mats, reproductions of billboard posters, so-called "teasers," the availability of one-minute radio interview transcriptions and material prepared for television broadcast, as well as billboard advertising extending from "one sheet" to "24 sheets." Universal Pictures Corporation designates this press book as a "Showman's Manual," and attached hereto, marked Exhibit F, is the back cover of such press book indicating the billboard posters featuring "Alfred Hitchcock's Sex Mystery *Marnie.*" The entire press book will be presented to the Court for inspection upon the hearing of application for injunction. My last picture, *Torn Curtain,* has received similar coverage, and I am attaching hereto, marked Exhibit G, original advertisement appearing in the *Boston Herald* for Friday, July 10, 1966, advertising my last picture, "Alfred Hitchcock's *Torn Curtain.*"

It would needlessly encumber this record to attempt to include the hundreds of thousands of newspaper clippings, articles and paid advertising which have been utilized to exploit my name in motion pictures, television films and otherwise, although I will make available to the Court any amount of such material which the Court may desire, reflecting the enormous coverage which has been accorded me in every media for more than twenty years.

Needless to say, I consider the possessory use of my name above the title of a film as of extraordinary value to the producing company as well as to myself. Every producing company has informed me that my name has "box office value" and part of the benefit received by such producing company is the right to use, advertise and exploit my name in order to advertise to the general public a motion picture film or television film of unusual nature and quality.

As to myself, I have always considered my name and reputation to be the most valuable property right owned by me. My name has continuously been used as a personal trade-mark on every film produced or directed by me since 1948, and if I am prevented from using this trade-mark identification in the future, I shall be deprived of my most valuable asset.

I should like to stress the fact that in the suspense psychological mystery field, direction is peculiarly creative; timing and so-called "stage business" are of the utmost importance. The director is required to utilize a special skill in molding and welding the various elements of plot, characters, lighting, music, props, sound effects and all of the other diverse elements into a single integrated whole which will convey to the audience the precise psychological effects and dénouements without which the picture would be a complete failure.

Without in any way detracting from the importance of the contribution made by the writer of either basic story material or screenplay, the writing is but a *single element* in the production of a film. It is the director who bears the primary responsibility to produce the integrated film and to edit it in such a manner that the various elements are perfectly combined. This has sometimes been referred to as "creative magic," but in everyday terms it is not magic but tremendously hard work and effort on the part of the director which creates the film. I might add that not more that fifty directors to my knowledge have ever been granted possessory production or presentation credit, although there have literally been thousands of persons who have directed motion pictures during the past sixty years. The possessory credit which I have enjoyed for more than twenty years is the lifetime goal and ambition of literally hundreds of directors who are presently directing motion picture and television films. In my view, they should be given the right to achieve that ambition; it is an enormous incentive to better direction and better pictures, and in my opinion the right to bargain for such possessory credit should never be denied to them.

I declare under penalty of perjury that the foregoing is true and correct. Executed this 2nd day of May, 1967, at Los Angeles, California.

[signature above typed name]
Alfred Hitchcock

INTERVIEW WITH ALFRED HITCHCOCK

"Interview with Alfred Hitchcock" was originally published in *Antaeus* (Summer 1973): 121–33.

In the fall of 1971, the Film Division of Columbia University proposed to the University that Mr. Alfred Hitchcock be awarded an honorary Doctorate of Humane Letters for his outstanding contributions to cinematic language. The degree was approved by the various committees at Columbia, and Mr. Hitchcock was contacted to see if he would indeed be able to come to Columbia for the June 6, 1972, graduation to receive such a degree. Mr. Hitchcock agreed.

When he arrived in New York, one of the students called him to ask if he would come to speak to the film students before the graduation ceremonies started. Mr. Hitchcock was happy to oblige by coming to the Film School itself for one and a half hours with the students before the day's ceremonies began. Since most of the students had seen a sneak preview of *Frenzy* (to be released a few weeks later), the centerpiece of potatoes and neckties was appropriate. The students began the interview by asking Mr. Hitchcock how he began in the film world.

ALFRED HITCHCOCK: I worked in advertising, designing advertisements, before going into film. I started out designing art titles, since that was back in the days of the silent pictures when we used narrative titles, character titles and spoken titles. Both the titles and their drawings were, of course, terribly naive. For example, if the title said, "By this time George was leading a very fast life," you'd have those words and underneath a candle with a flame at both ends. But this is where I learned script writing.

QUESTION: *Do you think that the studios have learned what "cinematic" is?*

HITCHCOCK: No, they haven't. There are too many films with what I call photographs of people talking. When they get translated into a foreign language with superimposed titles, the audience spends their evening reading. They never get a chance to look at the picture. You see, most people get confused; they think that galloping horses are cinema. They are not. They are photographs of galloping horses. Pure cinema is montage, the joining together of pieces of film and creating an idea. It's like putting words together in a sentence. From that comes the audience's emotion. *Rear Window,* possibly one of the most cinematic pictures that anyone's ever attempted, depended upon cutting to what a man is seeing, then cutting back to his reaction. What you're doing is using his face to create a thought process. A novelist would use words to get this effect. I do it visually. I did the *Encyclopedia Britannica* motion picture section some years ago and in it I cited an example of cutting from the close-up of a man's face to what the man sees, and then his reaction. This was to illustrate how by a little change you can alter the whole thought process. The example I used was of a man looking out and seeing a woman nursing a baby. When you cut back to him, he smiles. That makes him a rather benign gentleman. Now, leave the two close-ups in and take the middle piece away and substitute a girl in a bikini. Now he's a dirty old man! Just by that one change, you see!

QUESTION: *When you write a scene, do you keep in mind the place of the actors on the screen?*

HITCHCOCK: The size of the image on the screen and its composition is really orchestration. It's no good throwing a close-up on the screen just for the sake of a close-up. It's like music, you know. You have loud brass when you need it. The same applies to the size of the image. This side of the technical situation is almost completely ignored these clays.

QUESTION: *I wasn't thinking of the size so much as the position of the actors on the screen.*

HITCHCOCK: Well, I wouldn't look at it that way. I would say it's a question of whether you're using the subjective treatment. Truffaut was interested in the way I used this subjective treatment. In other words, you make it from one of the actors' point of view. That governs the position and size. I'll give you an example. In the rape scene in *Frenzy* you go to the woman first—she looks up and there's the man coming in the door. It's all from her point of view. It's only when they get very close together that you have to become objective and look at them in profile: if you continue the man from her point of view, it would look too ugly. You'd have this size thing on the screen and she would be almost cross-eyed looking at him.

QUESTION: *In* Frenzy, *how long did it take to shoot that potato truck sequence?*

HITCHCOCK: Being an ex-art director, I'm an old hand at the technical end. I dictated every cut in that scene to a secretary. It came to 118 from beginning to end. Then I had a platform built about as high as an average table, so that the camera and all the lights could stay on the studio floor. Both the lights and the cameras would have had to be constantly lifted if we had used a real truck, and that would have been a waste of time and energy. So I just had this platform built with four springs at each corner and loaded it up with the sacks. We could move it around, do whatever we wanted. This is all based on the theory that it's what you're putting on the screen that counts. So many directors are conscious of what they're shooting on the set, that they go to enormous trouble. They've got to have the real truck. I knew that the cutter would have a problem with the 118 set-ups that I dictated because of the similarity of the shots, so I had numbers made on yellow cards. The cutter only had to refer to my dictated script. But to answer your question, the whole scene took about four days.

QUESTION: *In* Frenzy *you give us the feeling that one is being speared into a funnel. You start out with wide open spaces in the first shot, and at the end you focus on about an inch of a trunk.*

HITCHCOCK: I think what you're really saying is that you start story-wise fairly loosely, and as the story develops, your own concentration becomes sharper and sharper and sharper. That's called script structure. One of the things that pleased me about *Frenzy* was that the background was a character. You see, I've never believed in using a background and then playing something else against it. In this case your background is a produce market, as I'm describing it in the trailer—selling fruits of evil and the horrors of potatoes. But what happens is that here you are in a produce market, and it eventually leads you to potatoes, from the potatoes comes the dust, the dust gets into a brush, and there's the undoing of the murderer. So, that produce market background played a very vital part in the story. It's like when I wanted to do Mount Rushmore in *North by Northwest*. I wanted to use that dramatically, but the Department of Interior wouldn't permit it. I wanted Cary Grant to slide down Lincoln's nose, then hide in one of the nostrils, and then get a sneezing fit. Cary Grant, not Lincoln!

QUESTION: *What attracted you to the story of* Frenzy?

HITCHCOCK: The potatoes, of course!

QUESTION: *It seemed that a lot of things you had done in earlier films were pushed even further in* Frenzy.

HITCHCOCK: Well, I did a few little experiments with sound. In the market, when the police sergeant comes up and talks to the salesman, the red-haired fellow, he suddenly turns around and says, "Oh, meet my friend . . ." and the man's gone. I took every bit of sound out of the track.

QUESTION: *What about when he steps out of the doorway?*

HITCHCOCK: Same thing. I took every bit of sound right out, just to emphasize the words from the man: "Is there anywhere to sleep tonight?" And when we tracked out the second murder, down the stairs and into the street, I brought that traffic noise up three times the volume, so that people subconsciously would say, if she screams, nobody's ever going to hear it.

QUESTION: *What about the use of music in your films?*

HITCHCOCK: A lot of my films don't have any music. *The Birds* had no music. In fact, the bird sounds were entirely electronic from beginning to end. I took the film over to West Berlin. They had a machine there, a huge console, that is guaranteed to give you any sound you want. They gave me an example of a tank battle all done on this machine. Anyway, all the bird sounds were made that way. You know, sometimes you can do without music altogether, and working with musicians is not easy. The trouble with all musicians is that you have absolutely no control. I remember Tiomkin used to say, "Oh, do come down and tell me what you think." And I'd go down and there would be seventy musicians and they'd play a passage and I'd say, "Well, I don't think it's right because . . ." And Tiomkin would then say, "We can't change it now! It's already orchestrated!" There never is and never can be close collaboration between a director and a composer.

QUESTION: *There's a shot in* The Birds *that I'm curious about. It's the beginning of the bird attack on the gas station. You have a high angle shot from out in the middle of nowhere as the gas station goes up in flames. From where was this shot taken?*

HITCHCOCK: When we were filming *The Birds* Universal was building a new car park. They had cut the side of a hill away. We put the camera on top of the hill and just had the burning car in the car park, with a few people running; all the rest was blacked out. Then the matte artist made a matte of the harbor and the town, as seen from above. So you got your action movement and your burning car, but the rest of the town is on a fixed matte. Now the problem was how to get the birds in; the rest of that shot was now complete—you actually did look down and see the town and the burning car. We went out to a cliff over the ocean and got a lot of fish and bread and stuff and threw it over the cliff. The gulls behind the camera went down after it; they were constantly going down, chasing the food. When that film came into the studio, we discovered that now and then you could see the surf, the beach, the cliffside—everything. So we used what is called the rotoscope method. Two old ladies spent three months copying each bird onto a plain background and then copying the silhouette. (When you double print you must have a silhouette first. They used the travelling matte system.) It took them three months to do fifteen feet, ten seconds. This footage was then printed into the scene. You saw the birds going down over the town. I've often wondered why so few people ever question that shot. They take it for granted, I guess. They never say, "Did you have a balloon for that?"

QUESTION: *You expressed to Mr. Truffaut a desire to shoot a film about a city.*

HITCHCOCK: I'd love to, but I can't find the story.

QUESTION: *Don't you think you did that at all in* Frenzy?

HITCHCOCK: No. The idea that I have in mind is much more ambitious. It's the whole of the thing that makes the city work, starting in the morning and going right through to midnight. The difficulty is getting the material. You have to be careful not to get a cliché story.

QUESTION: *Would you focus on one character?*

HITCHCOCK: That's the problem. It ought to be one character. The chase story is the obvious choice, but it's too obvious.

QUESTION: *From the films that I've seen, it would appear that* Marnie *is the most brilliant in terms of color. The tones and values are the most carefully controlled. Did you spend a lot of time designing sets with specific colors?*

HITCHCOCK: I think that with all color you should start with black and white. In other words, to repeat the simile, it's like music: you can orchestrate color. Speaking of using color in films, I actually shot *Psycho* in black and white for one reason only: the flow of blood down the drain. I knew that if the film were in color, that scene would be quite repulsive.

QUESTION: *Are there any films that you've shot in color and after seeing the final print wish you had shot in black and white?*

HITCHCOCK: No, I think color is all right today as long as you control it. This, however, is often difficult. Unfortunately, there isn't enough coordination in the studios between, say, the dress designer and the set dresser. I mean, it's quite possible for them to have a green settee and for a woman to come in in a purple dress and sit on it. I think a set dresser ought to be as knowledgeable as a writer. He ought to know the economics of the character who owns the room, what sort of pictures to hang on the wall, what sort of books, what phonograph records. I usually overcome these problems by sending out a photographer to photograph the quarters of an equivalent character, and all the details around his room. Otherwise you can get some very absurd things; you get somebody who puts a Modigliani on the wall and the character has never even heard of Modigliani.

QUESTION: *That recalls something in* Suspicion, *where one detective walks over to a Picasso.*

HITCHCOCK: Yes, I had him do that. That particular painting always reminds me of a cartoon I once saw about a rather mild country couple who are in a museum. They are staring at an abstract and suddenly the abstract thrusts an arm and a pointing finger at them and says, "I don't understand you either!"

QUESTION: *How did the convention of your appearing briefly in each film begin?*

HITCHCOCK: When we ran short of actors! It's always very brief. That's because I don't want to suffer the indignity of being an actor for too long.

QUESTION: *Last night the women's film festival began. It's a two-week event with many features and shorts directed by women or written by women. They hope to demonstrate that women have had a considerable creative function in film. What about the role of women in film-making?*

HITCHCOCK: Strangely enough, there have been very few female filmmakers in the history of movies. Lois Weber was one; Ida Lupino was another. For some inexplicable reason, there have been very, very few women.

QUESTION: *You say inexplicable. Is there a possible explanation in terms of unions and male domination?*

HITCHCOCK: No, it has nothing to do with that. I don't think men will take orders from women. I think that's your root problem. But it is a strange thing that in the whole of the history of movies, there have been two, at the most three, women directors.

QUESTION: *What kind of working relationship do you have with your editors?*

HITCHCOCK: Well, I shoot a pre-cut picture. The editor has to put it together as I have shot it. Somebody wanted to have a look at the outtake material on *Rear Window*. He went into the cutting room and there was a small roll of film on the floor. That's all that wasn't used, because I make a film on paper. I never understand this business of shooting from all angles and getting millions of feet of film. I've never been on other directors' sets, so I wouldn't know. I've been asked, "Well, don't you ever improvise on the set?" And I say, "No, I prefer to improvise in an office!" I think the main reason for people not doing this is that they lack the sense of the visual, they can't visualize things ahead of time. I never look through a camera. What for? To confirm or to find out whether the cameraman is a liar? There's no reason for it, because you're dealing with a rectangle, just as much as any painter with a canvas. You have a rectangle in a theater, and that is the thing that you're visualizing all the time.

QUESTION: *You say that you don't look through the lens on your camera when you're shooting. Do you admire directors like Sternberg, who had exquisitely framed films?*

HITCHCOCK: Yes, well, there are very good pictorial directors. It's like saying do you admire Mexican cameramen like Figueroa; you say, look what they have to photograph. They've got missions which are white against a black sky with white clouds all done with filters and God is the art director. I don't think it's all that difficult.

QUESTION: *In terms of making pre-cut films, didn't you shoot alternative endings to* Topaz?

HITCHCOCK: Yes, I shot a scene that was true but never to he believed. That was a duel in a football stadium. I was fascinated to see a duel fought in a vast stadium with all the ads for Dubonnet, these two little figures and a man up in the stands with a high-powered rifle. The moment when they start to fire, the man in the stands shoots one of the men in the back. You know, very often you see things that have actually occurred in real life and nobody will believe it when you put it on the screen.

QUESTION: *Why did you shoot the ending you finally used?*

HITCHCOCK: It was a matter of, shall we say, disagreement with the front office. They always have the last word because they say it's their money. But I have complete artistic control over everything. I'm very familiar with the top men. They often send a story down and say, "We think this will be a very good picture for you." And I read it and it's horrible. But it's very difficult to go back and say, "You're a jerk for sending this to me." You have to be very tactful in how you handle it. I remember years ago when I was working on *Rebecca*. David Selznick, one of the biggest producers, said, "I've got a good idea for the last shot of the picture." I said, "What's that?" And he said, "When this house Manderley is in flames and smoke is rising into the sky, wouldn't it be a good idea for the smoke to form the letter 'R'?" What do you say, you know? Very embarrassing. You have to go around it some way. I thought it out and said, "Look. I've thought that thing over and I think it would be nicer and more realistic if you go into this Rebecca's room and the sheets are initialed, and you close in on the flames consuming the initial." He said, "Yes, yes, that might be good, too."

QUESTION: *How do you feel about previewing a film before an audience?*

HITCHCOCK: I don't believe in seeing previews—little boys pick up the cards and write "Junk It" or other rude remarks. And yet, directors take them seriously, they really do.

QUESTION: *When you were in England, before you came here, did any specific director appeal to you? When I saw* Young and Innocent, *I immediately thought of Lubitsch. I thought the congenial nature of that film was somewhat atypical of the sort of humor that you do deal with.*

HITCHCOCK: Yes, I think that Lubitsch was one of the principal men that I admire. He made all kinds of films long before he came to Hollywood. Lubitsch had made very big spectacular films long before he did his early films here. The first time I saw him, he was playing the part of a clown in a wordless play called *Sumurun*, in 1912.

QUESTION: *Do you miss working with the kind of professional actors and actresses that were around Hollywood in the '30s and '40s?*

HITCHCOCK: You mean the "Stars"? No, I think I'm much better off to use first-class actors from the theater, to be able to use them while they are playing leads in the West End of London, as I did in *Frenzy.*

QUESTION: *Has the front office ever pressured you into using big stars?*

HITCHCOCK: Yes. That's why people like Julie Andrews got into pictures, which is ridiculous. She is a singer. But they say, "Oh, she's so big at the box office." In one movie she's supposed to be a scientist; every time I came across a line which had some scientific meaning, I had to cross it out because I just didn't believe it when she said it.

QUESTION: *What is your preparation with actors in terms of rehearsal?*

HITCHCOCK: No rehearsal, no rehearsal! I always start a picture with the writer and dictate a treatment. In other words, it's a description of the film as though you ran it with no sound, describing every action and indicating lots of shots, but in narrative form. Sometimes I end up with 100 pages, which are very difficult to read because it is a purely visual description of everything that takes place. You can't ever put in words like "he wondered" because you can't photograph "he wondered." When this is finished, the writer goes off to write the dialogue. This is the method I prefer.

QUESTION: *What about preferences as far as shooting? Do you go from beginning to end?*

HITCHCOCK: It doesn't bother me because I know the film by heart.

QUESTION: *Isn't it difficult for the actors without a rehearsal?*

HITCHCOCK: Actors are there to do as they're told. Actors in movies cannot have the same freedom as actors in the theater, because in the theater you have a proscenium arch and you have a room and they wander around. But in the case of film, you're cutting. That's why in a film where cutting is an important factor, the Method actor is of very little help.

QUESTION: *When you have a moving camera throughout, don't you have to pace your actors very carefully?*

HITCHCOCK: The trouble comes when an actor has the nerve to say, "Well, I wouldn't do it that way." I have to say to him, "Well, you better or else! This is because I'm stuck, cutting-wise. You cannot let an actor tell you what he's going to do; the film won't cut together.

QUESTION: *Doesn't this cause a good deal of conflict on the set?*

HITCHCOCK: No, no.

QUESTION: *What attracted you to do a film in 3-D?*

HITCHCOCK: It was the fashion and the custom. In fact, somebody at the studio once said to me, "Oh, you should do some of that multiple screen stuff." I said,

"What for?" He said, "Well, they've done a film and it's got three images at once." And I said, "Well, Méliès did that in 1898."

QUESTION: *Did you think at the time you were doing* Dial M for Murder *that 3-D would become an accepted convention like color and sound?*

HITCHCOCK: I didn't mind one way or the other. I didn't care. You knew 3-D would never last unless they could get it without the polaroid glasses.

QUESTION: *Do you think there's any future for it now with the new laser process?*

HITCHCOCK: Only if they develop the holograph, which is lensless photography. I suppose they'll always prod you to extend this sort of thing, so that you can have Indians shooting arrows at the audience, and so forth.

QUESTION: The Wrong Man *is the one film of yours that stands out as being a sort of semi-documentary feature film.*

HITCHCOCK: The mistake I made in *The Wrong Man* was letting the director intrude anywhere in the film. It should have been strictly impersonal.

QUESTION: *Are you particularly satisfied with the film, other than that?*

HITCHCOCK: Not entirely. You see, I had the moment when Henry Fonda was whispering a prayer to a figure of Christ on the wall, and then I slowly dissolved to a street in Queens and the figure was coming along until it came and superimposed its face over Fonda and you saw that this was the real man. I should never have done that in the film because it never took place.

QUESTION: *So you prefer an entirely realistic situation?*

HITCHCOCK: You have to stick to it.

QUESTION: *In so many of your English films you have these expressionistic touches which are very powerful, and yet you now say that you prefer very realistic qualities.*

HITCHCOCK: But I mean in *The Wrong Man,* because we're dealing with an event that actually took place. It's not a fiction story. It's totally different. With fiction you can do whatever you like. The mistake I made with *The Wrong Man* was that I put things in that never actually occurred.

QUESTION: *Yes, but don't you feel a sort of mystical hold and attraction between the two men? I mean that technique is experimental . . .*

HITCHCOCK: Oh, I prefer to experiment with the technique of storytelling, but not with true stories. After all, what are you doing? You're pulling an emotion out of an audience. That's our purpose. That's why I'm not a self-indulgent director in terms of "I'm only going to make a film to please myself." I think the whole power of film is that it belongs to so many people on a given night. You create an emotion through film and you have the possibility of having an audience in Tokyo, West Berlin, London and Paris, all going through the same emotions at a given time. I don't think any other medium can do that. Stage can't.

QUESTION: *Speaking of stories, how do you feel about adaptations from well-known literature?*

HITCHCOCK: I think it's always a risk. A well-written book doesn't necessarily mean you get a well-made film. You're dealing with literature, which is another medium altogether.

QUESTION: *But do you need to make a film of a well-written book?*

HITCHCOCK: Not necessarily, no. Ideally, when you're adapting a novel to a film script you read the book once, and then put it aside.

QUESTION: *Of all the things you've done, do you have a favorite film?*

HITCHCOCK: Yes, I liked a film I made called *Shadow of a Doubt*. That was written with Thornton Wilder and was really done in the right way. We went into a small town. We lived there for a bit, got to know all the people, and chose the house that we wanted to use. Thornton thought that the house looked too big for our character, who was only a bank clerk. I said, "Look, Thornton, look at the door, it's peeling, but let's send an assistant to the real estate company and see what rent he pays." The assistant discovered that the rent was correct, so we went back and wrote the script. When I returned to shoot, I discovered that the man was so proud that we'd chosen his house that he had it all repainted. He ruined it. We had to put on an army of painters and dirty it down again.

QUESTION: *You've always had a very benevolent attitude toward villains. How did this come about?*

HITCHCOCK: Ah, villains. I think villains should be very attractive men. Otherwise they'd never get near their victims. Most people cast heavies in a very obvious way. I think it's a big mistake. If you look at most of your cultural murderers, they're rather gentlemanly sort of fellows.

QUESTION: *You even make them family men.*

HITCHCOCK: Yes, why not?

QUESTION: Suspicion *seems such a good example of that. The villain is tremendously attractive. I heard there was another ending for that movie, too.*

HITCHCOCK: Yes, the big mistake in a story of that kind was to cast Cary Grant. In those days the idea of Cary Grant being a murderer was ridiculous. That was the day of the Star. I had an ending whereby the wife really came to the final conclusion that her husband was a murderer, but she was so much in love with him that she didn't want to live. She knew he was going to kill her and she wrote a letter to her mother to this effect, and added, "But, Mother, I think society should be protected." So she seals the letter and puts it beside the bed and then he brings up the fatal glass of milk. She drinks and dies. Then you fade in on one quick shot of a cheerful Cary Grant walking down a street and popping a letter into a mailbox. But they wouldn't do it to Cary Grant. As a matter of fact, to show you the idiocy of front offices, the ex-head of RKO came in from New York and said, "Oh, you should see what the new studio head has done to your picture." He said it with a grin on his face, knowing how ridiculous it was. This new studio head, in my absence, had taken *Suspicion* and reduced it from one hour and three-quarters to fifty-five minutes, taking out everything in the picture that might point to the man being a murderer. Everything. Ridiculous. I had to sit down and put it all back again.

QUESTION: *The wonderful thing about that film is the ambivalence; one moment you're sure he's the murderer and then the next moment he does something that kind of neutralizes it. Was that intentional?*

HITCHCOCK: Oh yes, that was all quite deliberate. It was the woman's mind and what was happening to it.

QUESTION: *You made quite a point in your book that you wrote with Mr. Truffaut about Janet Leigh's bra in* Psycho, *especially that it stayed on her chest throughout the movie. In* Frenzy, *I noticed a couple of scenes where this wasn't the case. I wondered what persuaded you to begin removing ladies' clothing on the screen.*

HITCHCOCK: Actually, in *Psycho,* she should have never been wearing a bra at all. She was having an affair at three o'clock in the afternoon with a man in a bedroom. She should have been stripped, but then we weren't allowed. There wasn't that "permissiveness." I'm not a great believer in just showing nudity for the sake of it. Somebody asked me the other day how long did I think nudity would last on the screen and my reply was, "Well, all breasts sag eventually!"

HITCHCOCK AT WORK

INTRODUCTION

In his comments on film, Hitchcock was often theoretically imaginative, speculative, and even abstract in expanding the horizons of what could be done in his chosen medium. But he was ever the pragmatist, and his relentless thoughtfulness about film was not an exercise in pure theory but a key part of his effort to outline and negotiate the challenges of making pure cinema in an impure world. The articles collected in this section illustrate that theory and practice are inseparable for Hitchcock and broaden our understanding of what the phrase "Hitchcock at work" means: he was in a very real sense at work making films when he was theorizing about them and theorizing about films when he was making them.

One of his earliest articles, "Making *Murder!*," is very informative on several levels. Especially at the beginning it is a charming and witty personal profile, showing him in a domestic setting with his daughter, "who regards me as a joke," and his wife, who appears primarily in her professional role as the full partner in "the Hitchcock combination—Mr. and Mrs." that prepares the scenarios for his films. Ironically, their delightfully idyllic country cottage distracts them from that labor, and he feels an urgent need to escape back to the true retreat for a committed filmmaker: that is, the noise of the city.

Once he is safely back at Cromwell Road, which is home, sweet home, because it is the place of work, sweet work, he turns to describe his methods in detail. Even though he has been asked to focus specifically in this magazine article on his most recent completed film, *Murder!,* his current project, *The Skin Game,* based on a play by John Galsworthy, is very much on his mind, and it is not surprising that he concentrates first on the adaptation process and the complexities of turning literature into film. After repeatedly emphasizing Alma's vital contributions at this stage, particularly the "masterly ease" with which she is able to "revise" or "invent" what he "expound[s]," he states what we now recognize as one of his defining principles of pure cinema: the overriding concern "to visualize the story kinematically." While later in his career he tended to downplay his reliance on the specifics of literary texts, here he is quite willing to highlight two key ways in which even pure cinema benefits from and leans on literature. First, the source text is a wellspring of "incidents, scenes, dialogue, and all else necessary to the making of a genuine screen version." And more generally, the careful analysis of literary structure and technique provides valuable ideas that can be applied to cinematic structure and technique. Hitchcock differentiates between the challenges posed by adapting a novel and a play and notes some particular assets and liabilities of each: for example, the "expansive detail" of a novel like *Enter Sir John* provided much interesting material for him to work with but many difficult choices when it came to shaping "the most effective episodes for consecutive and balanced groupings" in *Murder!*; and the "brilliantly clever stagecraft" that is one of the main attractions of a play like *The Skin Game* turns out to be "no end of trouble" when it comes to "finding the true screen equivalent" and fitting the story to its audience. As different and problematic as they are in some ways, both literary genres provide models of the "elusive" but essential elements that he wants to incorporate in his films: "the full popular flavour plus intelligent treatment."

Both of these elements are necessary to establish cinema as a serious art but more practically to allow it to address and satisfy its "universal audience." Much to his credit, Hitchcock avoids the condescension that more than occasionally creeps into discussions of a mass and inevitably hybrid audience: the counterpointing of "popular" and "intelligent" doesn't lead to any talk of "groundlings" that must be pandered to, and we are a long way from his references to "moronic masses" and anti-cinematic "plausibles." Here he is realistic and respectful in noting that some in the audience will "miss the finer details, but grasp the dramatic whole," and others will "enjoy" subtleties "to the full" without looking down their noses at "the popularity of the subject matter."

In his discussion of *Murder!*, it is clear that the challenge of "intelligent treatment" is what really engages him, and he illustrates this concept with a tour de force description of the blend of theorizing, serendipity, and improvisation lying behind the construction of one of the key sequences in the film, the entrance of Sir John. He decided that he would frame "the crux of the story" not as a trial scene, which "the public is weary of," but as a jury scene, and the inspiration for how to shape this sequence came when a "gramophone burst into song" while he was at work, giving him the idea of picturing the repeated "ding dong" assault of the other jurors' voices that "bewilder" and "numb" Sir John into submission. It may be a bit of a surprise that after such a stunning description of the origin of a sequence most viewers would be tempted to call expressionistic that Hitchcock goes on to emphasize that "intelligent treatment is not necessarily something strikingly original" but rather is linked more closely to "absolute naturalness" than "exaggeration in tone and gesture," which he specifically labels "unintelligent treatment." His intention, though, is not to exclude or downplay what have since become identified as highly stylized "Hitchcock moments" but rather to stress the importance of nuance, subtlety, texture, and a hunger for reality: the thoughtful handling of the "dozen and one little things which have no bearing at all on the story, just the sort of things which occur in real life." Intelligent treatment at work in *Murder!* is thus equally well illustrated by the memorably inventive jury scene and Hitchcock's probably unnoticed but nevertheless careful attention to detail in having Sir John "occasionally sucking a lozenge to ease his throat," as a real character like Sir John would do in real life.

As much as this essay focuses on defining Hitchcock's approach to filmmaking, from beginning to end he also points out that what he outlines is "characteristically English," and the triumph of intelligent treatment in cinema is not only personal but also national. His concern here is to make good—and well-received—films as well as to enhance the reputation of English cinema and, more concretely, to recapture a larger part of the market from American films, a much-discussed topic in British film journals at the time. This last effort may be part of the reason why instead of holding up American films as the models he learned from and emulated, a recurrent claim in many of his early and late writings and interviews, he uses them here as his prime examples of "unintelligent cinema," all "paint and plaster," "beautiful sets," and "elaborate dresses, with all the gilt and pomp of fabulous wealth and dominating power." Hitchcock envisioned himself as the custodian of pure cinema, but he was also frequently described as the great hope of his country's filmmaking operation. He takes both of these responsibilities seriously in this essay, not only thoughtfully defining intelligent treatment as a fundamental artistic goal and strategy, but also confidently proclaiming that it will trump the Americans' "highly-polished banality" and "will prove the salvation of the English film industry." While this essay is accurately titled "Making *Murder!*," it might also have been subtitled "The Care and Handling of English Cinema."

We have just seen a particularly good example of how polished anecdotes about his working method frequently enliven Hitchcock's writings published in popular magazines and newspapers. But we get an even closer glimpse of Hitchcock at work when reading the archival records of his discussions with various collaborators, often dutifully transcribed despite not being meant for publication. While it is somewhat of a stretch to label the document titled simply "Hitchcock Notes" (which I have modified slightly to indicate the specific subject), evidently a complete transcription of a conversation about *Stage Fright* between Hitchcock and Fred Ahern, the production supervisor, as one of his "writings" or "interviews," it nevertheless deserves a place in a volume like *Hitchcock on Hitchcock* because of the detailed extensive backstage view if offers of Hitchcock at work.

As much as he complained, "I wish I didn't have to shoot the picture," as we'll see at the end of this section, the comments here show him—typically, I think—fully energized by the prospect of executing the visual plan of his film. The epigraph for the entire conversation might well be Hitchcock's comment, "We've got to be fairly ingenious as to how we set these little pieces up," and ingenuity turns out to be a matter of logistics as well as cinematic imagination. As Hitchcock and

Ahern go through the script scene by scene and sometimes shot by shot, we get a close and clear view of the numerous considerations, negotiations, and complex decisions that are the essential but most often invisible components of the work of art. The challenge is daunting: how to create a high level of suspense, pictorial effect, atmosphere, and accuracy—and stay on budget.

To do all this successfully, he must be part Murnau, part Kuleshov, and part Selznick. Like Murnau, Hitchcock is very attuned to frame composition in tracking his characters' movements through interior and exterior settings; not at all hesitant to use process shots in tandem with more straightforward "realistic" techniques; and also aware that while some scenes call for meticulously assembled and arranged objects, others revolve around suggestion rather than detail, with the part standing for the whole: a doorway instead of an entire building, for example. Like Kuleshov, Hitchcock was a great proponent and practitioner of "creative geography," constructing a unified cinematic space by combining shots from separate settings. Much of the discussion here focuses on the careful planning required to join shots of a character in front of a projection plate, at a real location, and on a studio set into a seamless sequence. And like Selznick, a mentor as well as an adversary, Hitchcock rarely forgot that a dollar sign is behind every cinematic decision. (Some years later when he described to Truffaut the mechanics of one of his most celebrated shots, the combination zoom and dolly in *Vertigo,* he was particularly proud to note that he was able to do it for "only" nineteen thousand dollars, rather than the first estimate of fifty thousand [246].) Again and again in his conversation with Ahern, the first or last consideration in figuring out a camera angle or in deciding to shoot on location or build a set or to include a particular visual element or prop was whether it would cost or save money.

Despite the omnipresence of budgetary concerns, it would be misleading to frame this conversation as pivoting on art versus accounting. More broadly speaking, the production meeting is about finding ways to confront "all the contingencies," to use Hitchcock's own phrase, connected with turning what he has envisioned into something that can be captured on film. Reading these notes allows us to witness the extensive preplanning and multilevel decision making necessary to overcome the innumerable problems that lie in the way of fulfilling his main goals: to create visually effective frame compositions (like a seaside shot that he sets up as thoughtfully as any painter would, calculating the percentage of land, sky, water, and silhouettes); intricately choreographed sequences; striking special effects (with much attention to process shots integrated with live action and fully inhabited spaces); and atmosphere (established by careful use of physical detail but also sound design, especially traffic and background voices).

This production meeting shows not only how Hitchcock works but also what he is after. He may well have been one of the most imaginative and formally inventive of all filmmakers, but his constant emphasis on research in this conversation confirms and illuminates his efforts to "make it real" and "get it right" (not his phrases but surely his aims). It is important for him to gauge how far Jonathan's car would have traveled during the half hour he tells his story while driving so that when they cut back to the present, he will be shown in a part of London that he would have arrived at in reality after such a drive. The pub sequences will be shot on a set but one "based on research of an actual pub." And Scotland Yard should be consulted extensively, to get accurate information about "the behavior of our man, the police procedure and so forth," but also "diplomatically," to be sure not to "put ourselves in their hands so that we tie our own hands in the matter." The underlying message throughout this production meeting is that "the detail is very important," and careful research is necessary to add texture, accuracy, and authenticity, all while preserving artistic autonomy. A close look at his working method illustrates that he is, and knew himself to be, a "literalist of the imagination," to use Marianne Moore's well-known phrase.

While his meeting with Fred Ahern focused on budgets and bolts, Truffaut and Chabrol steered him in a much different direction in their conversation published in *Cahiers du Cinéma*. This interview is translated for the present volume by James M. Vest, who has already summarized and commented on it extensively in his comprehensive study *Hitchcock and France* (94–98), stressing how revealing and valuable it is on several levels. The dynamic between interviewers and interviewee is particularly complex. For all their nervousness in approaching the revered master of cinema, Truffaut and Chabrol do not hesitate to voice their undoubtedly novel and surprising critical opinions about Hitchcock's works, framed as leading questions calculated to generate assent. The interview is in many respects a Socratic spectacle, set up so that Hitchcock repeatedly says "yes" to the interrogative statements of Truffaut and Chabrol, and so his further responses confirm that the fundamental elements of his cinema are exactly as they propose.

Ultimately, though, Hitchcock is far more than Glaucon to their Socrates, and even in the presence of such master ventriloquists, he is no mere dummy. He steers the discussion at various points to topics that are not centrally important to Truffaut and Chabrol: for example, the color scheme and British humor of *The Trouble with Harry*, his most recent film, and especially the incorporation of concern for the audience as a major component of his artistry. He affirms that "a cinema is a big screen with a whole lot of seats," even as his interviewers make clear that they are primarily interested in an aspect of his "conscience" different from the one that drives him to make commercially responsible films. And when they want to talk about his recurrent theme of "the idea of domination," he comments instead on what he feels is more important to him, the challenge of creating "strong emotion" in the audience watching his films. Even when Truffaut and Chabrol narrow and enforce the agenda, he often modifies the terms they offer. He is willing to accept their definition of him as a "serious" filmmaker but is at the same time wary of being "overly serious" and seems to agree with "a lot of people" who "find a blend of the dramatic with the comic" in the "true Hitchcock." And he is simultaneously agreeable and resistant, honest and coy, when he responds to their claim that his films have an "'added dimension,' somewhat, or entirely, metaphysical," by rephrasing their claim as "It's my soul getting into the subject"—indicating that he will define "metaphysical" in his, not necessarily their, way.

Complementing the banter that characterizes this interview is Hitchcock's recognition of how often Truffaut and Chabrol are right on target about his films, followed by his thoughtful and insightful responses to their provocative, if leading, questions. Their insistence on the serious thematic and moral figures in Hitchcock's carpet linking his works prompts him to give a fuller version of what in other interviews sometimes comes across as his commitment to a rather simple formalism: "It's the way of treating things that counts most. But still, if I were a painter, I'd say 'I can only paint with a message.'" Their focus on his "certainty of framing and blocking" leads not only to a somewhat familiar demonstration of how he uses sketches to convey his ideas to the cameraman but also to a somewhat surprising revelation that his framing is guided by "the first thing that people will notice: the faces." He confirms their remarks on the development in his framing by noting, "I use a different technique for each story," purposely avoiding "boring" and predictable closeups, as in *Strangers on a Train,* when he showed "a menacing crazy man" by using a deep-focus shot in front of the Jefferson Memorial "that was the equivalent of a closeup"—a striking way of expressing that for him the true measure of a shot is not so much spatial as emotional. Finally, although he initially resists their attempt to set up *I Confess* as the model of the "true Hitchcock" film, all inclusive and uncompromising, he ultimately agrees with their assessment, by admitting that his "ideal" film would indeed be closer to *I Confess* than *The Lady Vanishes* but then also by outlining in detail his plan for *The Wrong Man.* The simple response of the interviewers ("That's like *I Confess* but pushed much farther . . .") says much more than, in effect, "We rest our case." A dual triumph is masterfully evoked here and in fact throughout the entire interview: the proper celebration of Hitchcock's genius and the acknowledgment of Truffaut and Chabrol's expertise in appreciating and articulating that genius. This interview is a tour de force for all involved, and the value of Hitchcock's numerous confessions throughout the conversation is not at all undermined by his concluding remark— Truffaut and Chabrol generously give him the last word and, it turns out, the last laugh—that what he says in an interview "depends [on] what press it was." Hitchcock affirms the freedom to say what he wants in different circumstances, even if he contradicts himself, but there is little doubt that in the presence of Truffaut and Chabrol what he reveals about his work is more than provisionally true.

Although the subject never comes up in their discussion, at the time when Truffaut and Chabrol were interviewing Hitchcock he was deeply involved in plans for his new television series. Not surprisingly, he actively prepared for the premiere of *Alfred Hitchcock Presents* by an extensive advertising and publicity campaign that included thoughtful comments on "the Hitchcock approach to television," captured nicely in his syndicated article "Alfred Hitchcock Brings His Directing Techniques to the Medium of Television." One of his main efforts here is to show how well prepared he is for this endeavor, and he begins by pointing out that the "new medium" is in fact not so new to him: the technique he used in filming *Rope* is very much the same as that used in contemporaneous live TV dramas like *Studio One* and *Climax!* His shows, of course, would not be presented live, but his experience with *Rope* illustrates that despite his reputation as "the calm, complacent Hitchcock" accustomed to leisurely shooting schedules, he is perfectly capable of "mov[ing] around rapidly when the occasion demands."

Hitchcock's careful analysis of the differences between film and TV underscores his confidence that while TV work requires a potentially stressful "rapidity," the nature of the medium makes it possible to shoot quickly and efficiently. Filling a small rather than a large screen simplifies lighting, "one of the most time-consuming elements in filming a motion picture," and precludes the use of "large sets" and "elaborate long shots," which are not only "unnecessary" but in fact also "disturbing to the home viewer." Hitchcock seems comfortable with and perhaps even relieved by the technical limitations of television that rein in what can be attempted and accomplished in the medium. In the spirit of his oft-noted fascination for the challenge of restrictions (shooting a film in a phone booth, for example), he seems intrigued by doing on television what he couldn't normally do in film. Technically, television "tells its story best when the camera concentrates on the faces of the performers." This guides him not only as the producer and overall consultant for the show, enforcing a close visual style suitable for the medium and the budget as well, but also as a director of some episodes, now with an opportunity to shoot in a way that he hadn't done before. There are also new opportunities in subject matter, and he is pleased that the perfect match between the thirty-minute television show and the short story allows him finally to get to the extensive "store of fascinating yarns which, until now, I have never had the opportunity of committing to film" and which would not be suitable as the basis for full-length motion pictures.

Hitchcock offers a detailed analysis of some of the key requirements of the television medium, a glimpse of his working method, and a pitch for the show outlining exactly what the viewer should expect: "interesting half-hour dramas which will concern themselves with startling, shocking, suspense-filled stories having a surprise twist at the end." Without specifying it, he also introduces one additional part of the show, which turns out to be one of the major components of this latest incarnation of the Hitchcock brand that will become an essential part of his legacy: himself—that is, his very carefully cultivated persona. Hitchcock is a "presence" from the beginning to the end of the article, and in the manner that will become familiar to millions of television viewers through the next decade, he allows himself to be envisioned as bizarre and beleaguered, "beset by the frantic frenzy commonly associated with television," even as he asserts and conveys his ultimate detachment from and control over the surrounding circumstances. This article can be taken seriously as a source of some of Hitchcock's ideas about the two visual media in which he worked, but it is also wonderfully entertaining and revealing as perhaps the first of his appearances as the host of *Alfred Hitchcock Presents,* giving a full preview of the blend of self-mockery, drollery, and bravado that characterizes his on-camera role that was a central part of the show.

The final piece in this section is not what it initially seems to be. Even the title given to this interview, "Hitch: I Wish I Didn't Have to Shoot the Picture," seems to announce that it will be a reprise of some of his most well-known statements, and indeed, especially at the beginning, the interviewers guide Hitchcock into familiar territory. They warm up by saying, in effect, "Tell us the one about avoiding cliché or preplanning your films or not looking through the viewfinder of the camera," and so on, and Hitchcock complies. But there are numerous moments where he rethinks, adjusts, and embellishes some of his favorite credos. He avoids the cliché even as he talks yet one more time about how he tries to avoid clichés by explaining that he does so not only to stay one step ahead of an audience, "now highly educated" by mass media (especially in the real details and cinematic conventions of "all forms of mayhem [and] crime"), but also to challenge himself to "find new ways to do the same thing." His brief analysis of this "same thing" that he tries to accomplish is subtle and insightful: playing with audience expectations and generic norms by building off both suspense (what an audience knows) and mystery (what it doesn't know) allows him to create a "mad tension," a stunningly accurate and memorable phrase describing one of his most characteristic efforts and effects. Even as he characteristically emphasizes careful preplanning, which more than occasionally—and I think mistakenly—reinforces an image of him as a coldly methodical filmmaker, he also highlights his belief that "you can improvise all you want," but "in the office," not on set. This stage of preparation is "the most enjoyable part of making a picture," holed up in an office, "searching for freshness" with a writer who "becomes more than a writer; he becomes part maker of the picture"—a startling admission for Hitchcock, who often stressed his involvement in the writing process but rarely gave much credit to the contribution of the writer. And he glosses one final Hitchcockian commonplace in a manner that simultaneously broadens our understanding of the witty comment used as the title of this piece: his reluctance to indulge in what is often considered the emblematic gesture of a director—looking through the camera while on the set—is in part a way of distinguishing himself from other directors, part an expression of confidence in his camera operator, and perhaps most of all a subtle reaffirmation that cinema is fundamentally more a matter of cutting than shooting the picture.

His annoyance at the conventional figure of the director leads him to a very precise and balanced definition of his approach to filmmaking: "The whole art of the motion picture is a succession of composed images, rapidly going through a machine, creating ideas." When soon thereafter he adds story to image and orchestration—"You have to have the story because, you see, you need shape"—he completes a masterfully brief summary of what for him is pure cinema and confirms that he has much more than the same old responses to offer when interviewers ask him about "challenge," "stimulus," and "inspiration" as he "go[es] from picture to picture."

MAKING *MURDER!*

"Making *Murder!*" was originally published in *Cassell's Magazine,* August 1930, 56–63.

After wrestling for three weeks with the scenario of Galsworthy's *The Skin Game,* surrounded by the too-pleasant distractions of life in my little cottage hidden in five acres of coppice near Guildford, I held council with my wife.

"Alma," said I with the dictatorial authority of a film director, "we go to London at once. We need solitude; we need a retreat, a sanctuary from the birds of the air, the animals of the field, from all mankind and from the sights and sounds these things torment us with. We need the sights and sounds we can ignore; we must have *peace.*"

That concluded the council.

"Blackmail," that costly contrivance which is dear even when locked up in the garage, was hiked out in readiness for the trek. We filled up with petrol and oil, packed in Patricia (who is two and regards me as a joke), my secretary (who is a bit older and manages to take me a little more seriously), and a maid. My wife and I were also "among those present."

Within two hours, having skillfully avoided all traps *en route,* we reached the seclusion of Cromwell Road, Earl's Court, and I rubbed my hands with the grim satisfaction of a determined man who has at last got his troubles by the throat and is on the point of wringing the life out of them. Oh, happy man!

Here was I, perched on the roof of London in my fourth-floor flat, a helpful gramophone waiting to subdue the noisy war of hooters versus klaxons waging battle in the outside regions. District underground trains went clattering by, one hundred feet below but in full view, at the back. Coming from the far distance was that conglomeration of indistinguishable sounds which go to make up town life.

"Peace! Full-throated glorious peace! And now to *The Skin Game,*" thought I. "We"—that is, my wife and I—"will do six weeks work in three."

Scarcely before I could hang my hat up in the hall and certainly before I could sink into that fruitful reverie induced by the District trains, I was faced with an emissary from the Editor of *Cassell's Magazine.*

Would I write something about *Murder!*?

"You did say *write,* didn't you?" He edged a bit towards the door as he assured me I had heard correctly.

Had the Editor come in person . . .

And now I have shelved *The Skin Game* for half a day while I set down something about *Murder!* If I appear to digress at times and mention matters affecting films in general, let it be understood that I have *Murder!* at the back of my mind all the time, as one of the films I would use to illustrate the point.

According to the critics—and they know everything—it is the best of my dozen films. And the more daring of the tribe have hazarded that it is the best English crime-story yet told on the screen. I intrude with this flattery only because I hope to make it clear that I have at least aimed at making this film what I regard as characteristically English.

I have sought to combine in it two elements which are, disguised and expressed differently, in the most successful American films. Given these two elements, which I will describe later, I am convinced that English films will more than hold their own with Americans. And, because the combination is actually more natural to the English, I am sure that our own studios are destined to supply the cinemas of England with the bulk of their programs.

The scenario of *Murder!* is jointly the product of the Hitchcock combination— Mr. and Mrs. When I refer to the scenario I shall be bound to adopt the editorial plural.

This seems to be a fitting place to let you into our domestic secret. Mrs. Hitchcock knows a great deal more about scenario writing than I am ever likely to know. I only put my masculine foot down with a thud when I want the scenario draft brought into line with a particular idea of Mr. Hitchcock's. I will explain that delicate operation later. All I need to say now is that, when I expound Mr. Hitchcock's idea, Mrs. Hitchcock will revise or invent with masterly ease.

Murder! is our film version of a best seller by Clemence Dane and Helen Simpson, known to the reading public by the title *Enter, Sir John.* Following our usual method, we learned the story by heart before putting pen to paper on the scenario. The intention was to visualize the story kinematically, if I may invent a word. Then we returned to the original to select incidents, scenes, dialogue, and all else necessary to the making of a genuine screen version.

It happens sometimes that it is impossible to make an absolutely faithful reproduction of the story but departures from the original are less likely to be necessary in dealing with a novel than with a play. For this reason: the play is, in a sense, life in cameo, whereas the novel is life in expansive detail. In the play, rigid economy must be practiced in many ways; entrances, exits, curtains, are of supreme importance. So much so that the dramatist often finds his story shaped out of his own hands by the exigencies of stage technique.

It has been found that the technique demanded by the stage rarely lends itself to the screen. The result is that the story must be treated differently, divided and told in a different sequence of episodes, scenes and acts. And when one is compelled to make all these changes and at the same time present a faithful adaptation, the problem is far from easy.

The more perfect the stage technique, the more difficult becomes anything like a faithful screen adaptation. Galsworthy's brilliantly clever stagecraft in *The Skin Game* is giving us no end of trouble in finding the true screen equivalent.

Converting *Enter, Sir John* into *Murder!* presented difficulties of another kind. Our main concern in preparing the scenario was to choose the most effective episodes for consecutive and balanced grouping. We were unhindered by the rigid grouping which characterizes a play but we had to bear in mind all the time those two elements to which I have already referred.

There were many hours during the two months we were working on the *Murder!* scenario when even the solitude of our London drawing-room failed to inspire a single useful idea. They were blank hours when we wandered in and out amongst pieces of furniture, biting knuckles and strumming tunes on the piano case.

What I wanted—and it was my wife's business to plan the scenario accordingly— was an adaptation which moved forward with increasing tempo yet never losing the rhythm. I wanted, too, those elusive elements, the full popular flavor plus intelligent treatment.

I had chosen the story because of its popular appeal. In this I had my popular subject. Now I had to introduce that other element, intelligent treatment. It was not enough for film purposes merely to picturize a collection of events related in the novel. And here let me digress again to emphasize the necessity for giving *Murder!* (and every other English film) intelligent treatment.

The producer has got to bear in mind all the time that he is working for what I would call a universal audience. That is, one which is made up of every class in the community.

Theater audiences are different in that they are individual. You have the St. James's audience, the Haymarket audience, the Lyceum audience, each positively characteristic and individual. Result, the management of the Haymarket wouldn't look at a Lyceum play and the Lyceum management wouldn't give two hoots for a Haymarket show. The Haymarket likes its detective stories (or plays) vellum bound, gold tipped, with that nicety of expression which its patrons pay for. If I may particularize, I regard A. A. Milne's *Fourth Wall* as a typical Haymarket production for that reason. *The Bells,* strong, fierce, gripping in its intensity, belongs naturally to the Lyceum.

Film producers dare not produce for one theater or one audience. They are bound to produce for the West End deluxe cinema and the picture house at the other end of the scale. There is the universal audience and to satisfy that audience there must be combined in the film popular subject matter and intelligent treatment. One element in the universal audience misses the finer details, but grasps the dramatic whole. The other element, that section demanding intelligent treatment primarily, will enjoy that to the full, and is not offended by the popularity of the subject matter.

I have tried to appeal to both elements in *Murder!,* and portions of the story set me some hard thinking. For example, how could I emphasize the pressure to bear upon Sir John to make him agree with the rest of the jury that his protégée was guilty of the murder. He was reluctant, although all the evidence pointed to her guilt. She was found by the side of the body of the murdered woman, who had been no friend of hers. Blood was on her dress and a blood-stained poker by her side.

Eleven of the jury were for conviction; Sir John alone stood out even in the face of overwhelming evidence.

I felt here that it was vital to the success of the rest of the film that intelligent treatment should not be lacking. Trial scene? No! Emphatically no! The public is weary of the trial scene and my opinion is that you cannot get it over on the screen really successfully. It is liable to fall terribly flat. Besides, here Sir John was the central character and here is his entrance—*Enter, Sir John.* It is, in a sense the crux of the story.

A jury scene, then, it had to be. And while Mrs. Hitchcock was curled up in an armchair, nibbling the end of a pencil and gazing into space, I toyed with the gramophone, which, like my thinking apparatus at that moment, wouldn't go. Suddenly the "juice" arrived and the gramophone burst into song. Almost simultaneously my thinking apparatus started into life.

"Got it," I exclaimed. "We'll have all the jury repeating single phrases. We'll make 'em ding dong, ding dong, ding dong into Sir John's ears till he's bewildered. We'll numb him with monotony and stun him with crescendo. That'll make him give in and everybody can see him crumbling. We'll have a rehearsal."

I washed my hands in jubilation while that practical wife of mine set to on questions about rehearsing in a drawing-room, how was it to be done and by whom.

In a few minutes I had commandeered the maid, hauled in my secretary, gathered them in a family circle with my wife, and allotted each one line. And there, in our lofty London drawing-room, the four of us rehearsed the jury scene.

"Red-handed!"

"Poker by her side!"

"Dress all over blood!"

"Head bashed in!"

Over and over again we repeated each our own line, maintaining the rhythm but increasing the tempo. The effect was marvelous. At least, I thought so, and after that rehearsal I could go to the studio with the whole thing cut and dried.

Intelligent treatment is not necessarily something strikingly original. I call it intelligent treatment when the players are called upon to behave with absolute naturalness so that they do a dozen and one little things which have no bearing at all on the story, just the sort of things which occur in real life.

Exaggeration in tone and gesture, common enough on the stage and in some films, is unintelligent treatment. Stiff formality, where in real life there would be informality, is unintelligent treatment. In real life a character of Sir John's physique and temperament would take the mild precaution of occasionally sucking a lozenge to ease his throat. He does so in the film.

The American idea of intelligent treatment of a popular subject is to polish it up with paint and plaster—that is, with beautiful sets, elaborate dresses, with all the gilt and pomp of fabulous wealth and dominating power. American producers have provided what I call highly-polished banality. At home they cater for a nation which is as mixed as our cinema audience. The same films make their appeal in England because they please more people than do those English films which have neither intelligent treatment nor polished banality.

If English films have subject and treatment to recommend them, they will beat the American, with their subject and glitter. I believe the recognition of this difference and making the most of it, will prove the salvation of the English film industry.

It took eleven weeks in the studio at Elstree to produce *Murder!* in two versions—German and English. About my German production I will say nothing. For the other I can only add that I have done my best to make it characteristically English.

HITCHCOCK'S NOTES ON *STAGE FRIGHT*

"Hitchcock's Notes on *Stage Fright*" is printed from a typescript transcription (c. 1950) of a production meeting on *Stage Fright* with Fred Ahern, the production supervisor for the film, and is housed in the British Film Institute. All ellipses are in the original.

HITCH: *You saw in the opening, Fred, we opened with some top shots of a car going through London by St. Pauls. You remember the streets by St. Pauls where it is all devastated on each side? Well, I thought we would have a very high camera shooting down, so that we see these streets at that time of the evening 7 or 8 o'clock.*

FRED: Including St. Pauls Cathedral?

HITCH: *If we can get it in—you know. But I thought we could probably get two angles shot from a high building looking west. Our backs are to the east of London looking west with St. Pauls, and see this car rushing through. Then we need, to follow that, a low shot as it comes towards us. Then as the car fills the screen we cut inside the Studio on to a back projection shot, a process shot you see. Then we'll have process plate as he starts to talk and he describes how he was in his apartment, you see. Now his apartment is a room above a garage. A street is there with rows of garages each side, and there is a narrow staircase up the side that leads to what I think he would have two rooms. A sitting room in the front, maybe a little kitchen between and a little bedroom at the back. Now I don't think we want to make it a combined set, because it means putting a whole set-up on a platform just for the sake of getting the stairs. I think we should break those two sets up—just have the two rooms, a couple of front windows, you know, the little kitchen between and the bedroom at the back. Then build the narrow staircase on a separate set with a double clad door on the outside of the staircase so that we can do that shot when he runs from the Police. You know?*

FRED: Your idea is so that we can build the set on the floor and not have to worry about big platforms?

HITCH: *Forget the platforms. Build a little narrow staircase as a separate thing. Because you save a lot of money that way, don't you?*

FRED: Oh, sure you do.

HITCH: *Now, I won't pick up the part where the Police come and he gets into the car outside. We'll jump now from story continuity when he leaves his house and goes to the Charlotte Inwood house to get in. Well, I thought there that we would make up the front door to start with, but the exterior we ought to do on a real exterior.*

FRED: What type of an exterior is it?

HITCH: *Well, it will be in Mayfair by the back of Piccadilly there. You know the Ritz Hotel?*

FRED: Yes.

HITCH: *That section between the Ritz Hotel and Hyde Park Corner. Well this district would lie to the back of there you see, and we'll have . . . as I say we'll shoot the real exterior there, then just make up the front door in the Studio. Now the inside of the Charlotte Inwood house is what we have to deal with. First of all we need a hallway. We've got to build a hallway because you know when he runs out down the stairs—that's quite a bit of action. The downstairs rooms we needn't build actually, although they'll have to be dressed through the open door. But upstairs the whole set should be very similar to the one we had in Paradine, what was known as Keene's house. Very similar to that.*

FRED: That's the interior?

HITCH: *Interior. And upstairs there should be a couple of rooms. The front room is Charlotte's room and the back room is her husband's room, the man's bedroom. Now, where the bathrooms are I don't know. They don't concern us in our action. But what is important for our action is that she, Nellie, appears in Charlotte's room in the front while Jonathan is in the back faking the burglary. Remember that scene?*

FRED: Yes, her dresser.

HITCH: *Yes, Charlotte's dresser. Which means that from the landing you can get into Charlotte's room and from the landing, through another door, you can get into the back, which is Inwood's room. And the veranda window that he breaks, you know, they are windows which open out on to a little balcony that opens on to the back of the house. So when the Art Director builds that set, he must add the bathrooms where ever it is convenient, you see. Now here again we could build the hallway and the upstairs rooms separately just as we did in* Paradine, *except in that particular set we had the two rooms downstairs, didn't we, in addition to the hallway. This we won't need, we'll just need a hallway.*

FRED: We'll just need an entrance hall downstairs and the staircase and the hallway upstairs and these two bedrooms and the bath.

HITCH: *Yes, that's right. Well, the bathroom isn't used, but I'm just saying from the point of view of architecture, we may have to indicate it.*

Now of course you will need a platform above though, because you know when the girl comes out on the landing we look down, don't we, and see Jonathan running out. So we'll need to shoot from above.

FRED: Just the one shot of his exit.

HITCH: *Yes, I think, I can't remember, are there any others?*

FRED: That's all I remember.

HITCH: *Now, the outside—well, now let's see. That completes his action, eh. He comes outside and just drives off again casually. So we might have to build a little bit each side of the front door, you know, so that we don't overshoot. We cut down our exteriors as much as possible, except we are going to be faced later on with quite a big exterior job there.*

Now, back of the mews when he gets back there and plays his scene with Charlotte, there is no more change in set there. There's a kind of a flashback over his face, isn't there, when he wonders what's happening. Well, that can all take place up in Charlotte's room or Inwood's room. Remember when he sees them opening the Telephone Directory and all that? Well that could take place on the desk in Inwood's room you know, the back room. Now, down in the street, he runs away, doesn't he. He runs down . . . the stairs and lets the police in. Then he doubles back, doesn't he, he lets them come in and he locks the door on them and jumps into his car. Well now I think we ought to shoot that on the real exterior, because shooting up and down that mews or garage street . . . I think it's quite unnecessary to build all that.

FRED: What was the time of day on that?

HITCH: *Late evening, but it's daylight . . .*

FRED: Still daylight.

HITCH: *But, if you like, what we could do, that exterior door at the foot of the staircase, we could put enough set on each side, its only garage doors and shouldn't be too expensive to build, and a bit of cobblestones in front, enough to take the width of the car—so that the little scene where he locks himself in the car just before he drives off, you know, we could do outside that door, and maybe the reverse we could shoot down on the cobbles or against doors the other side. In other words, use our same background, possibly, and bring the car in the foreground and use that as the other side of the street as well—double it up. Couldn't we Fred?*

FRED: They nearly all look alike anyway.

HITCH: *They all look alike and we could paint them another color. Slap a different coat of quick drying paint on those garage doors and then we've got the other side of the street. I shouldn't think it would be too expensive to build. And then you see we are only left with our lock shots there.*
What do you think?

FRED: I think that's good. It would be better to have it inside. Then we have control of our light and our weather.

HITCH: *Well we could even . . . yes, that's right. We should make a special note that in the case of the shots shooting out of the staircase of Jonathan's apartment, that we have cobbles to cover a downward shot. For example, when the woman arrives with the bloodstained dress, we are actually shooting down so you are going to get a cobblestone background. When the police arrive, if we can we should shoot down, but be prepared to have cobbles for a good width across and maybe a bit of a painted backing beyond. Now, I think we have discussed the little scene inside the car, haven't we, and all that.*

FRED: I don't think we covered the little scene for the recording.

HITCH: *Yes we did.*

FRED: Oh.

HITCH: *Well I'll repeat you the scene. Yes, we use the background . . . we make up the garage doors each side of the staircase and use that as a background for the little scene in the car. Remember I said we should take a width enough to take the car.*

FRED: And then double that with a repaint job for the reverse shot.

HITCH: *Sure. For the reverse shot.*

FRED: I see.

HITCH: *Maybe it might be necessary just for these little intimate shots around that car to have a couple of process plates up and down the street. You know, just to . . . because they'll all be very intimate shots there. Now, for the escape of the car . . .*

FRED: Oh, excuse me Hitch. We will need to be covered down one side of the street to catch the moving around of the police car when they try . . .

HITCH: *Well that should be done on the real street.*

FRED: Oh.

HITCH: *That should be done on the real street, you see. But the stuff to be done in the studio—I think we ought to do the real exterior with some doubles in the longer shots, and leave the studio stuff for merely our intimate shots of where the police peer in the car and try to unlock it and so on and so forth. Then we'll need a final Top shot of the car driving away—the little car—followed by the police car, and we've got to choose a location where we are high enough to see the car go all the way down into the garage street or mews out into the main traffic, possibly around by the Dorchester Hotel, or somewhere like that, and out into Hyde Park and away.*

Now, the next thing we pick up is the Royal Academy of Dramatic Art. Of course we will have to use the real exterior for that.

FRED: I have forgotten now, is that the stage door entrance?

HITCH: *No, that's the Royal Academy of Dramatic Art where the rehearsal's going on.*

FRED: Oh, that's right.

HITCH: *Well now we shoot all that on the exterior, as much as possible. Now the only query is whether we have to make up the outside of the entrance to this little rehearsal theater. I'm a little hazy myself as to the exact geography, but the police car goes by and sees the other boy's car with the broken window waiting outside, so they wonder where he is. So we might do that on the real exterior until they go down those area steps which lead to the rehearsal room, and then we have to build a set inside, which will be a rehearsal room like a little auditorium and a corridor beside it which leads on to the wings, you know. Then there will be a reverse on that auditorium.*

Now later on I'll talk to you about research for that particular set.

Now the only other problem—when the police are outside talking about the escaped man, remember they are outside and they say to one detective, "You better stick around here, he may have abandoned the car or he may turn up for it"—so we leave one man out there. Now where that scene plays could be against the front door, but I don't know whether that should the real exterior or not. Maybe we'll have to build that little section, you see. If so, we have another . . . we could do the piece where they pass the policeman when the couple come out—you know.

FRED: The moustache gag.

HITCH: *The moustache gag, you see. Now, of course, actually the only way to stage that to get the suspense out of it is to shoot down the street with them coming towards us, so it really in a way ought to be done on the real exterior, because we don't want to build a whole length of street just for that shot—and then pan them around to the police, you know. We could pan them by the policeman at the crucial point, stay on the Closeup of the policeman and then we can cut, shooting the other way up the street on the real exterior to them approaching their car. Well, once they get in the car, that's from the policeman's viewpoint, we then don't actually show them getting in, we lap-dissolve and we are back in the car again. In other words, he has finished telling his story so that will need another back projection plate but in a different part of London, not near St. Pauls, because this narration would have taken about . . . well, let's assume we get the illusion of it taking about half an hour . . . so now we want a plate about a half an hour's drive in the east of London away from St. Pauls, because that's the direction they're going, you see.*

FRED: Now we're back in the girl's car again.

HITCH: *Back in the girl's car, just a straight back process shot. That fades out and now we fade in on a pictorial shot on the coast at the mouth of the Thames, where its very, very low flat country. In other words, your proportion on the screen will be about twenty-five percent land at the bottom of the picture and seventy-five percent sky, and silhouetted on this low land, with the sea beyond (it will be like a promontory, you know), will be the silhouetted house and one or two boats in the water nearby—sort of one or two masted private yachts. It should be a moonlit-sky—very pictorial—and you see the silhouette of the little car arriving. This is location as well. Then we cut to a Close Shot and we see our couple getting out of the car. They can still be silhouette; we know who they are, so these can be doubles on the real location, and they tip-toe towards the boat. We've got to find a location where a boat is right near this house so we see where they are going. And then we cut to the window or the doorway of the house, which should be built on part of the set that we're coming to next, that's the inside of Eve's farm house. So he comes out and he calls out something, you know, "Bring him in the house." Now, where they suddenly stop at the sound of the farmer's voice, there we can use a stereo or a Shipman backing with a moonlight effect behind it and the sea beyond. Or, we can make it a back projection plate later on when we do back projection. We don't have to do any continuity. That will be about a waist shot of the two people, and then at that point it lap-dissolves again. Now we are inside, the Commodore—we'll call him the Commodore—his house. Now that set should be a big living room with a big open fireplace in it, logs burning, a great atmosphere of the nautical, one might say, and a staircase off, going upstairs—because the boy goes off upstairs, do you remember? And maybe a couple of rooms or one room off above the staircase. The window should be a long window opening out onto the sea, so that we can use a moonlight backing out there for that, and we can avoid it in the daytime and just have the effects of that window. Now the whole of the action takes place there. Now, the question is, when father and daughter are walking along the jetty, you know after the boy goes to bed, I think we could do that against a couple of stereos, tight two, and dolly away from the stereo with the house in the background, you know. Because they could stand there and talk, and then take another stereo or a back projection plate shooting out to sea so I get two angles— I get the angle towards the house and the angle towards the sea. Now that should be sufficient because I don't want to show any Long Shot there. If necessary, when we shoot the Long Shots in the moonlight, which will be, I imagine, infrared stuff, I can shoot an establishing shot of the couple strolling along that jetty towards the boat, up and down there, with doubles. So we pick that location, establish the action, and the Second Unit will take care of all that stuff there, stereos or the process plates. For example, where the girl looks back to the house there's a light in the window. We produce a stereo for that.*

FRED: One can't use stereo though if they do any walking or any moving around.

HITCH: *Yes, straight back, providing I don't pan on it. I think a couple of stereos will give me all I want there. Because the nature of the scene is intimate enough to be very close on them once I've established where they are. There was something of this nature, I mean the house on the flat country and the big sky, in the opening shot of* Great Expectations. *Did you ever see that film?*

FRED: Oh, I remember.

HITCH: *Where the little boy ran along? Well, I know that out by the mouth of the Thames, by the estuary there, there is a place called Brightling Sea, in Essex, where they call them the Essex Flats—they run right out to the sea there. And you would obviously have to shoot this sort of thing not in moonlight but in the very, very early morning sun, because you are looking east, it's the east coast you see, so it would have to be shot in the very, very early morning. On the other hand, you see, if you've got the right silhouette and back light you can matte in the sky. Now there is a little scene where she pushes her car out of a garage. Well that we should do at the house. I don't think it is necessary to build it, although of course Miss Wyman is the leading lady, so maybe we ought to consider either building it or getting some little garage near the studio, you know . . . exterior, it's daylight, it's not like moonlight like this, so that we could either pick a studio garage or something or a little house near the studio in Elstree somewhere for the Close Shot. I don't think it warrants building a set for it. She finds a note on the seat, do you remember, and then she gets in and drives away. Then we go back to this shot, when we see the little car driving away from this house. Now, if we have a bit of luck, you know, maybe we can have the car pushing done in the distance by a double so that we have got practically no background when we shoot our Closeup. But let's examine that in detail with the Art Director. I just hate to go to the trouble of building this kind of set, you know, of which there are hundreds to be got anywhere.*

FRED: Well, we can surely find a location.

HITCH: *Now there is a little scene of her driving back to London. Well, that's a plate again. A Closeup of her in the car against a countryside plate, going away from the house. If necessary, we might make a plate of this location, with the sea and the house in the background, from an entirely different angle, and then there is a shot, I think, looking ahead, or something, you know, beyond the hood of the car.*

FRED: Well, we'll have to cover it so you can choose what angle to use.

HITCH: *To cover it, yes, that's right.*

Now, of course, comes the big problem set. We pick our girl up, coming around the corner of the street. In other words, we have our camera on a street corner shooting away from Charlotte's house. Our camera has its back to Charlotte's house—so that we want to get a street going by and just the corner of the building on the right hand side of the screen—maybe the telephone booth is there, I don't know. So that you get traffic going by behind, which should be a plate, and the corner of the building built against the process plate. And she comes round and stops dead. It probably should be a knee shot or maybe we can get it fixed up so that the curb cuts at the bottom of the screen, or something. So she comes round the corner and comes towards us in waist shot, then she looks. Now is the big problem because this is what she sees. The important thing about it is it's a very busy affair. Normally, you know, if we were shooting it here, we would stage all this on the back lot, because we have police cars, other traffic going slowly, crowds (we've got a crowd of about sixty or seventy people), press photographers, all that curious crowd outside the Inwood house. And I want, if possible, for the Inwood house to be one that goes up steps. I don't exactly mean as rough as a brownstone house, but nevertheless one where we can see the passage of people in and out of the house. So, if it rises up a few steps, don't you think so, photographically it's much better than going up on the level, you see. Now, the question is how to stage that because I think it will be much too big an area for us to build—and I don't know, do any of the back lots have street stuff as big as this?

FRED: No, I think you will find that we have to go into London and pick a location, the same as we did the house on Portland Place.

HITCH: *The only point is, you see, it looks to me as though we ought to do it on a Sunday or something, so we get a clear street, but I don't know what the situation will be. The longer views of it can be Second Unit. The only trouble is that I can't send anybody out there to do it because I'll have to stage all this myself. The detail is very important. This I regard as one of the most difficult scenes in London. We have no problem here, you know, we go out on the back lot and do it, but in London we have a problem, and again I don't feel like spending the money at all to stage it. Now we have the problem, Fred, we also have the problem of moving the girl along from that position, that process position there, she has got to move along the street and get a little nearer to it before she crosses, do you remember? So what we could do, we could build a small section of street, but only what we need for a waist shot, you know, head high, enough to take her along maybe a walk of ten feet—twenty feet say.*

FRED: Well this is all silent.

HITCH: *Silent, yes.*

FRED: So if we can find a good place for this, for Charlotte's house . . .

HITCH: *Yes, but you don't want to take Wyman out there,—you don't want to take any principals out there see. That's why I'm suggesting we build this set, in other words she comes round the corner, looks, we cut to what she sees and she walks along, you see. Then at a certain point she stops and we again photograph across the street from her view point. Now she exits the picture in the Close Shot and a double, the back view of a double, can go across away from us towards the front door. Then we pick up a very close view of the principal, Wyman herself, on our own made up door with the crowd matched in to the real exterior. See what I mean Fred?*

FRED: Let her push through and get into the house on the built up exterior.

HITCH: *Built up exterior. You see, then I think we don't have to take her on the exteriors. Now she is told to move along, isn't she, and so forth. Now we've got an angle looking down the street with a crowd looking on, right? Well I think for that set-up if I put the camera low enough we could use a Shipman so that she is pushed into the gaping crowd. It can either be a Shipman or a process plate. Now, if we want to have moving traffic in the distance this is a process shot, but if we want to shoot up a bit, so that we shoot above the tops of taxis and cars, then it's static and it can be a Shipman set-up right near the real exterior.*

FRED: You know we might find it advisable, if weather conditions are bad, to put the money into building this exterior with just false fronts on the street, some construction and some painting . . .

HITCH: *On the back lot at Elstree you mean?*

FRED: . . . and have them right on the back lot where it's available to us whenever decent weather arises, then we don't have the location problem.

HITCH: *Yet it's Second Unit anyway, Fred.*

FRED: That's right.

HITCH: *You see it's Second Unit anyway, that's why I'm working it out that way, so that you don't have any question of going out with your principals. The only question is myself. Now, what we may consider doing around that period, if . . . you better look into the cost of the set. If we can photograph the particular house we like in London and reproduce it on the back lot, then the Second Unit can line that up, can't they. But then there is this awful business of calling the Extras and all that. Now we've got a scene where she goes on the telephone to her father, do you remember that?—right at this point. Well, that I think calls for a process plate because through the glass of the telephone booth you can see the activity outside the Inwood house beyond. Now we can locate that anywhere we like as though it's on the opposite side of the street, so there's no problem there. As she comes out of the telephone booth she looks across the street and sees some activity—that's the Scotland Yard men coming out of the house. Now I imagine that it could be shot either the same angle we started with when she came round the corner and put the booth near there, or put the booth further up the street. In any case it should be process while she is on the phone and another angle when she comes out so that she looks out in profile, and then we cut to what she sees, which will give us Second Unit stuff, then she exits the picture in Close Shot, just as we had earlier on, and then a double crosses the street again.*

FRED: Then what she does will be a three-quarter shot.

HITCH: *Yes, it will be an independent shot. That's in order that we disassociate her with the major exterior. Now we've got her on the other side of the street outside the house again, and here's where Smith, our leading man, the detective, detaches himself and goes on his own towards the pub. Do you remember that? Well now if we do that shot of her in the crowd, starting to follow Smith, we could do that on our built exterior of the front door of the house. Then we can actually, if we got a couple of good doubles with a camera on the location, pan them down the street with he ahead and she slightly behind him until they got to the outside of the pub. Now that will have to be built double clad, in other words the pub itself and the outside, only just the complete width of it, so that we can go close enough to get her on the sidewalk with a few passers by. But of course what would be nice, and I remember I did it once in Notorious, would be in the pub window to reflect the activity of the street. I did that by a process screen and a process plate reflected in the plain glass window of the exterior. If It didn't cost too much it would certainly tie our pub in with the real exterior, do you think so?*

FRED: Yes, it's good.

HITCH: *It worked very well then when I did it over at RKO.*

FRED: Well it shouldn't be difficult to do.

HITCH: *It shouldn't be, but you know I'm just scared to know how long process is going to take over there.*

Now inside the pub, of course, we've got a straight set which ought to be based on research of an actual pub. The most important thing, why I mentioned research in connection with it Fred, is we want a Mayfair pub, a pub that has a slightly different clientele to one in another part of London. I mean, as it's written in the script, there'll be chauffeurs there, maybe a couple of butlers from a neighboring house, you know. It wouldn't be too big a pub but the saloon bar wouldn't be too tatty, you know. Anyway that's a matter for research and that we'll take up later on under the heading of research.

Now we come to the outside of Eve's mother's house. That's got to be a small Georgian house in the back streets of Westminster. There is a place called Smiths Square, which is typical, but they are not big, they are small Georgian houses behind Westminster Abbey. We will have to build just the exterior of the house, the front door and maybe the two windows, so that the car that pulls up outside, can just get it in the picture. I imagine the whole width of it will be about 20 ft.

FRED: Probably we'll just have to build the first floor.

HITCH: *That's all.*

FRED: The ground floor height.

HITCH: *Ground floor only, that's right. Now the little scene there between her and the detective and she goes in the house.*

FRED: And that's where he takes her home and she invites him to tea.

HITCH: *Yes, yes. Now there is a little cut of Smith going down the street away from her and he stops on the corner to turn and glance back. Now of course that looks like a real exterior again with Smith, but there are lots of opportunities actually, if we can work it with Second Unit, to do that because we have got lots of scenes without Smith which will fit in anytime. Only I would like to get that in. It's just the first intimation that Smith is falling for the girl.*

Well we have nothing to discuss on the next sequence which is in the pub again, where she makes her deal with the actress's dresser, a character called Nellie, you know. Now we have Eve back at her home sitting at a dressing table. And now we better discuss the inside of Mrs. Gill's home. Now what is called for on the screen is a hallway, front door, shooting outside the front door, which we better cheat with a Shipman or something, the downstairs sitting room and a room at the top of the stairs, straight in, which is the study or Eve's room. It's the room where Jonathan eventually hides. Although Eve's dressing table is in another little bedroom, so I imagine that will be a little two-sided set. And I don't think we want to show her passage from her bedroom all the way down when she goes in that disguise, but it looks to me as though we've got to build a hallway there, you know, straight stairs. It's not anything like as elaborate as the home we had in Paradine. *That on a much smaller scale. But again I think the hallway can be built separately, and the sitting room downstairs separately, but double clad the front door on to the hallway, and the study a separate set upstairs and her bedroom a separate little two-aided set.*

FRED: There will be no necessity of taking anyone up the stairs and into this bedroom.

HITCH: *Well we can cut. I don't think . . . you know, Fred, we often go to a lot of expense in building combination stairs and room up top or down below, but actually of course to save building platforms to hold whole rooms saves a lot of dough, doesn't it?*

FRED: Oh, a lot of money.

HITCH: *Eh?*

FRED: I should say so.

HITCH: *And a cut is just as effective, don't you think?*

FRED: As long as there's not a continuous scene . . .

HITCH: *I don't think there is. Well, all these are based on the treatment at present, and I don't think when we come to the actual script it will change—I know it won't change.*

   Well now the next episode where Eve goes to the house as the character, Doris, it's pretty well a repetition of what we showed in the first place, except that there is not so much activity outside the house. She comes round the corner just the same, you know, it's a repeat. In other words, where she came round the corner and looked on the first day of the crime . . . well it's really the second day of the crime, when all the activity was going on. Now she comes round as another character and the activity has died down. So the same corner set-up with the process will be wanted and I've no doubt . . . I don't know whether it will be too long to change her make up . . . but we could knock off that same shot at the same time with a make up change, what do you think?

FRED: If it isn't too much of a change, we should be able to, yes. In this second trip of hers to the house, there will be a police sergeant outside the door . . . I think it's in the treatment.

HITCH: *Yes, it just says . . . all it says is that only a solitary constable will come down in front of the house to stop the curious from looking in. That's all. So she crosses and goes in, front door bell, and now she is inside. Now set-wise she waits in the hallway. Now the only problem is, I am not clear how we shall handle it, whether we see outside this door of the Inwood house. If so, we're shooting down steps, aren't we?*

FRED: Could be.

HITCH: *Yes, but that means putting the whole thing up on a platform just to get a glimpse out of a door, doesn't it?*

FRED: Hitch, if we could shoot from somewhere near eye-level we could do this again with the painting of the stuff across the street or a Shipman.

HITCH: *We could go into that. On the other hand, Fred, if we didn't shoot out the door, you know, and shoot across the hallway, so we never actually saw out the door,—but of course all this is dependent on whether there is a porch in front of the house.*

FRED: Well the drapery man will help us a lot on this too because most of the windows are covered.

HITCH: *I wasn't thinking of the windows, I was thinking of the hallway itself—do you remember like the Keene hallway?*

FRED: Yes.

HITCH: *Shooting out of that door—it's just a question of what you see out there. But I think we should avoid, in any case, going to the bother just for a glimpse. You see, it isn't as though we shot actually out into the street. After all for all we know we might, if we really need it seriously, we could go into the doorway of a house and shoot something on a real exterior, couldn't we? Shoot out. Anyway that's a matter of deciding finally with the Art Director what sort of house we're going to have and so forth. But I still think for our purposes to start with it should be up steps. Upstairs, of course, the action of the new maid, the dressing, the visit to Charlotte by the detective—all take place on the same set, so there's nothing there, is there?*

FRED: Nothing now, no.

HITCH: *The next sequence, of course, is the visit of Smith to tea, where the Commodore comes to tell Eve about Jonathan's escape. Well that takes place in the sitting room in the Gill house, so there is no change there. This, of course, is outside the stage door. Well, I think we'll have to stage that, don't you? That bit of stage door there, too. And we've got to have the interior of the stage door so that looks like a stage door—interior and exterior—maybe an alleyway or something. And it's daylight, because of the long summer evenings.*

FRED: That isn't an expensive set anyway.

HITCH: *No, it isn't, is it?*

Now we come to our big problem, Fred, the theater. Generally speaking, taking in the two sequences there, we need the following sets. We need the auditorium, the stage and the wings—in other words, the offstage atmosphere of the quick change dressing room, the stage door entrance and the stairways, you know, from the stage to the stage door, and the pass door that leads to the auditorium. Now I suggest that we build only the section including the stage door, you know, the outside of it, the inside of the stage door, the turn in the stairs that go up to the dressing rooms and just one corner of the stage only—one side, I'll say—from one edge of the proscenium arch to the inside of it, not the auditorium side, to show the pass doors, switchboard, or whatever they have, the quick change dressing room, which is a little room off the stage—a little square room. Then the door that leads to the stage door and to the dressing rooms should be the same door. Now for the rest of the stage and auditorium, we should do a real theater.

FRED: Well, in our set we need the one dressing room at the top of the stairs.

HITCH: *I'll make that a separate scene.*

FRED: Oh, I see.

HITCH: *That's a dressing room and the corridor outside. That's a separate set. That's Charlotte's dressing room.*

FRED: Yes. Well, we don't take anyone clear up the stairs . . .

HITCH: *No, we cut down to when we turn . . .*

FRED: We cut them in on a set on the floor.

HITCH: *You see, it's dead footage, Fred. We've got no walking shots in the script except along the corridor outside. They turn a corner and we pick them up below, you see, so we make our geography as short as we can. The other piece of set we shall need comes at the end, where Jonathan breaks away. He dashes out through the crowd going home and he goes down some stairs and he pushes open the door, so when the detectives burst their way through, they see the open door that leads to the street and they go through that door, where he's hidden himself around the corner. And Eve comes down there and suddenly she sees him and leads him on down under the stage. That little bit of set we may have to build because geographically there are certain requirements, Fred, which I doubt whether we'll find in a real theater. So they, as far as I can see, are the main pieces. Now, for example, shooting at the stage proper should be done in a real theater. Shooting across the auditorium—we're never going to shoot into the full auditorium, there's no need for that—that's a dull shot anyway, it's been done so many times. Now I'd like to get a light effect so strong on the stage that when you look out into the auditorium it's practically black—maybe a few faces in the boxes, and maybe the first couple of rows or something, but nothing beyond that. We'll have to rig up our own loudspeakers in the theater—a proper rig to suit ourselves, you know—and underneath the stage shots, the prop room. We'll have to build this, don't you think? You don't think we can do it in a real theater for the underneath the stage shots? I hate to build that for two people just walking across that little orchestra pit door.*

FRED: Well, it's possible we might find one that we can shoot it in. We'll have to investigate that.

HITCH: *I'd like to find a theater because that . . . you know, the prop room is all right because you've got atmosphere to put over there—we'll have to dress it anyway. But just the passage from the prop room across the underside of the stage to that orchestra door, I think if we could do it in a real place, it would save the cost of that set—just for two people to walk across, you know, there's no action beyond that. The safety curtain coming down and all that action we want to shoot on a real stage, because the auditorium is open beyond that, you know. I mean, to build one would be quite ridiculous.*

FRED: Let's see. Eve, when the safety curtain drops . . . I've forgotten, was she in the auditorium side, or the back stage?

HITCH: *No, no, no. She went underneath the stage, locked him in the orchestra pit and she ran back under the stage and came round the way that she originally went down.*

FRED: So she sees it from back stage.

HITCH: *She sees it from the door that leads off to the stage door, near the dressing rooms. Of course you'll make a note that Charlotte's dressing room includes the bathroom for the open window when Jonathan gets through there.*

FRED: OK.

HITCH: *Now we have a little problem of Eve and her father where they walk home after the theater. Now that could be a treadmill and a plate, you see, and we walk them out of that shot into the front door of their house. Now I don't know what time of the day it is—but I'm not certain how late this is, Fred. This is probably about 10 or 11—10 or 10:30 at night. It may be dark. Now if it's dark then what we ought to do is to make a plate from a stereo. In other words, make up a stereo, a night shot. I don't see any point in taking lights out, you know. It's late at night and the streets are deserted. Or, we might make it a half-light plate, you know. But we'll have to figure some way of getting that plate done.*

FRED: It's too bad we can't figure some way other than a treadmill. A treadmill is always so artificial. Maybe when we get there we'll find that we could find in one of the smaller towns—maybe out somewhere near the studio—where we might find a place where there aren't lots of people to bother you where we might be able to do the walk right out in the open.

HITCH: *Well, of course, we've got dialogue there. It's a very important little scene.*

FRED: Well the dialogue could be wild track.

HITCH: *There is difficulty with the acting of it on an exterior.*

FRED: Yes, it might be difficult.

HITCH: *Now on the other hand, Freddie, I don't know what size screen they have but if we could get a stereo made up I shall be so close on them, we'll put traffic sounds on, we've no need to show traffic in the shot . . . Their footsteps, and we could have the noise of a car in the distance, you know. Let our dubbing provide our atmosphere rather than try and show it. If we could get that and stick it up in the studio, then I could walk them away from the stereo, couldn't I?*

FRED: Yes. How long a walk do you see?

HITCH: *Well, I see it a walk of about 20 feet. Now alternately, we could add, just head high, a length of brick houses of windows along the Eve Gill house, you know, around Mrs. Gill's house, enough to travel along a three-quarter shot.— Rather like we did in* Capricorn, *you know, two men coming out of the Bank and walking along to Crown Lands Office. That could be done.*

FRED: For our traffic there again we might use your idea of process reflecting in the window where ever they pass.

HITCH: *Yes, but you keep on moving.*

FRED: Oh, that's right, the whole thing has to move.

HITCH: *Better count that out. Well, Fred it's a night shot. I would like to get the feeling of them walking through a London street if we could. Of course you know what we ought to do, don't you, we ought to do that scheme we did on* Paradine *and Selznick got jealous of or something and didn't want to use it. Walk them right along that street and turn them into the house—you know that? That would be a wonderful shot. Make the plate and do it on the treadmill and take them right through the door of the Gill home. We've only got to put them through that doorway, you know they close the door behind them, and we pan them and they go right in the sitting room.*

FRED: Well, we can investigate that and see what we can do.

HITCH: *Look into that and see because it might be effective you know.*

The next sequence is with Jonathan in the room with Mrs. Gill. That's in the sitting room again so there's no change there, unless we combine it with that hall set, you know, but it's just a question if we have the stairs running up. We could quite easily put that downstairs sitting room because that's on the floor level, isn't it? So that wouldn't add to the expense just tying that in with the stairs, would it?

Well, the next scene is the day of the garden party and we've got a shot of a taxi pulling up on the corner of Whitehall, you know, with the Houses of Parliament and Big Ben in the background. She would have come from West-minster, he would have come from Scotland Yard, which is nearby. Now we could show the cab pull up and we could do it again Second Unit. And when she puts her head out of the window we can cut close against a process plate there. He comes out and gets in the cab and goes off with her. Actually, again if it weren't for the question of taking principals out that could easily be done with Jane Wyman and whoever played the man—you know with a concealed camera on the sidewalk or something. It would really establish her, you know—work in a London setting.

FRED: Well, we may have to change our plans about not taking her out.

HITCH: *Well, we can keep that in reserve, Fred. We can make a longish shot of the taxi pulling up and as she puts her head out of the window we cut close to it, you see. As she steps out on the sidewalk, well, that can be a process shot, we can have people walking in the foreground and have quite a good effect with traffic in the background. He can come dashing up—we can flash to him running across the road, if we go on exteriors with the principals. If we don't, he can walk in the picture by process. Well, they get in the cab and then they drive off. There is our process plate inside the cab, and that process plate should be made from where they stop, Houses of Parliament and Whitehall, up there you know and so forth. You tie up the dialogue and see how much plate we want then.*

Now we are at the garden party. This is our pièce de résistance. Well, as you know, Fred, this is based on the annual Theatrical Garden Party which took place last year I think at Roehampton Club and of course I haven't been to it for years and years and years, but it used to take place in the Botanical Gardens in Regents Park. The reason for doing it in the rain is because I felt that photographically it would be more amusing, more interesting, you know. The umbrellas are fresher looking as a pictorial thing—and just to shoot a garden party in the sunshine, well, there's nothing fresh about that you see. And I think this, Fred, that our photography will look better if it's a little drab there rather than trying to reproduce sunshine in the studio which as you know is a devil of a thing to match up. Now the question is, how to shoot it. Now obviously it's going to have to be a process deal, don't you think? I mean the idea of going there on a London exterior and shooting intimate scenes is out, because of the weather situation. Now the question is how to get our plates and our Long Shots. Now there are three ways. One, the ideal way, is to pray to God it rains on the day of their garden party, which is an unkind thing to say, but that would be ideal. Second possibility is to shoot it on the day following the garden party using all their props and their things; take a crowd there and shoot it and if it's a fine day then let's take smoke pots and smoke out the sun as much as possible and take some sprinklers. You don't have to cover the whole area as you know with sprinklers. You cover the foreground and maybe in the background here and there where it shows up, maybe on some water or some tent and any buildings that show water on the top, you know, they can be hosed over or something, and then make the plates of that. Now the third alternative is to stage the Long Shots on the back lot at the studio. You know you can make a deal with the fairground people, to bring their stuff and stick up the tents . . . You still might make a deal for the people to bring the stuff from wherever the garden party took place, similar stuff, and stick it up on the back lot, and we might make all the plates there. But I certainly think for all the dialogue scenes, we've got to do them inside against process. No question about that. Then you see the garden party calls for a couple of tent interiors. Well, that's straightforward, isn't it. There's no problem there. And perhaps we might do some of the tent interiors against some of the plates. I don't know what else to discuss. I think this—I think we ought to consider also in view of the fact that we're going to photograph people against the plates under umbrellas, now the cameraman may say, "I can't light the people." Well, I think we should consider using sort of umbrellas with three-quarter shapes so that they can get some light through the top of the umbrella don't you think, or on very close shots have an umbrella with a hole cut in the top. Some of the umbrellas of course they use aren't black at all, you know, they're made of light cellophane. We could give Eve one of those and maybe the Commodore a black one, that should be all gone into, but I hate to arrive there to shoot, then the camera man who hasn't been consulted at all says, "Well, how do you expect me to light people under an umbrella?" Because the fault I've found with all this kind of thing is that the departments never face the problems until the day of shooting when it's presented to them on the set. Haven't you found that? All the contingencies connected with this garden party should be faced as early as possible. Just the same, while we are on the subject, the question of the stage stuff. That number that Charlotte does, you know, whether we see it from the front or the wings, has to be

*rehearsed so that we don't hold up production while the number is rehearsed.
That's got to be ready-made and stuck up there so we can photograph it. And there
is also a question which I'll have to examine with you at a separate time and we
must make a note of it, what actual stage stuff we're going to need not only for the
Charlotte stuff but for any other background stuff that we need during the scenes
in the wings, especially with the arrival of Jonathan and so forth. I think, as far as I
can remember it's mostly Charlotte. So that we ought to have a look at it. And then
you've got to go into the question of what numbers we're going to use, whether we
take numbers from here, and also whether we can get costumes shipped from here
to save us buying them. I mean there are musicals being made all over this town,
there must be costumes that are available but we can't tell what we want until we
get the number. But in any case I think to go to the trouble of having those things
made in England is fantastic. Won't they allow us to ship them in?*

FRED: Yes, we can ship them in.

HITCH: *So I think it is a very important thing to get the costumes lined up so that
we can ship them once the number has been decided upon.*

*Well you see there are some shots in the garden party which need not be
process. For example, there's the scene where Nellie, the blackmailer, is taken
behind some tents, you know. Now that could be played against some bushes or
trees. On the other hand, I would prefer always to keep the garden party
atmosphere going, even though we may show a couple of pieces of tent in the
foreground and through the alleyway between the two tents, then we see the
garden party beyond. So we've got to be fairly ingenious as to how we set these
little pieces up. But the whole point is that all these various meetings and settings
that have been written that way you see—you cut from one thing to another—
and each little set-up should either have a bit of tent in the front or a tree
processed behind it, you know, so that we preserve the atmosphere of our garden
party continually, and if you watch the treatment carefully you'll find they are
cut from one thing to another.*

FRED: We can make lots of use of trees in this.

HITCH: *Well I would say make use of tents as much as anything . . . well now look
at the tree in* Capricorn—*it took years to do and was never finished, so I hope to
God we don't get anything like that because that was really ridiculous, wasn't it?
Well that's the general survey of the garden party. The actual shots are pretty well
indicated in the script, where they take place and so forth. It's just a matter of the
Art Director making various little setups and using bits of tent as I say and
process combined with it. And obviously it's a dub job, you realize that, because
there's the sound of rain all the way through.*

*Well the next sequence is back in the house, isn't it, with Jonathan. That's in
the study upstairs, which I've already talked about, you know that's a little room
. . . I'll have a talk with Whit and see if we can't cut out that set and make that*

*Eve's bedroom back there. It wouldn't actually be Eve's bedroom . . . no I don't
like the idea of showing Jonathan hiding in her bedroom. Rather, when we have
a dramatic scene with him at the end there, you know when he starts giving
himself up and all that, it better take place in the study—so that it would need to
be a little sort of characteristic room of a young girl, you know,—a fair amount
of books and photographs—school days and all that sort of thing.*

FRED: On the order of an upstairs sitting room?

HITCH: *Yes, sure. In fact it could be partly the mother's study, it needn't be Eve's
own study—a general little sort of poor man's library, you know, that kind of
thing. Well there's a scene downstairs in the sitting room with Smith. Smith goes
off to the theater. Now the rest of the sequence at the end is in the theater, isn't it,
which we know pretty well. We know it's in the auditorium. You see I've written
it to save expense so that we don't have a finale going on on the stage, you know.
We see the orchestra leave, which establishes our orchestra pit door,—(ingenious
huh?) the last of the audience leaving—(the camera will be up in a box so that it
will look down and see our group pan round to the loudspeaker)—and I've
described to you the different pieces of set: back stage, stage door, exit, that
special turn in the stairs we require for the little bit of set where Eve takes the
man on down through into the prop room. Oh the prop room—that shouldn't be
an expensive set, should it?*

FRED: No, the only thing expensive about that would be the rental of props.

HITCH: *Supposing we borrow them from one of the theaters?*

FRED: Or perhaps the theater that we're going to use for the shot will have an
established prop room with lots of old things in it. We might find it far better
to just go right down there and shoot.

HITCH: *We might find even that we could get permission to use a prop room of a
big theater like Drury Lane, even though we may not use the theater itself. That's
a question and we must go into all that.*

FRED: I think that's worth checking because it will certainly save a lot of money
if we can find a place that's already outfitted.

HITCH: *Well I think I have covered the sets and location pretty well. Now shall we
talk about research required? I'll run through the movie again on the question of
research.*

*Well obviously, Fred, the first research we want, it would seem to me . . . I mean this
is stuff that you can do before I get there . . . maybe some photographs of stills of
that Essex exterior house with boats nearby, you know. Maybe some photographs of a mews, especially that top shot which shows the car driving away.*

FRED: You mentioned in the first part of the last recording what district you
thought this mews apartment is in . . .

HITCH: *Mayfair. Then some selections for the house for Charlotte—that's Mayfair.
That should be a pretty good class place, you know fairly elegant.*

FRED: And your main requirement is that it has steps up to it.

HITCH: *Yes, so that we can see the procession of people going up and down. Now here's a thing I want to find out. I would like to get, maybe from the newspapers or the police archives, some photographs outside the scene of a murder,—see how many people they got around there, you know—so that we get some idea of what the atmosphere is like. There'll probably be many murder cases on the actual location, but they should be taken . . . or the photographs that you secure from the newspapers should be taken on the day after a murder has been committed in London somewhere. I'd like to get that research done. In regard to the theater—well, we ought to get some different photographs of different theater interiors. Now the most important thing about the theater is that the stage is a big stage so that we can get far enough back to photograph it.*

FRED: You mean the depth back stage.

HITCH: *And the depth on each side, so that when we're shooting across the wings we can get far enough back. You know what I mean? That's very important. It's no good having a stage that is so small we've got no room to shoot around it. So I would say myself we ought to go, regardless of the auditorium, for the biggest stage we can get that gives us a lot of shooting room. That's very important, Fred.*

FRED: Then we might also get some photographs of the back stage of those theaters . . .

HITCH: *We want to get a lot of research on back stage because in assembling our quick change room and the stage door, you know, we may have to make up our own to suit our purpose of our action. But we should get a lot of actual research of what they all look like—detail, the signs, electric wiring and everything. I don't want any guesswork on the art side as to what those theater wings look like. I want it based on actual photographs all the way through, you know. Now I want photographs taken of an apartment over a mews—over a garage.*

FRED: Go right inside and take photographs.

HITCH: *I want photographs of that, I want photographs of the staircase and everything, you know. That's very important because that's an unusual thing and I don't want any guesswork on that. Now the same applies,—we've got to choose a nice house and maybe some interiors—photographs of interiors of the little house in Westminster, you know. Now for research on the garden party, we should get all the newsreel we can for the last couple of years—they're well covered by newsreel—all the newsreel we can and all the stills taken last year and maybe the year before—Long Shots especially. There should be plenty of those in existence.*

FRED: I know where to get that.

HITCH: *Now, here's a very important thing. I want to get some help from Scotland Yard on the behavior of our man, the police procedure and so forth. Now this has to be done very diplomatically because you know our character, Smith, operates*

*an awful lot on his own at the end, you know, and I don't quite know how that's
to be handled. I don't think it ought to be handled officially yet and I don't think
it ought to be handled from the bottom through the press representative . . .
public relations man I mean at Scotland Yard. When I was on* Paradine, *you
remember, I went to the Editor of the* Daily Express, Christiansen, *and asked
help and he put me on to some fellow who had no entrée whatsoever. He took me
down to the press public relations man and I found myself among a lot of
cigarette smoking reporters. Whereas somebody else told me that the Commis-
sioner of Police was the man who would have liked to have met me while I was
in London. Wasn't that a jerky situation to be in? So we've got to go right to the
top. I would like to have, if we can, a Scotland Yard man assigned to this
picture—but an important man to advise us on all the actual procedure. But I
want it to be done discreetly because I don't want Scotland Yard to say, "Well
hell, you can't have a man behave like that—in Scotland Yard they don't behave
that way." You know, I don't want to put ourselves in their hands so that we tie
our own hands in the matter, you see. You'll have to discuss that with Mr. Clark
over there. But it's a very important thing because I don't want to do a lot of
things that are wrong; on the other hand I don't want to have Scotland Yard tell
me well you can't do this and you can't do that.*

FRED: I think that's a connection we should make after you're in London.

HITCH: *Well you know that Sam Ingle, the Fox Producer, is over there at the
moment. He is lining up a Scotland Yard picture, you know. Zanuck wants to do
a kind of a FBI thing—*House on 92nd Street *over again with the help of
Scotland Yard. I don't think they'll get the same facilities—I'm not certain, but
I'm wondering whether you ought to discuss this thing with Tenny Wright as
soon as you can and tell him of our angle over there and see what we ought to do
and see whether we ought not to put a phone call through to Clark in London—
have Tenny Wright call him and say that we shall require facilities from Scotland
Yard and we'd like somebody to get to the top and, if necessary, beat Fox to it. It's
very important that, Fred.*

*Now, I don't know what other research we wanted for the Royal Academy of
Dramatic Art—photographs of all that down there?*

*Now there's another very important thing we will need. That is the coopera-
tion of the Actors Orphanage for us to be able to photograph the Theatrical
Garden Party and all, and the cooperation of the Royal Academy of Dramatic
Art for us to reproduce their rehearsal room and call our character a student of
the Academy. That will have to be taken up with Kenneth Barnes. And the
Actors Orphanage I think is a Noël Coward matter. Now it would seem to me,
(this has to be discussed with Clark when you get there), whether we don't
donate the premier of the picture in London to the Actors Orphanage in return
for these facilities. For example, if we were fortunate enough to get some shots of*

the Garden Party, (and if we put rain on it afterwards, in some way or other printed rain on it), showing the well-known actors and actresses—that's why I say the ideal would be if it really rained and we were actually able to get the real thing because then we would get all these London actors and actresses, all the film stars, in the thing, because they couldn't refuse if the Actors Orphanage were the beneficiaries—at least I don't think so. On the other hand, Rank may kick at letting his stars appear in a rival company's picture.

FRED: Well that's something also Clark can deal with.

HITCH: *He can deal with that. The idea I don't think is so much of a problem. We've got to give some donation there, but after all we don't bring them into disrepute at all. The only thing we do with the Actors Orphanage is to make their Garden Party a wash out. I don't know who knows Noël Coward well enough, I mean I know him, but somebody might know him a bit more too. Maybe Sidney might help us in that matter by ringing up and talking to him. But they are the two main things that we are actually . . . well there are three things. We're putting Scotland Yard into the picture, the Actors Orphanage Garden Party and the Royal Academy of Dramatic Art. They are actually going into the picture, so we have to get full approval on all those matters. Again, you see, we've got to give some bait to the Actors Orphanage to let us do it in the rain.*

Now in regard to the set-ups and continuity of shooting, naturally I don't think we can shoot this thing in continuity. It depends upon how your stage space situation is. But I think one thing we've got to shoot out of continuity is the theater, so I'd like to leave that till last. Everything in the theater left over till last.

FRED: And all of our main characters appear there too, so that will mean we have to watch the time on our actors very closely.

HITCH: *Yes, but what I don't want to do, Fred, I don't want to bring the end near the beginning of the picture. I'd rather [take] things that belong to the beginning of the picture and put 'em when we're near the end of the picture. Do you see what I mean? Now the garden party, that can be shot in continuity pretty well. And otherwise I think that if we could leave . . . the most important set to be left standing that we could leave and go back to is Mrs. Gill's house. Because I think that the shots in the Inwood house can be done both together. We needn't jump out of that set you know—in other words, Jonathan covering up the crime and the maid can be shot just before we do her first day of work as the dresser. But I'd like her first day of work as the dresser to come into the continuity. See what I mean?*

FRED: Well I'll put this show on a breakdown board so that we can juggle it around for shooting.

HITCH: *Yes, but you see, as a general principle, Fred, when we shoot out of continuity, the things that come at the end I'd like to shoot at the end of the schedule. And anything in that same set that did come at the beginning, I'd like to tack that on to it. Is that clear?*

Roughly, it would seem to me—I don't know, but a rough schedule—it would start in sets in the studio I mean—sets and the arrangement of them in Jonathan's place, you know. Then after Jonathan's scene, the Royal Academy of Dramatic Art scene—or maybe that could go at the end if necessary, because we've got it at the end of the picture as well. So if we didn't do that then you'd go right to the father and daughter scene with maybe a process between—you know, the journey down. Then the father and daughter scenes, then the Inwood house interior. And where the exteriors come in all the time,—I don't remember— maybe they could come between. Maybe the exterior of the Inwood house could come before the interior. And after the Inwood house . . . or we can get the pub first, then the Inwood house, and knock off the two pub scenes together. But the set we should dance in and out of is the Gill home I think—that is spot it through.

FRED: As far as exteriors are concerned, we'll have to just lay out our work to be done exterior and shoot it as we can.

HITCH: *As we can and shoot it even ahead—start it ahead of our schedule. The exteriors we can start as soon as we get our plates done.*

FRED: It would be well, too, to have the exteriors done before we do the interiors, for cutting purposes.

HITCH: *That's right, sure. And the plates and all that. Now how long, in black and white, does it take to get plates through? In other words, supposing we were to do the Long Shots of the Garden Party, how long would we have to wait for those plates to come through?*

FRED: Here, we have to wait about four days for black and white.

HITCH: *Do we, as long as that? That means to say that I've got to shoot the Long Shots of the Garden Party . . . but they can be done Second Unit again Fred, can't they? So they wouldn't affect our main shooting.*

FRED: Of course we may be able to push rushes on particular plates that we need and get them faster too.

HITCH: *Well it isn't a question. If I could shoot the Long Shots one day and get the plates the next day . . .*

FRED: Well that's impossible, I know.

HITCH: *Well I'll have to fill in with something else then. Well if we have to fit in with that kind of thing it would be well to preserve some kind of pieces of action, you know, outside the Royal Academy of Dramatic Art or one of those odd pieces with the police or something, or fill in with all those odd kind of pieces, you know.*

FRED: We can tell when we get it all down on paper and see where we stand as far as that goes.

HITCH: *Now you've got enough in the treatment to get all the shots out, haven't you.*

FRED: I think I have.

HITCH: *Oh yes, well they're all clearly indicated there.*

FRED: That I have to get on to right away.

HITCH: *That can be got on to quickly, you see. Nothing else, is there?*

FRED: Nothing else I know of.

HITCH: *OK.*

INTERVIEW WITH ALFRED HITCHCOCK

François Truffaut and Claude Chabrol

"Interview with Alfred Hitchcock" was originally published in *Cahiers du Cinéma* 8, no. 44 (February 1955): 19–31. It was translated from the French text for the present volume by James M. Vest. I have added the headings *"Cahiers"* and "Hitch-cock" to identify the speakers. All ellipses are in the original.

HITCHCOCK: My most recent film is called *The Trouble with Harry.* I started it immediately after *To Catch a Thief.* I finished *To Catch a Thief* one afternoon at 5:30, and at 7:30 *Harry* was underway. There's a reason for that. *The Trouble with Harry* was to be filmed in the East of the United States, at the time when the trees were in full autumnal color. It's the first time, to my knowledge, that a film has been made in color specifically for the season in which the action occurs. So I brought together actors, cameramen, a whole crew and we left for Vermont. There we waited for the leaves to deign to transition from green to yellow and from yellow to red. But, you see, we were forced to start production very quickly, because the leaves might very well have not waited for us. It's very interesting because during the entire film the color scheme will be that of the trees: yellow and red. *The Trouble with Harry* is a comedy about a corpse. This corpse is named Harry and causes numerous difficulties for various people. One man, who has gone rabbit hunting, thinks he has killed Harry. With the help of a friend, he buries the corpse. Then he recalls that he had only three bullets and, since he killed three rabbits, he says, "I've not killed Harry. Let's dig him up!" In the course of the film, the body is buried and disinterred three or four times. It's macabre but very funny. I made this picture in thirty-one days and it was edited at the same time as *To Catch a Thief,* by same editor, and thus the two films will be finished around the same time.

CAHIERS: The Trouble with Harry *seems to resemble your English films.*

HITCHCOCK: Yes, it is rather like a British comedy. Do you recall *Kind Hearts and Coronets*? It's a film of that sort, you see.

CAHIERS: *Is it more like recent films from England or like your films from before 1940?*

HITCHCOCK: More like current British films. You know, Londoners especially like comedies about corpses: jokes about cadavers and things of that sort are *de rigueur.* In other countries, in Germany for example, the public takes death very seriously and never joke about it. I think the French understand this sort of joking; they are more like the English in terms of humor, aren't they?

CAHIERS: *Perhaps. To return to our main topic, we must confess that we prefer— by a large margin—your American films.*

HITCHCOCK: Maybe because they are meant for a wider audience?

CAHIERS: *That's not it. We think they are more serious.*

HITCHCOCK: With more depth and background?

CAHIERS: *Yes.*

HITCHCOCK: They doubtless have more character. I was very young when I made my English films, and I made them with all the fervor of a young filmmaker. Now I must make them more substantial. It is very likely that I will remake one of my old English films, *The Man Who Knew Too Much,* but this time it will be with an American starlet, and, keeping the same subject matter, I'll treat it a little more seriously.

CAHIERS: *So you made comedies when you were a young filmmaker and your recent films—particularly* I Confess—*are completely serious. We would call that an "evolution"!*

HITCHCOCK: Yes, because, you see, today I believe we must create a different cinema, give more substance to our stories. In other words, we used to treat stories more superficially, while the difficulty nowadays . . . Take for example a spy story. Today we must pay greater attention: What story? And why? The public asks many more questions. Formerly it sought only a sort of superficial tension. Now one must have that tension plus much more reasoning behind it.

CAHIERS: *Is this an imperative for you, from within you or for the public?*

HITCHCOCK: Both, I think. Personally, from the perspective of a technician, I am not deeply interested in the moral or the message of the film. I am like, let's say, a painter who paints flowers, or this table, or this tape recorder. It's the way of treating things that counts most. But still, if I were a painter, I'd say,

"I can only paint with a message." It's just that this message is too profound for a painting.

CAHIERS: *What's curious about your American work is that all your pictures treat the same subject matter, or rather that one finds in each of them comparable relationships among the characters.*

HITCHCOCK: Yes, I know.

CAHIERS: *Always the stronger and the weaker; always the idea of domination. Why?*

HITCHCOCK: I believe it's for the following reason: in my opinion, viewers must have a strong emotion while watching the film. They expect that I should raise their anxiety concerning what will happen. And that is possible only if I succeed in making the audience identify with the characters. If they remain indifferent, sitting there—if they remain only observers—there isn't sufficient emotion, and no anxiety at all. That's why the content is always better when the audience can experience the same emotions as the actors on the screen.

CAHIERS: *We think that you began to change your style with your first American picture,* Rebecca?

HITCHCOCK: Yes, that's right.

CAHIERS: *All your Hollywood films can be found in* Rebecca, *and for the first time. For example, Laurence Olivier's confession is like a preliminary sketch for Ingrid Bergman's in* Under Capricorn.

HITCHCOCK: Yes, exactly. They both had to pace up and down in the room as if on a stage. You understand what I mean? Olivier did that quite well. I don't know whether Bergman did that properly in *Under Capricorn*. Not so well, I think. That was Hitchcock disarmed in the hands of the actor. No good can come of that.

CAHIERS: *The films we prefer are* I Confess *and* Under Capricorn.

HITCHCOCK: I find them too serious. *Rear Window* too: overly serious. Have you seen it?

CAHIERS: *Not yet.*

HITCHCOCK: The ending is very nerve-wracking. American audiences scream and can scarcely stand the suspense of this film. The viewers scream and that makes me very happy; that pleases me. Even now that sort of thing amuses me enormously. I'm not so serious as the public in that. I must admit that, hearing them cry, I find that comical.

CAHIERS: *No doubt, but a film like* I Confess, *you did very seriously?*

HITCHCOCK: Yes, because it was a religious film. But a lot of people said this is not true Hitchcock because you don't find a blend of the dramatic with the comic.

CAHIERS: *For us the true Hitchcock is much more than that. And for you?*

HITCHCOCK: Oh, there's no doubt. I would very much like to make a picture based on Dostoyevsky, *Crime and Punishment,* for instance. That would be very easy for me. I tend to make serious, deep films and that's easier than the pictures that I must make commercially. Commercial movies are difficult for me because they involve perpetual compromise, lots of it. And it's much, much easier to make a film without compromise.

CAHIERS: *It seems to us that* Rope *is a draft, a first sketch of* Under Capricorn, *as* Strangers on a Train *is for* I Confess. *If we especially like* Under Capricorn *and* I Confess, *it's because you seem to have included the very best from your other pictures just, as you say, without "compromise."*

HITCHCOCK: Yes, I see what you mean.

CAHIERS: Rope *is the first film in which you used the ten-minute take.*

HITCHCOCK: Yes, I experimented in *Rope.* I created a new technique because I said to myself here's a story that takes place in a single setting, in an hour and a half. Consequently I'll have to come up with a special film technique that will be continuous, without stopping, with no cuts at all, in order to create this exact sensation of continuity.

CAHIERS: *And you returned to this technique and refined it in* Under Capricorn?

HITCHCOCK: Yes, that's right. It was a very difficult technique, because one had to . . . Certain people thought it was a mistake and that it wasn't truly cinema. Yet it's pure cinema because you must do the editing in your head, in advance. Then the movement between scenes is made continuous by the movements of the actors, not of the camera alone, but of the actors *and* of the camera together. Thus the camera roams about while the actors change positions, and together they establish various framed compositions. In my opinion it's a purer cinema, but not enough people agreed. Still for me, it's nevertheless a purer cinema because the cut was a necessity in olden days when one could not move the camera about.

CAHIERS: *Certainly when you were making* Rope, *were you already thinking of* Under Capricorn?

HITCHCOCK: Uh . . . no. *Under Capricorn* was not in pre-production. I made *Under Capricorn* because I wanted to apply the concepts of *Rope* to a different sort of story to see what that would yield.

CAHIERS: *One might even say that this technique is pushed to new limits in* Under Capricorn, *because you took on a set with many rooms, a fourth wall, and even an upstairs level.*

HITCHCOCK: Yes, you're right. It was terribly difficult for the technicians.

CAHIERS: *Similarly you took the techniques of* Strangers on a Train—*lighting, framing, editing—and applied them, in a somewhat purified manner, to* I Confess.

HITCHCOCK: Yes, it was much purer from every point of view. It was not so commercial. The settings, the characters, everything was purer.

WHY WOULD I GO SEE THE RUSHES?

CAHIERS: *Is it necessary for you to make commercial films?*

HITCHCOCK: It's really a matter of conscience. My conscience forces me to make commercial films. Because, you know, a lot of money is involved, other people's money loaned to you so you can express yourself. And my conscience tells me: One must tone it down so "they" don't lose their money; or else the industry will die peacefully. There's my reasoning.

CAHIERS: *Were you your own producer on* Rope, Under Capricorn, *and* I Confess?

HITCHCOCK: Yes.

CAHIERS: *Were those stories really close to your heart?*

HITCHCOCK: Yes, that might well be. Yes, that could be so. Look, in England "they" made a lot of non-commercial films and there is no longer an industry: "they" no longer have money to make films. You have to drum it into your head. . . . After all, what is a movie theater? A cinema is a big screen with a whole lot of seats to fill. Surely, if the cinema were different, if things took place in a room, like a picture one looks at on a wall, that would change many things. But you have to recognize facts. That's exactly what makes filmmaking difficult. It would be infinitely more pleasant if one could film in 16mm and then, as with all the other arts, if deemed necessary to reach a bigger audience, to expand to 35mm for wider distribution. It would reduce upfront costs to a trifle, and then, as in the case of a manuscript that one edits for publication, it could become something big. But as things are, it's a bit like a painter who would have to pay a million dollars to paint his picture and frame it.

CAHIERS: *Jacques Becker once said, "Of all directors, Alfred Hitchcock must have the fewest surprises during projection."*

HITCHCOCK: That's true. I don't even view rushes. I'm asked, "Why don't you go to rushes?" I answer: "Why would I go to rushes?" I have seen what happened during filming; in my head, I know the framing in detail, and if there is some problem with lighting or in the camera, the cameraman will tell me. But as for the acting and the composition of shots, I know. So it's not necessary for me to view rushes.

CAHIERS: *This certainty of framing and blocking appears to us to be growing since* Strangers on a Train. *It seems that the results are closer to your sketches. Is this exceptional precision due to Robert Burks, your usual director of photography since* Strangers on a Train?

HITCHCOCK: I use Burks now because he facilitates my work, because with him I never look into the viewfinder. I'm asked: "Why don't you look in the viewfinder?" But after all I know what lens is in use and its aperture; I can see the position of the camera and the actors. I tell Burks, "Frame tightly, OK?" and he answers, "Right." I have all that in my head, their placement, their size, everything. He knows the framing I want and, if there's the least doubt, I draw a little sketch. Hand me a pencil. First I draw a rectangle in the shape of the screen, you see, and I say: there's the frame; a little drawing for each setup. Look: a man there in front; now here's the girl and there's the guy watching from a little farther off. The position of the characters determines the framing. Good. The first thing I draw, no matter what the framing, is the first thing people will notice: the faces; so, above all, the position of the faces. You see. I first draw in the heads and that dictates the framing.

CAHIERS: *Yes, exactly. Since* Strangers on a Train *the framing has seemed different, as has the lighting: more rigorous, sharper, clearer, with more grays . . .*

HITCHCOCK: That depends. I use a different technique for each story. It changes every time. For instance, in *Strangers on a Train* I had to show a menacing crazy man. I couldn't use close-ups all the time: that's boring. So I had the idea of using a small silhouette. The grandiose Jefferson Memorial in Washington, all white, with a little silhouette, oh so black. That was the equivalent of a close-up.

CAHIERS: *It was better.*

HITCHCOCK: Oh, yes! I think so too.

I'M INNOCENT!

CAHIERS: *Do you dislike being labeled "the master of fright," "the king of suspense," "maker of thrillers," etc.?*

HITCHCOCK: In America one is quickly typecast, once and for all. I'm obliged to do suspense; otherwise, people are disappointed. In other words, as I often say, if I were to make a movie of *Cinderella*, "they" wouldn't be happy unless there was a corpse in the carriage.

CAHIERS: *But would you like to do* Cinderella?

HITCHCOCK: *My Cinderella*. That might be interesting from the standpoint of composition, of framing.

CAHIERS: *Some years ago you were offered a curious project: a modern* Hamlet *with Cary Grant, from a psychoanalytical point of view.*

HITCHCOCK: Yes, yes. But do you know why I didn't follow up on that project? It's funny. A fellow sent me a registered letter, by courier, stating he had written a considerable number of modern Hamlets, and that, if I were to do mine, he would sue me for $1,250,000. I went to court and I won. But the fellow was a poor man and was judged non-accountable for costs. I paid the court costs and, after all was said and done, that set me back $10,000.

CAHIERS: *That's awful.*

HITCHCOCK: It's horrible. So for the moment I've abandoned the project, but I may take it up again. A modern Hamlet but with exactly the same problems.

CAHIERS: *That would be a serious film?*

HITCHCOCK: Yes, a very serious film.

CAHIERS: *A large number of people prefer your British films. And you?*

HITCHCOCK: I prefer the current American Hitchcock genre, with a little more humor than the English films.

CAHIERS: *For you or for the public, that humor?*

HITCHCOCK: For the public, I'm afraid.

CAHIERS: *Your ideal film, the one you'd like to be able to project like a painting on the wall, would it be closer to* I Confess *or to* The Lady Vanishes?

HITCHCOCK: Oh, to *I Confess.*

CAHIERS: I Confess?

HITCHCOCK: Yes, certainly.

CAHIERS: *This is very important for us.*

HITCHCOCK: Yes, it would be closer to *I Confess.* For example, I'm thinking about a film idea that is terribly appealing to me. About two years ago, a musician at the Stork Club in New York was returning home and at his doorway, at two in the morning, was hauled off by two men who dragged him around to different places like, for example, a bar, and showed him to people, saying: "Is this the man? Is this the man?" He is eventually arrested for robberies. He was completely innocent. He had to stand trial and all, and afterward his wife went crazy. She was put away in an asylum, where she must be still today. And during the trial there was a juror, convinced of the defendant's guilt; and while the lawyer was interrogating one of the witnesses for the prosecution, this juror stood up and said, "Your Honor, do we have to listen to all this?" That was a small procedural breach, but a mistrial was declared. And during the interval before the retrial, the real criminal confessed. I think that would make a very interesting picture, showing events from the point of view of this innocent man, what he must suffer, how he is put at risk by the actions of another. Everyone around him is so friendly, so kind; when he cries, "I am innocent!," people respond, "Sure, sure!" or "Of course!" or "You bet." Totally frightful. And I believe I'd like to make a film from this true story. That would be very interesting. You see, normally in this sort of film the innocent man in the story is in prison, but that is never shown on screen. It's always some reporter or private detective who works to get him released from prison. But no one ever shows—at least I've never seen—films from the point of view of the accused man himself. I would like to do that.

CAHIERS: *That's like* I Confess *but pushed much farther from the point of view of Montgomery Clift. What's curious is that although many of your films are rather faithfully based on novels, still your pictures return to the same themes and similar characters, even though there is little similarity among the sources.*

HITCHCOCK: You've seen *Dial M for Murder*? It's the same thing as the play, yet it's not the play. Everything is in the details: the key, the hands, etc.

CAHIERS: *Yes, quite different. Unfortunately we saw it in 2-D.*

HITCHCOCK: I made it in 3-D.

CAHIERS: *That seems important for certain details, for example the camera in the chandelier.*

HITCHCOCK: Yes, the chandelier was very interesting in three dimensions! I used the process to bring objects toward the audience only twice: first when the girl reaches out behind her for something to help her; then for the key under the carpet on the stair. I say to the viewer: there's the key. The only two moments when things come out of the screen.

CONFESSION

CAHIERS: *Let's return to that famous "Hitchcock touch." Is it merely a process of construction, or what?*

HITCHCOCK: Remember that I always make movies on paper. I don't rely on the writer. In fact I've never filmed another's screenplay. Never. I bring in the writer. I sit him down there. I sit down here. The film is constructed this way from beginning to end. The writer helps me a lot. He finalizes the dialogue and may even offer an idea. And when I begin to shoot the film, for me it's over. So much so that I wish I didn't have to shoot it. I've seen it all in my head: topic, tempo, framing, dialogue, everything.

CAHIERS: *It seems to us that all your films possess what we call an "added dimension," somewhat, or entirely, metaphysical.*

HITCHCOCK: Oh, that is me. That is my soul getting into the subject. That belongs to me. Some other story would not interest me in the least. If you said to me, would you like to make a film of some rather ordinary play, let's say *Four Colonels in Love*, I'd answer: Maybe, but that doesn't interest me at all. I could do it, from a purely technical perspective. Then that would become a Hitchcock film, in altering it, in rearranging it.

CAHIERS: *That change would not be entirely technical?*

HITCHCOCK: No, no. Not technical at all. It's something I make the characters experience.

CAHIERS: *So you have something to say and you say it?*

HITCHCOCK: I try. You've got the sense of it.

CAHIERS: *Certain critics don't realize that.*

HITCHCOCK: Not at all. That's very true.

CAHIERS: *Isn't that a little annoying to you?*

HITCHCOCK: Oh, you know, that doesn't have much impact. I continue and it all begins again, you see.

CAHIERS: *You've bought the rights to a French novel by Boileau and Narcejac,* D'Entre les morts.

HITCHCOCK: Yes. Oh, that will be interesting to film!

CAHIERS: *It's a perfect subject for you. One would think it had been written with you in mind!*

HITCHCOCK: It is likely to yield excellent results. The part I like the best in this story is when the man recreates the woman from among the dead.

CAHIERS: *Have you read the book or only a synopsis?*

HITCHCOCK: I've read the synopsis. That's enough for me. What if I don't read the book? I probably won't even glance at it. I'll make the film from the synopsis.

CAHIERS: *In France?*

HITCHCOCK: No. In America.

HERE'S WHAT I'D SAY

CAHIERS: *Among your projects you have the adaptation of the novel* Malice Aforethought *by Francis Iles.*

HITCHCOCK: Yes, that's something I'd love to do. You know the story? It's about a little old doctor. I'd love to make a film of that, but you see, no one in America or in Britain wants to do a film about an older man. . . . No one cares about the elderly. That's the big problem. I could see Alec Guinness in it.

CAHIERS: *Another project we've heard about is* Bramble Bush.

HITCHCOCK: Yes, but that didn't pan out. I started working on it because it offered an interesting situation, but I never finished. It was a bit too much like Raymond Chandler, private detective and all, and I don't like that. I don't like gangsters. I don't like police fighting gangsters. I prefer ordinary human beings plunged into risky situations, of course.

CAHIERS: *To come back to the subject of similar themes throughout your films, isn't there a direct connection between the Keller-Clift conflict in* I Confess *and the Peck-Valli conflict in* The Paradine Case? *In the one a guilty man and his confessor, and in the other a guilty woman and her defense lawyer?*

HITCHCOCK: Yes, but I was dissatisfied with *The Paradine Case* because there I had to make a very disagreeable compromise. Selznick had hired Louis Jourdan and, you see, the lawyer in *The Paradine Case*, Gregory Peck, was to fall in love with Alida Valli and discover that she was a terribly macabre woman, and sexually degraded because she had lived with a stable boy. And Louis Jourdan had nothing of the stable boy about him. He was not appropriate. But Selznick insisted: "I have Louis Jourdan under contract. Just change up the story!" Well the character was more Burt Lancaster. You see, he should reek of the stable, of horses. So much so that the lawyer realizes "What a horrible, repulsive woman! But I can't help loving her." A little like *Lady Chatterley's Lover,* but this woman is more dangerous for the man she holds in her claws.

CAHIERS: *Obviously the situation is different in* I Confess.

HITCHCOCK: Not completely the same. In *I Confess* it's on a higher plane.

CAHIERS: *But the conflict is the same?*

HITCHCOCK: Yes, it's temptation leading toward decline.

CAHIERS: *And the character usually does not sink. So your films seem to us fundamentally optimistic. The good triumph because they are just.*

HITCHCOCK: Not always; but that's the principle.

CAHIERS: *Since you're looking at the clock, a last question: during many press conferences you have said that your American films were all poor. Do you really think so?*

HITCHCOCK: No, no. That's not true.

CAHIERS: *Nevertheless, you said that. Why?*

HITCHCOCK: It depends what press it was. In London, for example, some journalists want me to say that everything from America is bad. They are very anti-American in London. I don't know why, but it's true. But I wouldn't say that. What I would say is that some of my American films are compromises, because of the public. That's what I'd say.

ALFRED HITCHCOCK BRINGS HIS DIRECTING TECHNIQUES TO THE MEDIUM OF TELEVISION

"Alfred Hitchcock Brings His Directing Techniques to the Medium of Television" was a syndicated article published in numerous places; it is transcribed here from the *Oakland Tribune,* September 18, 1955, B8.

Ever since it was announced that a new television program called *Alfred Hitchcock Presents* would make its debut on the CBS Television Network on Oct. 2, I have been asked many questions by many people about my approach to this new medium.

It had never occurred to me that I was expected to make profound pronouncements concerning "The Hitchcock Approach to Television," nor in fact, that I should do some serious thinking about any radical departures from my customary methods. After all, in filming a picture called *Rope* several years ago, I used a technique which, to a great degree, is quite similar to that being used in television studios on both coasts today.

Our performers went through their scenes without a stop; walls silently disappeared as the camera moved around for better angles and, in fact, all the movements of the camera crew, the stage hands and the cast were timed with great precision. Of course, there is one great difference between the technique used in · filming *Rope* and that of a "live" show like *Climax!* or *Studio One*. We used only one camera!

ANNOYED MAN

Several people, addicted to sadistic reflection, have quite pointedly asked me how, having been accustomed to working months filming a motion picture, I expected to commit a coherent story to film in a mere matter of two days. The very idea of Alfred Hitchcock, the calm, complacent Hitchcock, beset by the frantic frenzy commonly associated with television, seems to have provided many hilarious moments of contemplative amusement to those who have less important things with which to concern their thoughts. It annoys me, this notion that I cannot move around rapidly when the occasion demands. And I'm not so certain at all that the occasions will be as frequent as one might be led to believe!

For one thing, one of the most time-consuming elements in filming a motion picture is the lighting. Those enormous movie screens provide a medium which requires a certain number of large sets. Large sets require a great deal of careful lighting . . . and that takes time. Once the set has been made ready for me and the cast, I have always worked with rapidity.

Large sets requiring so much careful lighting, however, have no place in a medium where the resultant image averages but 21 inches in width. Elaborate long shots are not only for the most part completely unnecessary, but disturbing to the home viewer. I may discover, when we start production on *Alfred Hitchcock Presents* that I am whistling in the dark. But, at present, it is my belief that elaborate, time-consuming lighting is completely unnecessary when the camera is concentrating on the small areas used in filming a television show.

As well, I have observed that the deep blacks and shadows, so necessary for clear projection of motion pictures on large screens, seem unnecessary in television. The prime objective in lighting for television is to produce a sharp, clear picture, free of unusual lighting effects. These may be worth the time they take to achieve in the enhancement of the large screen motion picture, but they seem unnecessary and, in fact, often objectionable in the creation of the proper mood for television.

FACES VITAL

Television, as a matter of fact, by the very nature of the medium, tells its story best when the camera concentrates on the faces of the performers. If these faces are to be seen clearly on the television screen, they must fill the frame to a far greater degree than in making a motion picture. This very fact would seem to simplify so many of the problems encountered in filming movies, and, accordingly, producing for television has every reason to be achieved more rapidly.

The use of the proper story material in itself can contribute enormously to rapid recording for television. I intend to rely, almost exclusively, on short stories by famous authors for *Alfred Hitchcock Presents*. Obviously, in its original form, the short story is conceived with the prime objective of developing character and plot in a minimum amount of printed space. Obviously, therefore, any adaption for television of a well-written story should, I feel, provide smoother results with far fewer production problems than, say, an attempt to condense a long novel into a 30-minute script. I have observed, with mixed emotions, several television attempts to telescope into 30 minutes stories which, on the motion picture screen, could be presented properly in nothing less than two hours.

Conversely, since I believe few short stories can benefit by being padded and stretched to meet the length, timewise, of a good motion picture, I have accumulated quite a store of fascinating yarns which, until now, I have never had the opportunity of committing to film. And I've cherished them for years, these stories by Michael Arlen, Dorothy Sayers, Cornell Woolrich and others, with the frustrating knowledge that I could never do justice to them as full length motion pictures.

NO SHADOWS

In brief, then, the very requirements of achieving coherent interest on the home television screens seem to dictate the short production schedule that's supposed to terrify me. I regret that, having done an entire motion picture in a lifeboat and having photographed two hours of action through the rear window of a New York apartment, I shall not be able to oblige those who visualize me as a pathetic, though somewhat humorous figure, inventing new television techniques with wild-eyed frenzy.

I believe viewers who tune to CBS Television for *Alfred Hitchcock Presents* will witness interesting half-hour dramas which will concern themselves with start-ling, shocking, suspense-filled stories having a surprise twist at the end.

As for the "Hitchcock Approach to Television," well, I've never relied on creak-ing doors, or shadowy figures stealthily sneaking along the dimly lit sides of huge buildings, so I don't really anticipate any unusual problems in creating the proper mood.

HITCH: I WISH I DIDN'T HAVE TO SHOOT
THE PICTURE

Interview with Budge Crawley, Fletcher Markle, and Gerald Pratley

"Hitch: I Wish I Didn't Have to Shoot the Picture" was originally published in *Take One* 1, no. 1 (September/October 1966): 14–17.

Q: *How have you managed to find the same challenge, stimulus, the inspiration? How do you continue to find something new and worthwhile to do as you go from picture to picture?*

A: Well, I think that the main problem one has, in my particular field, is the avoidance of the cliché. You see, audiences now—with television, and having films for fifty years—are now highly educated in all forms of mayhem, crime: they're all experts—the public I mean. I was talking to a judge while I was making a film called *The Wrong Man* and he said that he wished they could have trials without juries, because juries were becoming—what is the word—something of a nuisance. They all want to know from the witness—if there's a police officer on the stand, they want to know, "What about the fingerprints, what about this, what about that?" They're all experts. So one has to recognize that you do have an audience today—with the increased facilities of communication, of television, films, paper-backs, and everything else—you have to be aware of this competition and meet it.

To give you an example of avoiding cliché: I made a movie called *North by Northwest* and I had occasion to use a situation (which is a very old-fashioned one) of sending a man—in this case Cary Grant—to an appointed place: He's what they call "put on the spot." And there, probably, to be shot at. Now, the convention of this situation has been done many times: he is stood under the street lamp at night in a pool of light, waiting, very sinister surroundings, the cobbles are all washed by the recent rain—you've seen that in many pictures—then we cut to a window and a face peers furtively along, then you cut to the bottom of the wall and a black cat slithers along, then you wait for the limousine to arrive. This is what we've been used to seeing. So, I decided, "I won't do it that way"; I would do it in bright sunlight, not a nook or a cranny or a corner of refuge for our victim. Now we have a situation where the audience are wondering. A mad tension. And it's not going to come out of a dark corner. So, not only do you give them suspense, but you give them mystery as well. He's alone and then a man arrives across the other side of the road, and he crosses to talk to him and this man suddenly says, "Look, there's a crop duster over there, dusting the field where there are no crops." Now, that's the first thing that you give to the audience: this sinister, mysterious comment. But, before it can be discussed, you put the man on the bus and he drives off, so you and Cary Grant are now—because you are identified with him—left alone. And then suddenly the airplane comes down and shoots at him all over the place. . . . So there you see an example of the very question you ask, "How do you keep up, how do you change?" Only by rejecting the obvious and then, out of that, you will find new ways to do the same thing.

Q: *You've been described, Mr. Hitchcock, not only as the master of the horror film, but also as master of preplanned production techniques. . . . How much improvisation is there in your films and would you talk to us about your methods of filmmaking?*

A: Well, in the first place I agree that you can improvise and should improvise, but I think it should be done in an office, where there are no electricians waiting and no actors waiting, and you can improvise all you want—ahead of time. Sometimes, I compare it with a composer who is trying to write a piece of music with a full orchestra in front of him. Can you imagine him saying, "Flute, give me that note again will you. Thank you, flute," and he writes it down. . . . A painter has his canvas and he uses his charcoal sketch and he goes to work on that canvas with a preconceived idea. I'm sure he doesn't guess it as he goes along. So, I am not in approval of the improvisation on the studio stage, while the actor is on the phone about his next picture and all that kind stuff.

Q: *Mr. Hitchcock, how have you been able to resist, over fifty years of direction, the temptation to look through the camera?*

A: I don't look through the camera. Looking through the camera has nothing to do with it. The ultimate end of what you're doing is on a rectangular screen of varying proportions—wide ones, tall ones, all those kinds of screens—but, nevertheless, what are you doing? You're using the rectangle, like a painter, but the whole art of the motion picture is a succession of composed images, rapidly going through a machine, creating ideas. The average public do not, or are not, aware of "cutting" as we know it, and yet that is the pure orchestration of the motion-picture form. So, therefore, looking through a camera has absolutely nothing to do with it at all. It's the rectangle where the composition arrives. I would say, if I looked through a camera, having asked for a certain composition of a given set-up, it would be as though I distrusted the cameraman and he was a liar, and I'm testing him out.

Q: *What about other directors?*

A: I don't know anything about other directors; maybe I'm a snob in that direction. And I've never seen other directors at work; I never have. I've heard about them: They tell me they dress up for directing. I've always worn the same blue suit everywhere.

Q: *What about seeing your rushes or your dailies? We hear that you pay little attention to them. Is this correct?*

A: Yes, it is correct, because I go and check them up after about four or five days, but I don't rush the same evening to see, "Has it come out?" That would be like going to the local camera shop to see the snaps and make sure nobody has moved.

Q: *Mr. Hitchcock, what about your editing methods? When do you start to edit your films, and are you able to edit them right through to the very end without anyone else interfering with it?*

A: Well I—following what I have said—do shoot a precut picture. In other words, every piece of film is designed to perform a function. So therefore, literally, the only type of editing that I do is to tighten up. If a man's coming through the door, going into the room, then you just pull that together by just snippets. But actual creative work in the cutting, for me, is nonexistent, because it is designed ahead of time—precut, which it should be. You don't agree with me, huh?

Q: *Oh yes.*

A: Oh.

Q: *Yes.*

Q: *Have you ever used a shot that, perhaps, might have been shot by accident on the set in a film of yours—that wasn't preplanned?*

A: Oh no, I don't think so. For example, in the film *Psycho,* I did a murder in the shower. I spent seven days on that—seventy-eight cuts for forty-five seconds of film. That meant you got pieces of film no bigger than two or three frames. And that was shot with the head of the leading lady; I had a nude girl—we shot a lot of her struggles—but more than that, what people don't realize in a situation like this, you had censor problems, so you had bare breasts to cover. So in order to measure this out, I had some parts of the scene shot in slow motion, so the girl moved like that to struggle and the arm covers the breasts there—which could never have been done had you shot it quickly because you couldn't measure it out.

Q: *Have you been up to date, shall we say, in your new film* Torn Curtain? *Do you have any love scenes in this which . . . uh . . .*

A: Oh yes, I have Julie Andrews and Newman in bed together discussing their wedding day. Although I must say—here's an example in this film, in this particular scene, of the avoidance of the cliché. I got so bored with seeing those English films with the nude couple in bed and that constant shot over the bare shoulder of the man, which is just covering the breasts of the girl— it's such a bore and so unimaginative that I took the trouble in the opening of *Torn Curtain* to show a ship in a Norwegian fjord and on board is an international convention of nuclear physicists, and I have turned the heat off on the ship. I have made the heat go wrong. The reason I did that was because I wanted all the people in the dining room to be wrapped in coats and freezing to death having their lunch. And then I go down below and show our couple in bed, covered with blankets, covered in topcoats, and your barely see them at all. For some inexplicable reason, my sense of propriety in this matter didn't seem to meet the approval of the Legion Decency; they complained that there were premarital occupations going on, and I don't understand why they said that because I can't see a thing.

Q: *Is the smallest period involved in production the shooting period?*

A: Oh yes. I wish I didn't have to shoot the picture. When I've gone through the script and created the picture on paper, for me the creative job is done and the rest is just a bore.

 . . . I think, to me, the great art of the motion picture is by means of imagery and montage to create an emotion in the audience and, therefore, the content is a means to an end. In other words, I would choose a story that would help toward that end rather than just photograph a story without any technique.

Q: *Would you approve of a film which involved only technique and no story?*

A: Oh yes, you have to have the story because, you see, you need shape. You see, the nearest art form to the motion picture is, I think, the short story. It's the only form where you ask the audience to sit down and read it in one sitting.

In the film, you ask the audience to stay in one seat for two hours. Therefore, you need a shape of the story that has a rising curve of interest. You know, Bernard Shaw once tried to figure out how long an act of a play would be based on the endurance of the human bladder. And that is our fundamental problem when we devise a film. We do ask a person to sit there for two hours and therefore the shape and story—shape comes into it considerably because, as you get toward the end when they, your audience, might begin to be—shall we say—physically distracted, you must increase the interest on the screen to take their minds off this kind of thing.

Q: *It's generally considered that films of mystery are best in black and white, yet you've photographed* Torn Curtain *in color. What have you been able to do with the color process and the photography which perhaps aids the mood you're trying to achieve?*

A: Well, when they talk about black and white, you remember that black and white itself is unreal basically. After all, we see color everywhere. The camera will photograph whatever you give it. If you want to give it a black and white set—a woman in a black dress and a white blouse, there'll only be one thing in color; that'll be her face, the rest will all be black and white so that you can create the same thing in your own way. In *Torn Curtain,* we decided that after we leave Copenhagen, which is the last location in the picture before we go to East Germany, to go grey everywhere—grey and beige—so we have a mood, a depressed mood, a sinister mood, in the general tones of all the sets and they're all painted grey for that purpose. So you see black and white or color really don't have any relationship. The only reason I made a picture like *Psycho* in black and white is because of the amount of blood.

Q: *Mr. Hitchcock, you're sixty-five and you directed* The Lady Vanishes *about '37. Do you find that it is just as easy now, in directing a picture like* Torn Curtain, *to keep up your enthusiasm as it was in the days when you were shooting* The Lady Vanishes, *and if not, why not?*

A: Yes, you have to do that. After all, the most enjoyable part of making a picture is in that little office, with the writer, when we are discussing the story-lines and what we're going to put on the screen, searching for freshness and so forth, and also always that lovely moment when we say, "Wouldn't it be fun to kill him this way."

. . . The big difference is that I do not let the writer go off on his own and just write a script that I will interpret. I stay involved with him and get him involved in the direction of the picture. So he becomes more than a writer; he becomes part maker of the picture, because the picture is being made.

Q: *If you were going to be murdered, how would you choose to have it done?*

A: Well there are many nice ways: eating is a good one.

Q: *Mr. Hitchcock, we have talked tonight a great deal about the technique of making motion pictures. We often hear a great deal said about the art of making motion pictures. Could you close by telling us just exactly where does the art come in. Is art a technique or does the technique become art?*

A: Well, I think that the art is in its basic form. The motion picture was the newest art form of the twentieth century and that is, its purest form, montage—pieces of film put together, shall we say, artfully, and creating ideas. But, you see, unfortunately, it's so little practiced today. We see so many films that are merely an extension of the theater: they are photographs of people saying lines and so forth. So I regret that enough films are not made using the pure art form.

HITCHCOCK SPEAKS

INTRODUCTION

On the surface, "Hitchcock Speaking," *Cosmopolitan*'s "exclusive interview," is framed as a light-hearted and entertaining celebrity and celebratory profile, featuring comments that "only a talented imp like Hitch could give." But there is a serious undertone rumbling throughout the interview, based on the repeated insinuation that the current time (the interview was published in 1956) was not only one of transition but one of crisis for filmmakers and the film industry. There is a palpable nervousness barely beneath the surface of many of the questions here that betrays deep-seated worries: about the "painful" effects of television on Hollywood; the need for American movies to "recapture the box office"; the damaging "conflict between art and money-making in the picture business"; and the various ways that "Hollywood frustrates anyone who wants to make quality pictures."

Hitchcock is indeed at his talented and impish best in responding to these challenges. Some of his buoyancy comes in the form of personal PR: he self-consciously plugs his previous film, *The Man Who Knew Too Much*, as a hit confirming the healthy state of American cinema and his latest picture, *The Wrong Man*, which features his new star, Vera Miles, "who, they say, is going to replace Grace Kelly," his icon of the kind of cinematic sexuality that he preferred. But in most other places his responses are not so much exercises in self-promotion as opportunities to express some of his carefully thought-out ideas about filmmaking in the new age of television.

Not surprisingly for someone who at the time had a big stake in each medium, Hitchcock is a great defender of both. For him, talk about the demise of cinema at the hands of television is unwarranted, and there is no need for filmmakers to rely, as some advised, on new technical devices for "survival." Hitchcock calmly keeps such devices in their proper place: he accepts the use of the wide screen, for example, as "a great advance in the presentation of a movie to the public" (he himself began to film in widescreen in 1954 with *Dial M for Murder*—also released in 3-D, another innovation meant to combat television), but it is an accessory, "an additional comfort, like plushier carpets or better velvet on the seats." The essence of film remains what it has always been—cutting, character, and story—and Hitchcock is confident that this combination in a motion picture is "unique, and whatever people may say, it is still a wonderful medium for bringing the peoples and backgrounds of the farthest points of the world into neighborhood motion picture theaters."

His praise of cinema does not come at the expense of television, which is by no means a markedly inferior medium, despite its mass audience, sponsors, smaller screen, and production constraints. These factors are sometimes advantages rather than obstacles. For example, far from devolving into a lumpen audience, the television public is an engine of "quality." It is "much more selective than it used to be" and "will watch only good TV shows," and its diversity creates not a "generalized simplicity" but an atmosphere of creative freedom that allows him "to use many more off-beat stories with unhappy endings than I had ever been able to use in movies." Working from the premise that "TV is a visual medium just as much as the motion picture is," Hitchcock expresses great confidence that he could do in television what he had always done in film: create suspense and art. The defining marks of suspense are constant, and there is no difference, he says, between the small and the large screen when it comes to fashioning stories that convey a "roller coaster" ride of "apprehensions and excitements" allayed by "the full knowledge that in one hour's time we are going to emerge into a normal world." He comments only briefly on the eternal struggle of art versus commerce but succinctly captures his pragmatic aesthetic by noting that in television, as in film, "art comes in whenever we can bring it in." He had a vested interest to defend, but he is undoubtedly sincere as well as a bit self-serving throughout this interview as he conveys how thoughtful and serious he is about his television work and the medium of television and how congruent all this is with his film work.

Hitchcock's long experience as a director qualified him, at least in the eyes of some reporters, as an authority on many subjects, including women, as that one-word title of a brief interview published in *Picture Show and TV Mirror* suggests. The specific subject he is asked about is "feminine fashion," and Hitchcock is not at all shy about affirming his oft-repeated personal preference for a woman who is "subtle in her dress as in her actions" as a general principle: "Men do not appreciate a woman who is loud in costume or manner." The insistent link of appearance and behavior leaves no doubt that fashion is of course a matter of far more than clothing: it is an index of identity, an embodiment of how a woman conceives of herself and is conceived of by others, and a key element in male-female relations. Fashion is a key part of the visual plan of a film but also an ensemble of "artificial means and devices to enhance a woman's appearance," a resource of "subtle deception" of which Hitchcock "approves wholeheartedly," according to the interviewer. It is not surprising that fashion is a site of struggle in his films and elsewhere, evident in the highly charged words that Hitchcock uses. The "most attractive woman is the one who exercises restraint," an elaboration of his witty, paradoxical, and constricting advice: "A woman who wants to subdue a man would do well to subdue herself first." He uses the term *panic* to describe what he takes to be a woman's self-defeating desire "to encourage attention," which may provoke a "wink" or a "wolf whistle" but won't help her "hook the man she wants." But his persistence in somewhat overheatedly envisioning woman as a spectacle of excess—"Too much of everything cramps her style; too much jewelry, too obvious make-up, too much, too tight, too loud"—suggests that there is panic in the mind of the beholder as well. We have passed quickly from the realm of haberdashery to that of female psychology and male fantasy and strategies of manipulation and control. All of a sudden we are at the heart of his greatest films of this time period.

The interview concludes with a brief mention of Hitchcock's current film, *North by Northwest,* which is indeed not only a stylish film but one that illustrates what might be called the deeper designs of fashion. As he notes, Eva Marie Saint's clothes reveal quite a bit: for example, her "heavy silk black cocktail dress subtly imprinted with red" figures her deception of Cary Grant, and her "basic black suit with a simple emerald pendant . . . intimate[s] her relationship with James Mason." But *North by Northwest* is in fact the last and in some respects least of Hitchcock's triptych on fashion, and this interview is, without ever mentioning them, an even better gloss on *Rear Window* and especially *Vertigo,* his most thorough dramatizations and examinations of the agonies of design and desire. Hitchcock's comments in the interview align him particularly closely with Scottie Ferguson, and our response as we read his comments might well be, as the saleswoman at Ransohoff's says, "The gentleman certainly knows what he wants," a hauntingly ironic phrase evoking the darker side of Hitchcock's insights into fashions and fashioning.

Given the popularity of *Alfred Hitchcock Presents,* its careful cultivation of Hitchcock as a genial but acid commentator on human foibles and eccentricities, including his own, and his penchant for wordplay, it was perhaps inevitable that he would be affectionately teased in an article titled "Alfred Hitchcock Resents," by Bill Davidson. This piece begins by noting that everyone recognizes him as the real star of his films, so much so that during the shooting of his latest film, *The Birds,* "he had to be smuggled into a moving van to protect him from his fans" while the star actors "moved about the streets unrecognized." The fact that his artistry and fame are so well established and unassailable, coupled with his prickly persona, means that publicity for him need not revolve around the puffery and coddling common to the genre and is free to be more inventive, honest, and playfully rough. Like the television shows, this profile begins with a caricatured sketch of his "odd physiognomy"—described here, astonishingly bluntly, as his "basset-hound countenance, mounted on his pear-shaped body"—and then features his distinctively "impudent vocal cords," his unmistakable voice, "spew[ing] a constant stream of delightful Cockney-accented vituperation."

The article aims to catalog the range of "Hitchcockian curmudgeonry," but there is substance as well as attitude in his assorted jibes and witticisms. His shorter statements are often familiar but far from throwaway lines. His comment on Walt Disney, for example—"I used to envy him when he made only cartoons. If he didn't like an actor, he could tear him up"—deserves the repetition that it gets in a variety of essays, interviews, and public appearances: it perfectly captures one part of Hitchcock's approach to filmmaking that emphasizes actors as basically visual elements in a director's medium. His remarks about the star system are also insightful as well as pointed. Stars, he says, are necessary for a successful enterprise "because of our mass psychology," but not sufficient, because "the star is no better than the story," and all this is true in public affairs as well as in show business. He mentions Audrey Hepburn and Marlon Brando, but his prime example is Churchill, "the biggest star on the world stage," and his description of the surprising fall of Churchill from office as a result of bad casting—"The script called for a domestic-problems hero instead of a war-problems hero"—is both witty and astute.

Sometimes edginess gets the best of him, especially as he dwells on the touchy subject of actors. We may be momentarily relieved not to hear the familiar refrain that "actors are cattle," but instead we get a troubling twist on the theme. "Actors are children," he says, and the evidence he provides is not pleasant: some are "good," some are "bad," many are "stupid," and he paints a picture of an actress unable to separate her role in a film from her real life to confirm his statement that actors "are children who never mature emotionally." When he gets down to specifics, he becomes more harsh: even five years after *Vertigo* he tears into Kim Novak, noting that he was "deluded" into thinking that she gave a "performance," when "actually she is just an adequacy" in a role that she got as a fill-in for the person he really wanted to cast. At this point his vituperation is far from "delightful."

But his "barbed utterances" mellow noticeably as the article turns to a detailed overview of his home life and his life in cinema. He seems much more soberly reflective than resentful in discussing his main worries about contemporary filmmaking, especially "the growing misuse of the movie camera." His brief mention of "a lot of young directors . . . after two pictures hailed as geniuses" perhaps betrays a bit of jealousy and anxiety, but his effort is not to ruin reputations; rather, he wants to reinforce the importance of "true simplicity . . . the elimination of all that is unnecessary," as opposed to "complicated fads," and to offer advice while ruefully reminiscing, "I just don't think the new people get as much basic training as we did in the old days." Finally, when asked "to comment acidly about himself, as he had about so many others," his responses are penetrating without being particularly corrosive. His softer side emerges as he admits, "Despite all my bluster and bravado, I'm really quite sensitive and cowardly about many things," including his work. He confesses an unsuspected fear of "going to see any of my pictures with an audience present," explaining, "I'm scared of seeing the mistakes I might have made."

Even greater than the fear of seeing his own films in public is his fearfulness about attempting several of his "favorite projects" because they don't suit the requirements of the film business or the interests of the young contemporary audience. He is not only fearful but also disturbed by giving in to his fears: "Most of all, I don't like myself for being afraid to make three pictures I've wanted desperately to do for years." (Within a few years, the worries that surface briefly here escalated into full-blown anxiety over and complaints about his inability to proceed with his most favorite unrealized project, *Mary Rose*.) Hitchcock at this time of his career was well known for frequently joking about "stories they wouldn't let me do on TV," but here, for a rare moment, he is not joking. Instead, he confronts not only the seriousness of being constrained but also his own hesitations and complicity: "A man in my position shouldn't be afraid of this, but I am." The invitation to exercise his "constitutional right to comment acidly on all the ludicrousness around me" thus concludes with a revealing and fascinating look at some of what lies within Hitchcock. In a twist ending worthy of his television shows, it turns out that beneath the persona of the vituperative curmudgeon is a person with deep fears, worries, disappointments, and self-doubts.

We get a much different view of Hitchcock in his interview with Richard Gehman, in which he is pictured as fully confident and in command. Gehman recounts how meeting Hitchcock is doubly "startling and surprising." The first shock comes when he appears as "the chairman of the board" (as Gehman titles the interview), "black-suited, banker-visaged, well-fed," and ensconced in a Hollywood office where "men deal with mortgages and money rather than mayhem and mischief." But an even deeper shock comes when he glimpses the true nature of Hitchcock's work, behind the scenes and far from the set. Hitchcock always defined pure cinema as the creation and manipulation of images, but Gehman perceptively recognizes that this extends also to the construction and deployment of the director's own image. While interviewing him, Gehman comes to understand that "when he speaks, it is as though there is another Hitchcock inside directing him," and the Hitchcock we see, whether on television or in person, is "fully as contrived as anything he does on the screen."

Gehman spends much time highlighting what Hitchcock doesn't do. He rarely appears on the set of his television series and delegates the hands-on production work of script selection, casting, and the hiring of writers and directors to skilled professionals like Joan Harrison and Norman Lloyd. But while "the truth is that Hitchcock has very little to do with the actual making of the Hitchcock show," he is unmistakably, if a bit ironically, a presence even in his absence, the prime mover of the show that bears his name, image, and indelible imprint. More than a persona and more than an auteur, "the gentleman has become a kind of institution, a fact of which he is fully aware."

But for all the emphasis on the creation and maintenance of Hitchcock's image and institutional "aura," there is also attention to some of the principles behind his script supervision, one of his key contributions to the show. He is nothing if not analytical and adaptable. In order to stay one step ahead of a new audience educated in the details and nuances of police work, the judicial system, and the usual dramatic conventions, he accepts the challenge of "outwit[ting] the audience to keep them with us." The twist ending is his creative and effective response to this challenge, the embodiment of his premise that audiences need to be fooled and misdirected—and the complete success of his strategy is illustrated by the fact that now his audience is "disappointed" if they don't get a twist at the end. He also broadens his familiar definition of suspense, his trademark, to include not just matters of life and death—"Is he going to be saved from the gallows?"—but also love stories: "Will they get together?" And he carefully considers the importance of structure as well as story, using a "tremendous analogy with music": even a relatively compact television drama can be symphonic, moving from an allegro through an andante to a climactic "final movement." As the interview concludes, Hitchcock radiates power and confidence: he even gives a slightly revised version of his memory of early childhood influences as being as much about his "fascination with the police" as his "fear of the police," adding mastery to the recollection of uneasiness, and goes on to describe himself as anything but fearful: "I don't get the jitters," he says. Hitchcock is indeed in all ways the unflappable and remarkable chairman of the board, and we are left with the vivid impression that image management—of his films, shows, and persona—is his business, and business is good.

By the late 1960s Hitchcock was well established as one of the most highly publicized and frequently interviewed film directors. But while the totality of material capturing Hitchcock speaking was enormous, most of the individual pieces published were brief, with the exception of Peter Bogdanovich's extensive interview and of course Truffaut's *Hitchcock*. We are fortunate to have a record of another occasion on which Hitchcock talked at length about himself and his films. On March 27, 1967, Hitchcock was the inaugural speaker in the new series of John Player Celebrity Lectures at the National Film Theatre in London, and while only a few selections from his remarks were published, the event was captured on video and broadcast by the BBC. The transcription that I include here is a valuable document that gives us Hitchcock speaking freely, at length, and unedited, enlivened and challenged by an appreciative and knowledgeable audience, prompted and occasionally provoked by a skillful and insightful interviewer, the British producer, writer, and director Bryan Forbes.

Interspersed throughout the evening are some set pieces and thrice-told tales. But Forbes is particularly good at holding to the plan he announces at the beginning: "I don't want to ask you any of the questions I'm sure have bored you over the years—well, I'll try to avoid them anyway." This, coupled with an audience that clearly indicates it wants to hear about Hitchcock's present and future as well as his past, helps steer him toward candid and revealing comments on both new and old subjects. Technical matters come up repeatedly, and Hitchcock offers precise and witty observations: for example, about his use of color in *The Birds* and *Torn Curtain,* in both cases emphasizing "restraint," "desaturation," and a visible contrast between the grim oppressive forces of life and "the flesh color of the face"; and about his use of sound, expressing his deep regret that the usual production routine precludes close cooperation with and power over the composer of the soundtrack and noting in particular that sometimes the best sound design features silence rather than music.

Other assorted questions revolve around getting him to describe the current conditions of filmmaking that he operates within. When asked whether or not he now has more freedom, he looks backward and gives a detailed description of the fascinating ending for *Suspicion,* showing a guilty Cary Grant, that he was apparently not allowed to use. But this is set in the context of his confession that the "complete freedom" that he now has is a "handicap" rather than a power he can easily exercise. As a director who is also a producer—and indeed a major shareholder in the studio, a "chairman of the board" even beyond what is envisioned in the previous interview with Gehman—he faces an ethical crisis and becomes "restrained by a kind of responsibility" that is fiduciary rather than aesthetic.

This is only one of a number of challenges he faces in adjusting to filmmaking in the modern age. He quickly dismisses "the current trend in the cinema towards nudity," and buried in his joking response is a subtle and serious insinuation that one can indeed deal with sexual issues and relations without a "zoom in to a close-up of the sexual act." But in talking about his plans to return to one of his abandoned projects, *Mary Rose,* he goes into unusual and unexpected detail about how he is keeping up with the times and audience expectations by "trying to attack it from a science fiction angle," including some kind of "solution" to the disappearance and then reappearance twenty-five years later of the main character, still a young girl, by reference to "the body being atomized." And despite his usual reticence to admit that he watched, admired, and was influenced by films by other directors, Hitchcock confesses that he does monitor what is happening in contemporary cinema. He graciously says "of course" when asked if he finds as much pleasure in Truffaut's films as he finds in his own, goes on to say that he has "pretty broad tastes," and mentions liking "some of the Italian films" in particular, specifically "Fellini and those fellows," and even praises the very recent Czech film *Closely Watched Trains.* What comes across as a charming openness to new cinema, though, is not entirely untroubled. This interview catches Hitchcock during a period of uneasy transition, something beyond his usual experience of "running for cover," and though here he seems resourceful and confident, we know from other documents and statements how worried he was about continuing to make films in an era when cinema seemed to be passing him by. Watching contemporary films brought him up to date but also made him feel irrecoverably out of date.

The two most important topics that Hitchcock talks about in detail here turn out to be linked in an unexpected way: by laughter. When someone from the audience turns attention from his well-known thrillers to his less well-known "very nice sense of humor" and asks, "How come you've never had any comedy?," Hitchcock responds to this perfect setup with a witty revelation that captivates the house and should launch a thousand articles: "But every film I make is a comedy." As if on cue, what follows on the evening's program is a clip from *The Lady Vanishes*, which prompts Forbes's acute appreciation of the timing not only of the comic duo featured in the clip, Naunton Wayne and Basil Radford, but also of their director, restrained, unobtrusive, and in all ways "impeccable." Hitchcock's ensuing close analysis of a sequence in Laurel and Hardy's *Bonnie Scotland* is one answer to the question "What makes you laugh?" but is also an illustration of pure cinema, without a spy or murderer or blonde in sight but filled with suspense, visual narration, pictorial inventiveness, and a snuff box rather than a bomb under the table that leads to a delightfully explosive dramatic payoff. He never worked with Laurel and Hardy, he admits to Forbes, but it is clear that he learned from them.

A film clip shown a bit later in the program turns the discussion to a darker subject: the sequence of the killing of Gromek in *Torn Curtain* is another touchstone of pure cinema but is palpably disturbing and initiates a fascinating discussion of violence in the cinema. One particularly bold audience member describes the sequence as masterly in terms of its direction but "a little bit tasteless," surpassing "even *Psycho* in its stomach-turning, nauseating quality." Hitchcock doesn't deny any of this and follows up his usual point that it is meant to show "what a horrible, awful thing it is to kill someone" by very specifically confirming what some critics have suggested about a scene set in totalitarian Germany that ends with someone dead in a gas oven: it does indeed and was meant to recall Auschwitz. This is an especially interesting comment given Forbes's earlier observation that Hitchcock's films "have never really been concerned with social consciousness" and Hitchcock's joking assent that "messages are for Western Union," which Forbes rightly notes earns both Goldwyn and Hitchcock "a cheap laugh." There is no getting around the fact that messages are for Hitchcock films as well.

The clip from *Torn Curtain* is interesting not only because of its violence and message but also because of the laughter it provokes, which Hitchcock, Forbes, and several members of the audience discuss extensively. Hitchcock is "pleased with that kind of reaction," not because "it's money in the box office," as one audience member suggests, but because it is "a release of tension" that people naturally crave and need. This well-known Hitchcockian notion of the paradoxical "enjoyment of fear" is explicated and confirmed by a group effort, with Hitchcock, Forbes, and members of the audience citing numerous examples of how our common response to horrifying and grotesque events is "laughter . . . tinged with hysteria."

The liveliness of this interaction perhaps contributes to the turn at the end of the evening toward Hitchcock talking at length about his understanding of as well as his relationship with the audience of his films. Rather than accepting the somewhat oversimplified premise that he derives "pleasure or power" from manipulating an audience, he instead emphasizes that his overriding concern, "what are the audience thinking now?," is necessary for him to plan and structure films that will have maximum impact. Often unstated, although perhaps implied, in his discussions of pure cinema is the point he states very directly here: "It's the collective audience, and their reactions, that is of interest, and must promote your endeavors." His vision of numerous audiences throughout the world simultaneously watching one of his films and "reacting in the same way" is not a fantasy of directorial control but a realization of the unique "power of the cinema." And his description of this shared experience as the source of "the greatest satisfaction one can have as a director" is a far from grudging admission of why one must indeed, despite his famous expression of regret, "shoot the picture": a film is "not complete without an audience."

It would have been nice to end this section with a piece capturing Hitchcock in high spirits and at top form, presiding over what Forbes rightly describes as an "inspired and urbane performance," but chronology dictates a somewhat more somber ending note. In his interview with R. Allen Leider more than eleven years after the Player lecture, Hitchcock is considerably less buoyant and engaged, insightfully commenting on his beloved art of cinema but from the perspective of someone who feels that it has been taken out of his hands and left to others who are poorly prepared and unworthy. Leider's questions prompt Hitchcock to review the formative influences on his life and career and also to conjure up a recipe for his artistry, with two ingredients figuring prominently. Emotion, properly handled, is crucial, and the cinematic experience of fear is not only enjoyable but also therapeutic: many spectators "live rather hum-drum lives and without the movies and TV to give them some emotional jolts they would crack up from boredom, I should think." These shocks should be visceral, but they don't have to be bloody: "I think *The 39 Steps* is much more effective than *Psycho*," he says, and later in the interview he laments that carefully prepared dramatic revelation has been replaced by reveling in violence. Emotion is also necessary in binding spectators to cinematic characters so that we identify with their situations, feel their pain, and care about their fate. Imagination is the other key element that Hitchcock emphasizes here, defined not only as the ability of the director to construct scenes that intrigue and terrify an audience and in general "make them feel," but also as a quality brought to the experience by the audience, which is allowed by the director to contribute to the overall effect of a sequence that is made more powerful by not being too graphic or explicit. A key part of his method is to get the audience "to fill in the blanks and fill their heads with images they create."

But when he looks at present-day cinema, he sees largely the spectacle of unprepared, wrong-headed, and disempowered directors and a style of filmmaking quite different from what he practiced and recommended. These days one is "helplessly in the hands of sales people, publicists, and others," and even if one is able to complete a film, it is then "turned over to the distributors," becoming "*their* film." These circumstances discourage him from further work and perhaps account for his grim judgment, "I don't think there is any quality in television films, nor in any of the recent theater cinema I have seen recently." He is particularly critical of the New Wave directors, dismissing them with the observation, "I don't think that they have really learned the business of making motion pictures," that is to say, "how to tell a story visually." Hitchcock is not alone in criticizing the coldness of some New Wave directors and the devolution of innovative style into modish clichés, but hearing him relentlessly portray one of the most vibrant, influential, and, ironically, Hitchcock-inspired and inflected movements of modern cinema as fundamentally amateurish, imitative, and gimmicky is painful.

Hitchcock's criticism of the New Wave is only a part of his broader portrait of a contemporary culture hostile to cinema. A key problem is "that many people, actors, directors, crew people, are entering the business nowadays with a total lack of knowledge of the business," and this means that there is no solid foundation for filmmaking as "an art form, not a money-making venture exclusively." The situation is so bad that he seems to have given up trying to make new films, in part to concentrate on protecting the ones he has made: for example, without his vigilance, a television screening of *Rear Window* would ruin the film by breaking up its rhythm and cutting up his scenes to allow for commercials featuring "toothpaste and mouthwash." Hitchcock also insists that the crisis of cinema is part of a far-reaching crisis of communications. An environment of information overload, graphic violence, "carnage without a message," and the spectacle of anonymous victims is not conducive to thoughtfulness, empathy, subtlety, and imagination. In such a setting, pure cinema becomes irrelevant, perhaps impossible.

This interview dates from and reflects a very difficult time in Hitchcock's life and career. His past was glorious but distant, and the present was, as outlined above, dismal. Unlike most of his interviews and writings, Hitchcock does not talk here about his latest film (he was four years beyond what turned out to be his last film, *Family Plot*); there is no mention of a current project (he was in fact still working on *The Short Night* but far from confident that it would ever be completed); and when Leider asks whether he has "a new project in mind for the future," he is uncharacteristically vague rather than, as he often was, prompted to talk enthusiastically about films he'd like to make. While we might have wished for something more celebratory, the mood is valedictory, and the concluding glimpse of the last days of Alfred Hitchcock, to use David Freeman's phrase, is subdued and sobering. Behind the master of cinema is the man ultimately mastered by life and the force of circumstances, confessing in his own words the haunting and poignant truth that Robert Frost, with Hollywood at least partly in mind, described with his usual uncanny perfection and precision: "No memory of having starred / Atones for later disregard / Or keeps the end from being hard."

HITCHCOCK SPEAKING

"Hitchcock Speaking" was originally published in *Cosmopolitan* 141, October 1956, 66–67. The bracketed explanation of the story "Two Bottles of Relish" occurs in the original publication.

Q: *Do you feel that television has in a rather painful way been good for Hollywood?*

A: Television has indicated to Hollywood that the public is much more selective than it used to be. Hollywood has learned that people will watch only good TV shows, and that on the nights when the quality of TV is not good, they will go out to see a selected movie.

Q: *Some people say TV has killed off the movie mogul. Is this true? How do you feel about movie moguls, after having dealt with them for so many years?*

A: TV has nothing whatever to do with movie moguls. The only thing that will kill off a movie mogul is extreme old age.

I love movie moguls.

Q: *Is television the only reason people are no longer going to the movies?*

A: The implication that people are not going to the movies any longer is a confounded lie. Look at the returns on my last picture, *The Man Who Knew Too Much.* (Plug)

Q: *Do you feel the survival of modern movies depends on improving technical devices such as the wide screen—or are they mere window-dressing?*

A: The wide screen was a great advance in the presentation of a movie to the public. It had nothing to do with technique. The wide screen was an additional comfort, like plushier carpets or better velvet on the seats. The technique of the motion picture is unique, and whatever people may say, it is still a wonderful medium for bringing the peoples and backgrounds of the farthest points of the world into neighborhood motion picture theaters. The actual technique has never changed. It is still a technique of cutting and pasting pieces of film together in rapid-fire succession, thus creating an excitement in the mind of the onlooker. Last and foremost there are the story it tells and the characters in the story. The story will always develop just as it develops now on the stage and in literature.

Q: *Do you prefer to work with name stars or with unknowns?*

A: I prefer to work with name stars so far as big audiences are concerned. The story you are telling is always improved when the hero or heroine who is in dire straits is well known: the onlookers experience a greater emotion from seeing a "relative" in trouble than they would from seeing a stranger. Big-name stars have become familiar to movie-goers and therefore are like relatives to them.

Q: *Do you feel that the growing trend toward independent productions makes for better pictures?*

A: Yes, definitely. The custom-made item, be it a dress or a sports-car, is always better than the assembly-line job.

Q: *Since TV hit Hollywood, have you—as a movie director and producer—had freedom to choose the stories and the stars that you wanted?*

A: I have always chosen stories and stars whenever, of course, they have been available. What does TV have to do with that?

Q: *Does the title of your recent book,* Stories They Won't Let Me Do, *imply that Hollywood frustrates anyone who wants to make quality pictures?*

A: This has nothing whatever to do with Hollywood. It has strictly to do with TV, and I don't blame the sponsor for refusing to let me do certain stories, because some of those I tried to sneak by him are horrible shockers.

For example, I tried to get in that "delicious" story by Lord Dunsany called "Two Bottles of Relish." The sponsor wouldn't "stomach" it, and in a way I don't blame him; I loathe relish myself.

["Two Bottles of Relish" tells of a mysterious murder in which the corpse was never found. It turns out that the murderer ate the body of his victim over a period of time, making it more palatable by the addition of two bottles of relish which he ordered from the local grocer.]

Q: *How do Hollywood's taboos differ from TV's?*

A: There is very little difference between the two. I found that taboos exist in all human societies—even in Africa, which I have just visited. In fact I am told that the taboo concept originated in Africa.

Q: *Whose approach to the subject-matter is more mature—Hollywood's or TV's?*

A: Surprisingly enough, where I expected to find in TV a generalized simplicity because of the enormous range in the age of the audience, I discovered that I was able to use many more off-beat stories with unhappy endings than I had ever been able to use in movies. The children love them.

Q: *How do you feel about the conflict between art and money-making in the picture business? Is it more or less acute in TV?*

A: These are two different questions. The answer to the first is that I think we ought to make money with movies so that with the income we derive from them we can make more movies. If we can squeeze in a little bit of art in the process, well and good. Shakespeare wrote to make money and not necessarily to make art—and he even insisted on a star in the leading role.

The other question, about TV, has the same answer, except that the reward of a successful TV show is not box-office returns but the sale of more of the sponsor's product. Again, art comes in whenever we can bring it in. Both of these answers will tell you that art has nothing to do with the money side.

Q: *Are there TV moguls? How does one deal with them (whether they be authentic or would-be moguls)?*

A: I love TV moguls.

Q: *What are some of the challenges a director has to overcome in TV, as compared to the challenges in movie-making?*

A: Time is an important consideration. The approach to making a TV film involves a complete change of thinking. A half-hour TV film must be made in three days, because the nice mogul who gives us the money can't afford any more than a certain amount. He is a poor mogul. In motion pictures the final return is greater, so that much more money is spent: and in any case the small TV screen does not require anything like the amount of expensive production that the modern movie picture demands.

Q: *What do you think is the finest movie scene—and TV scene?*

A: That's like asking Casanova which of his girlfriends was the finest.

Q: *Can a successful actor or actress schooled in movie technique be equally successful in TV?*

A: Definitely. After all TV is a visual medium just as much as the motion picture is, and we are looking at a screen with faces that give off expressions conveying certain emotions. From an acting standpoint, I would say that it is a tremendous advantage for a TV actor to have had motion picture experience.

Q: *Do you intend to go on making suspense pictures or will you try your hand at other types?*

A: I am so typed by the public that if I were to try my hand at another type of picture, let us say a musical, I feel sure people would expect the soprano, when she reached her top C, to turn it into a scream.

Q: *What is the difference between creating suspense in TV and creating it in the movies? Which is the more difficult, and why?*

A: There is no difference, because suspense is created out of the story you are telling and you are trading on the basic feeling that all of us have within us. We always enjoy suspense because we are able to suffer temporarily some apprehensions and excitements with the full knowledge that in one hour's time we are going to emerge into a normal world. People pay money to go on the roller-coaster. They scream with terror when it dips and rises, and for a brief few minutes they are enjoying fear. But how they giggle when they get out of the car and on to *terra firma*!

Q: *Some people feel that Hollywood is making too many masculine appeal pictures and has scared women away. Do you agree?*

A: It is impossible to scare women away on their own. When hands are linked together in a movie, both handholders would have to leave. And they rarely do. I do not think that women are scared by an excess of masculinity. On the contrary I would say they wallow in it.

Q: *Your movies have been noted for their lack of raw sex and innuendo. Yet Hollywood, in the desperate battle for the box office, seems to be emphasizing these. What is your comment on this?*

A: I do not believe in raw sex. I like my sex cooked, preferably with a delicate sauce. I felt there should be more mystery used where sex is concerned, and that it should not be thrown into your face *ad absurdum*.

Q: *What do American movies need to recapture the box office?*

A: Recapture what box office? Have you seen the returns on my latest picture, *The Man Who Knew Too Much*?

Q: *Finally, Mr. Hitchcock, what is Marilyn Monroe's future?*

A: Ask Arthur Miller.

The future of Vera Miles is also very bright. She is the girl who, they say, is going to replace Grace Kelly. She is in the latest picture I made, entitled *The Wrong Man,* with Henry Fonda.

WOMEN

"Women" was originally published in *Picture Show and TV Mirror,* September 12, 1959, 15. I have omitted the last two brief sections, which are not parts of Hitchcock's comments on women and fashion.

"If a woman is interested in catching a man's eye, or both of them come to that, she should be as subtle in her dress as in her actions. Men do not appreciate a woman who is loud in costume or manner."

Alfred Hitchcock, the renowned, rotund producer-director who has made a close study of women all through his long film career, has very definite—and sound—opinions on what constitutes the attractive female.

"A woman who wants to subdue a man would do well to subdue herself first," is his advice. "The most attractive woman is the one who exercises restraint in her use of beauty aids, as well as in fashion. In a panic to encourage attention, she may actually discourage in the way she doesn't wish. She may get the wink or the wolf whistle, but it is not the right kind. It won't hook the man she wants.

"Too much of everything cramps her style; too much jewelry, too obvious make-up, too much, too tight, too loud. It has ruined the appearance—and the chances—of more women than have sessions at the sink or stove."

Hitchcock's profession has made him an expert on feminine fashion. No detail escapes his eagle eye, and his film reel theories apply to real life, too. He firmly believes that what an actress wears on the screen is as important as what she says or does.

He believes that film fashions have an influence on feminine filmgoers; though the viewers may not be keenly aware of it as they *watch* the picture. None of his leading ladies step before the camera without a series of careful pre-production meetings of experts, not only on what they will wear but also why. The type of dress, design and color are all carefully considered. They must not overshadow the play or the acting, but they must have an impact. For this reason he has become an expert on what appeals and what does not attract the male viewer.

"And aren't all women looking to appeal to the male?" he asks, adding slyly. "For all that, most women dress for other women, to impress or outdo them."

Hitchcock has a great appreciation of black or white for women's clothes.

"A woman cannot go wrong, figuratively speaking, when she is wearing clothes in these faithful basic shades," he says. "I don't mean thick black hose, black pullovers and tight black skirts all together; they are a mere travesty of the theme. Black or white sets off the face to great advantage. Though, on the other hand," he hastened to add, "a woman might have a face that she does not want to show off. In that case, she'd do better to go in for one of the soft floral colors, pink, blue or yellow, tones that distract from the face and appeal to the eye in general.

"Never dither about a color. Try it against the face and contemplate the effect. If you are not sure, pass it by. You might find it effective when you wear it; you might not. Don't take the chance. The new lilacs and mauves are very becoming, but do make certain that you get the *shade* right for *you*."

Hitch—as he is affectionately called—approves wholeheartedly—and thinks most men do, too—the use of artificial means and devices to enhance a woman's appearance.

"I don't see why a woman should not correct or even improve on nature," he declares. "After all, the way science has progressed, it is hard to tell whether she wears false eyelashes or colors her hair. If there is something missing, why shouldn't she resort to a little subtle deception?"

Hitch points to his new MGM film *North by Northwest* which stars Eva Marie Saint—and Cary Grant and James Mason—to illustrate his concern with color.

"I suggested that Eva Marie should be dressed in a basic black suit with a simple emerald pendant (gorgeous with her fair hair) to intimate her relationship with James Mason. In a heavy silk black cocktail dress subtly imprinted with red she deceived Cary Grant; and we put her in a charcoal brown and burnt orange full-skirted jersey outfit for scenes of action.

"Yes," he concluded, "women can do a lot to make their lives more pleasant if they are subtle in clothes, make-up and manners. And go far to please their men, too."

ALFRED HITCHCOCK RESENTS

Bill Davidson

"Alfred Hitchcock Resents" was originally published in the *Saturday Evening Post,* December 15, 1962, 62–64.

In his 63rd year (and his 38th of film-making), Alfred Hitchcock holds two distinctions in the movie-TV industry—one centered on his odd physiognomy, the other on his impudent vocal cords.

First of all, Hitchcock's basset-hound countenance, mounted on his pear-shaped body, is far better known than many of the stars he directs. In fact, during the shooting of his latest Universal Pictures film, *The Birds,* he had to be smuggled into a moving van to protect him from his fans in the streets of San Francisco. Hitchcock and his cameraman worked behind one-way glass, which was built into the side of the van, while the stars, Rod Taylor, Jessica Tandy and Tippi Hedren, moved about the streets unrecognized.

The second and probably the most distinctive thing about Hitchcock is that in an industry noted for executives who gingerly avoid criticizing anything or anybody, he spews a constant stream of delightful Cockney-accented vituperation. He is such an outspoken curmudgeon that during the run of his old half-hour CBS and NBC television show, *Alfred Hitchcock Presents* (now replaced by a new one-hour series, *The Alfred Hitchcock Hour,* on CBS), one appreciative NBC publicity man labeled his interviews with the press *Alfred Hitchcock Resents.*

Following, listed by subject, are some examples of Hitchcockian curmudgeonry which he expressed to me:

DISNEY, WALT: "I used to envy him when he made only cartoons. If he didn't like an actor, he could tear him up."

FANS: "Most of my fans are highly intelligent people *per se,* or they wouldn't be watching my shows. Some, however, are idiots. One man wrote to me, after I had Janet Leigh murdered in a bathtub in *Psycho,* that his wife had been afraid to bathe or shower since seeing the film. He asked me for suggestions as to what he should do. I wrote back, 'Sir, have you considered sending your wife to the dry cleaner?'"

TELEVISION, COMMERCIALS ON: "Most are deadly. They are perfect for my type of show."

HITCHCOCK, ALFRED, GIRTH OF: "A few years ago, in Santa Rosa, California, I caught a side view of myself in a store window and screamed with fright. Since then I limit myself to a three-course dinner of appetizer, fish and meat, with only one bottle of vintage wine with each course."

ACTORS, CHILDLIKE QUALITIES OF: "There is no question that all actors are children. Some are good children; some are bad children; many are stupid children. Because of this childlike quality, actors and actresses should never get married. An actress, for example, attains the blissful state of matrimony and almost immediately goes to work in a picture with a new leading man. She plays a love scene with him so passionately that after three weeks on the picture she comes home to her husband and says idiotically, 'Darling, I want a divorce.' During her love scenes at the studio she has heard people say, 'Look, it's real,' and now *she* thinks it's real too. They are children who never mature emotionally. It's a tragedy."

TELEVISION, QUALITY OF: "The television set now is like the toaster in American homes. You press a button and the same thing pops up almost every time."

STAR SYSTEM: "Because of our mass psychology, we will always need stars. We need Winston Churchill, Bernard Baruch, and Roger Maris. In reality, however, the movie star is no longer important. The picture is. If you check, you realize that in recent years the biggest stars, like Audrey Hepburn and Marlon Brando, have disappointing records at the box office. The star is no better than the story. In the right picture the star will be as big as ever; put him in the wrong picture and you're no better off than if you used an unknown. There is a perfect analogy in public affairs. Right after World War II, who could have conceived that the great Churchill—the biggest star on the world stage—could be thrown out of office and rejected by the very people he had saved from disaster? What happened? The big star was in the wrong picture. The script called for a domestic-problems hero instead of a war-problems hero."

NOVAK, KIM: "With a girl like Kim Novak you sometimes delude yourself into thinking you are getting a performance. Actually she is just an adequacy. The only reason I used her in *Vertigo* was that Vera Miles became pregnant."

Such barbed utterances, in addition to his impudent gargoyle face seen on TV each week, have become two of Hitchcock's trademarks in the entertainment world. He has others, as well. There is, for example, the Hitchcock practical joke, and, like everything else he says or does, the joke frequently is a sly answer to something that Alfred Hitchcock resents. Not long ago he became incensed over the Hollywood party at which the seating arrangement is as excruciatingly important as that of a diplomatic affair. So Hitchcock threw his own lawn party, complete with delicacies and red-coated waiters from Chasen's Restaurant. "It was," Dave Chasen told me, "a shambles. Forty people showed up, but when it came time to sit down for dinner, all the place cards had phony names on them and no one knew where he was supposed to be. Jimmy Stewart's wife said to him, 'My Lord, we haven't been invited,' and they left. Everyone else shuffled about in embarrassment until Hitch got up and told them it was a gag. They all then sat down at the nearest place, catch-as-catch can, and we had a wonderful dinner. But Hitch, as usual, had made his point."

HITCH WASHES THE DISHES

Another Hollywood foible that Hitchcock resents is the extremely intramural and *nouveau riche* aspect of life in the film colony. He says, "I have no friends who are actors or directors, and my wife and I spend as much time as possible away from Hollywood in our country home in northern California; we bought it in 1938, the year we came here from England. I must confess that, like some of my colleagues in the movie industry, I collect paintings and I am proud to own a Klee, a Vlaminck, and a Dufy, but I keep them in the country house for my own enjoyment rather than putting them on display in our Los Angeles home for status purposes."

The Hitchcock Los Angeles home is comparatively modest as Bel Air mansions go. Here Hitchcock once again defies Hollywood tradition. While other filmland pads feature huge drawing rooms or outdoor patios, the most expensive and spectacular room of the Hitchcock home is the kitchen, the walls of which are lined with rack after rack of the rarest wines and liqueurs. Says Hitchcock, "My wife cooks every night and I help her wash up. Therefore I designed the kitchen so madame can cook in the most elegant surroundings and serve those of us who patiently wait there, sipping good wine, for her to complete her culinary masterpieces. We dine in the kitchen as well." The queen of this palace among kitchens, Alma Hitchcock, is a small, aristocratic, British-born woman who had been Hitchcock's assistant director on his first film when he married her 36 years ago. She compounds Hitchcock's Hollywood heresy by employing only one servant, a cleaning woman.

Chief among Hitchcock's resentments is what he calls the growing misuse of the movie camera, a mechanism which is as important to him as the palette is to the fine artist. "There are a lot of young directors coming up, and after two pictures they're hailed as geniuses," he said, "but they all have one common fault. They don't take the time to learn, as Somerset Maugham learned, that true simplicity is the hardest thing to attain—the elimination of all that is unnecessary. They all run to complicated fads. I just don't think the new people get as much basic training as we did in the old days."

Hitchcock's own training during the Golden Age of the silent films was as suspenseful and as harrowing as his own pictures, but, as he says, "I learned. There is no mill like this anymore."

The son of a poultry dealer in London, he had a strict education in a Jesuit seminary, and then, while he studied black-smithing, lathe-turning, screw-cutting and draftsmanship at the School of Engineering and Navigation in London, his hobby became the technical side of motion-picture making, which was flowering into a superb art form in the United States, Germany and Russia. The 17-year-old youngster read every movie trade magazine he could get his hands on, studied art at the University of London and finally backed into the infant movie industry in London as an artist, designing titles for the silent films. By the time he was 23, he was an assistant director and a writer.

"In those days," he told me, "my writing came almost exclusively out of my imagination. My first script, for example, was about a shell-shocked British officer and a French dancer who turned up with child. I was twenty-three and an uncommonly unattractive young man, and I had never been out with a girl in my life. With my background, I barely knew *how* the dancer got to be with child."

In 1925, after a couple of years of work as an assistant director with the great Emil Jannings in Germany, Hitchcock got his first directorial assignment from Gainsborough Pictures, then a comparatively new British company. He was 25 years old. He set out for Genoa with a cameraman, two actors, his future wife Alma and a thousand dollars. On the Genoa waterfront his money was stolen by a pickpocket, and he was able to continue the epic, *The Pleasure Garden,* on funds borrowed from the actors. At Lake Como he was joined by his star, Virginia Valli, then a big-name actress in America, and he promptly borrowed $200 from *her.*

"Throughout the shooting of the picture," says Hitchcock, "I spent more time worrying about day-to-day finances than I did about filming the script. Finally we headed back to Munich, my home base, and we missed our train in Zurich. I thought that was the end, because I didn't have enough money left to put my people up at a hotel. Then I discovered a fleabag near the station where the rate was only $1.50 a night, and I put them up there—my big American star and all. I carried everybody's luggage to save the tips, but I broke a window and had to pay a fine of 35 Swiss francs. The next day I hustled my people on the train. I told them, 'The food is terrible on these trains, so let's wait to eat until we get to Munich.' Hours later we pulled into Munich and I nearly collapsed with the relief of it. I, the big director, had exactly one *pfennig* in my pocket, less than one cent."

The Pleasure Garden was a success, and the following year—1926—Gainsborough gave him his first horror film to do. This was *The Lodger,* the story of London's most famous murderer, Jack the Ripper. The theme fascinated young Hitchcock, and, feeling his oats, he attempted many innovations which were inspired by his period of apprenticeship in Germany. For example, he opened on the full face of a hysterically screaming woman, and later in the action, through a specially constructed glass floor, he photographed Jack the Ripper pacing up and down in his room. Nothing like this had ever been done before.

When the film was completed, the Gainsborough executives looked at it and said, "This is dreadful. We can't release it." For several weeks Hitchcock's budding career hung in the balance as the film sat on the shelf. Economic necessity, however, forced Gainsborough to show it to the press and to a group of theater owners. The reviews were overwhelming in their praise.

One critic wrote, "This is the greatest British picture made to date." Another exulted, "Young Hitchcock is a national asset."

Hitchcock says, "One day I was a flop, all washed up at the age of 26; the next day I was a boy genius. So you can see I've had some personal experience in the field of suspense."

He went on to make such classic British thrillers as *The 39 Steps* and *The Lady Vanishes,* and then, after being summoned to Hollywood in 1938, he continued to add to his reputation as the master of suspense with *Rebecca, Spellbound, Notorious, Rear Window,* etc. Today, with his movies, his TV show and his Alfred Hitchcock mystery books and magazines, he nets close to $1,000,000 a year. He has long since become an American citizen, a designation of which he is extremely proud, and which, he says, "gives me the constitutional right to comment acidly on all the ludicrousness around me."

A TRAFFIC TICKET CAUSES PANIC

Not long ago, in the glow of conviviality engendered by a round of magnificent dinners with Hitchcock in his favorite San Francisco and Los Angeles restaurants,

I screwed up my courage sufficiently to ask him to comment acidly about himself, as he had about so many others.

He thought for a moment and said, "You know, despite all my bluster and bravado, I'm really quite sensitive and cowardly about many things. You'd never believe it, but I'm terrified of policemen and entanglements with the law, even though I make my living from dramatizing such situations. That's why I haven't been able to drive a car since I migrated to the United States. Even the thought of getting a traffic ticket throws me into a panic. Another thing I'm afraid of is going to see any of my pictures with an audience present. I only tried that once, with *To Catch a Thief,* and I was a wreck. I'm scared of seeing the mistakes I might have made."

He continued, "Most of all, I don't like myself for being afraid to make three pictures I've wanted desperately to do for years. They are *Malice Aforethought,* a book by the British author, Francis Iles; *We, the Accused,* by another Englishman, Ernest Raymond; and Kafka's *The Trial,* which Orson Welles has just made. Why am I afraid of them? Because I once did an arty picture in this category, *The Trouble with Harry,* and it was a disastrous flop. I've been afraid to try these favorite projects of mine, because they're about middle-aged or elderly people—which is death in our business, where the present world audience for movies averages between nineteen and twenty-four years. A man in my position shouldn't be afraid of this, but I am."

Then, as I took the master of the macabre home (I drove—he has his fear of police entanglements), he concluded with a Hitchcock parable: "I guess I'm like the murderer who is taken to the gallows, and he looks at the trap and says, in alarm, 'Is that thing safe?'"

THE CHAIRMAN OF THE BOARD

Interview with Richard Gehman

"The Chairman of the Board" is from an unattributed and undated item in Hitchcock clipping folder no. 2 in the Museum of Modern Arts Film Study Center. Internal references indicate that it was probably published in 1964.

To meet Hitchcock—one does not have to use his first name, so much a hallmark his last has become—is as startling and shocking as many of the visual surprises he has been providing so long for audiences across the world.

Outside his office on the Revue lot in Hollywood the morning sun, white and blindingly dry, transforms the twisted bougainvillaea and birds of paradise and other purple, orange and blood-red tropical flowers into a living abstract-expressionist painting. Stepping through it is like tearing a Grace Hartigan canvas . . . and finding oneself in the board room of a bank in The City, London's financial district. Hitchcock's office is in tones of solid mahogany, placid deep greens, subdued millionaire's reds. It is a place for men to deal with mortgages and money rather than mayhem and mischief.

At a small table with a leather top, Hitchcock sits like a board chairman patiently and imperturbably waiting for his fellow stockholders to file in. He is black-suited, banker-visaged, well-fed. His hands spread on the table top are like little pink clusters of sausages stuffed with the rich meat of thousands of gourmet meals at the best restaurants extant.

He is a most impressive gentleman, with a most impressively resonant voice. On television, when he introduces each segment of his show and the commercials as well, archness enters his manner. He twinkles, like a jovial undertaker.

In person, when he speaks, it is as though there is another Hitchcock inside directing him. It is a careful creation of character, fully as contrived as anything he does on the screen. The truth is that Hitchcock has very little to do with the actual making of the Hitchcock show. But the show (which moves from CBS to NBC next season) bears his name; the image must be preserved; the public must not be disappointed.

An actress had told me: "I worked in three Hitchcock shows, but never for Hitchcock. He never turned up on the set." Others said the same.

Joan Harrison, his protégée and producer (next season she will be one of a number of producers for the show), had said flatly, "He contributes nothing except script supervision." She added that she did the hiring of writers and directors and the casting.

But to say that Hitchcock has little to do with the Hitchcock television show is like saying that J. P. Morgan was not much involved in the banking company that bore his name.

Perhaps to preserve the image, Hitchcock maintains that he does have a lively interest in the proceedings at Revue. His own physical presence is not required often, he says; his appearances are filmed in groups of six or seven at a time.

"But I do insist on approval of all the writers' scripts. I read every last one and make whatever suggestions I can think of.

"And then—editing the final project, the film itself. It's a question of deciding how much of the original concept you can get on the screen. I've always figured that in a motion picture one's good fortune is to get 75 percent of the original concept.

"Don't forget, there are always compromises, in casting, in the quality of the direction, even in my own work . . . the minute you put a star into a role you've already compromised because it may not be perfect casting.

"Miss Harrison does the casting, yes, and Norman Lloyd. I try to put out fatherly words of advice without trying to—what's the word?—*usurp* their position. I think, myself, in television that we have a greater chance to cast more freely than in pictures. I'm not sure that star names mean all that much in television, at least in dramatic series."

As Hitchcock speaks in the measured cadences that make nearly every sentence sound as though it had been written for him by a 19th-century English essayist (the language is not all that grammatical, but the effect is there), one mentally reviews his body of work. It is as bulky as his real body.

Born in 1899 in London, Hitchcock went into the film industry at 21, working in a variety of learner's jobs—titling, gripping, etc. Having assimilated technique in this bound-boy manner, he worked his way into direction and scored his first hit with *The Lodger* in 1926. The first success to bring him to American attention was *The 39 Steps*.

Hollywood lured him in 1939. In 1940 he won the Academy Award with *Rebecca*. After that—well, the record is too long to set down. You could, in the classic phrase of another master, James Thurber, look it up.

The television record has not been quite as spectacular, the limitations of the medium being what they are, except in terms of length of stay. He went into TV nine years ago, which means that his is now the oldest continuously presented anthology on the air. The series, along with the televised reruns and reruns of old films, makes him the producer of more properties than there are pounds on him. He weighs around 190.

Thus the gentleman has become a kind of institution, a fact of which he is fully aware. He likes this position, for he feels it gives him an edge over newcomers. "Some people probably watch me out of habit," he said, like a banker contentedly surveying interest as it compounds. "There's an aura of institutional appeal about me—like Perry Como." The trace of a wink edges one eye.

"But I always regard the fact that we've got to outwit the audience to keep them with us. They're highly trained detectives looking at us out there right now. . . .

"I remember I was talking to a judge when I was making a little movie called *The Wrong Man*, with Henry Fonda. It was based on a real case, and he was the judge who'd heard it.

"He was saying that juries these days are such a nuisance because they've looked at television. They're all experts. They expect to hear a detective tell them about fingerprints, as they've seen it on *Perry Mason*.

"So, on our show, they're looking for flaws. We have to fool them. They think we're going in one direction, and we must have the twist at the end. When we had a half-hour show we could do short stories. Now, in an hour, we have to go to novels, crime novels, that sort of thing, but we still have a twist because they're disappointed if they don't get it."

Last season, Hitchcock continues, his staff went through 2400 novels to get 32 scripts. But sometimes they find they still have to expand short stories to get the material.

In judging stories, he says, "I work on the principle of a child sitting on the parent's knee saying, 'What's next?' I've got to make the audience wonder that. I'm noted for suspense . . . but suspense isn't necessarily 'Is he going to be saved from the gallows?'

"Suspense can be a love story, too. Will they get together? I always think there's a tremendous analogy with music. You start out with your allegro, go into your andante, then you build up—the shape of a symphony—and then you get your final movement, which is your biggest. I've always kept to that principle because by the time they've got to that last movement they've been sitting here a while, and your main problem has been to distract them from their discomforts."

Led into a discussion of his own boyhood and early influences, Hitchcock says, "I suppose one early one was fear of the police, or fascination with the police as a child. I had a very quiet, Jesuit education. I read a lot but was terribly scared of the Fathers. They were very strict.

"My father was a mild man, my mother was too, like me. . . . I don't get the jitters; that's why I'm overweight. I don't work or worry it off.

"That's the paradoxical thing about me, I have a very equable temper. Yet people get the impression, because of the work I do, I'm a monster."

He contends, as he discusses his alleged monstrosity, that the violence in his TV scripts and films is largely in the minds of the audience. Confronted by the fact of the horrendous *Psycho,* for which he was criticized in some circles, he declares that the early scene, in which a young woman was done in with a knife in a shower, was the only violence in it—and the rest of the effect was created because the audience expected more.

With a kind of amused world-weariness he admits that his mind turns to stories that will keep his audiences slavering to know what will come next. And he says there are some he never has been able to work out properly in television terms.

"I suggested a story about a fanatic old man who works in a baseball factory. He makes up one and puts dynamite in it. The ball with dynamite becomes the central character.

"The ball goes out on the field, we follow it to the umpire, who throws it to the pitcher, who then strikes out three men in a row to win the game. . . . Imagine the suspense! The ball is given to the club's director, and he puts it on a sideboard in his office with other trophies.

"At the very end I wanted to have a cleaning woman come in and jiggle the ball by accident, and it rolls and rolls toward the edge. It's about to fall down and explode, and she catches it in the very last shot."

He sighs. "We never worked it out."

The mind that can conceive of such a nerve-racking story of course has little time for family situation comedies, which, says Hitchcock, constitute about the only form of television he does not watch. But: "I watch almost everything else." He thinks the best future of the industry lies in documentaries, news and special events.

"Because, after all, you know, we may run out of stories. We only have a certain number of plots. Except . . . if one walks down Fifth Avenue, there are an awful lot of stories passing by."

There is a silence—a pregnant, suspenseful one. The expression does not change, but Hitchcock looks at his watch, significantly. He stands up. He has taken two hours out of his busy schedule of seeking scripts and preparing productions. He shakes hands solemnly and smiles precisely. The board chairman has brought the meeting to an end.

JOHN PLAYER LECTURE

The John Player Lecture of March 27, 1967, featured Hitchcock interviewed by Bryan Forbes. A very short selection of comments was published in "Hitch," *Films in London* 1, no. 7 (October 19–25, 1969): 6–7. My transcription of the entire event is based on the National Film Theatre audiotape cataloged as BFI Film History (Tape) Project, Hardcastle 7437.5149, and an undated BBC video, *Hitchcock at the N.F.T.* (59 minutes; an edited and slightly compressed version of the talk, with occasional voiceovers added to clarify inaudible remarks). I do not include the opening remarks before Hitchcock's entrance. I also omit occasional interjections as Forbes calls on people in the audience and false starts in the speakers' comments. Ellipsis dots within a sentence indicate a pause and, at the end of a sentence, an interruption of one speaker by another. On a very few occasions, brief indecipherable or fragmentary comments are silently omitted or when possible are replaced by my best guess (presented in square brackets) at how to reconstitute the statement or question. Film clips were shown at various points—including the trailer for *Psycho,* used as an introduction to the talk—and since they become reference points for comments and questions, I describe the clips briefly in brackets.

FORBES: *Ladies and gentlemen, it's my very great privilege and honor tonight to introduce to you in the flesh the director that most other directors would like to emulate, the director that most actors would like to emulate, and the director that most directors who fancy themselves as actors would like to emulate, if not equal, Mr. Alfred Hitchcock.*

HITCHCOCK: If I may say so, I wasn't too happy about the word *flesh.* And these steps were terribly awkward coming down—one had to step them one by one—and reminded me of the old lady who was walking with one foot on the curb and one foot in the road, and they said to her, "Why are you walking like that?" She said, "Oh, I thought I was lame."

FORBES: *This is obviously going to be my absolute downfall, this interview, so I approach you really as the depressed area's David Frost, Mr. Hitchcock. I don't want to ask you any of the questions I'm sure have bored you over the years— well, I'll try and avoid them anyway. What interests me, to start the ball rolling: I'm fascinated by writer's diaries, by writer's notebooks, and therefore as a fellow director, I'm fascinated at the point where you feel yourself committed. Is it in the script, is it the first day, is it long before the script? Where do you think it all starts for you?*

HITCHCOCK: Well, for me it all starts with the basic material first. Now, the question when you have, we'll say, basic material: you may have a novel, you may have a play, you can have an original idea, you can have just a couple of sentences, and from that the film begins. Now, I work very closely with the writer and begin to construct the film on paper. From the very beginning, we say, well, we roughly sketch in the whole shape of the film and then begin from the beginning, and you end up with, say, a hundred pages or maybe even more of narrative, which is very bad reading for a litterateur. I mean there are no descriptions of any kind, no, for example, "He wondered," because you can't photograph "He wondered."

FORBES: *And no "Camera pans right" or any of that garbage?*

HITCHCOCK: Not at that stage, no, not at that stage, no. It is as though you were looking at the film on the screen and the sound was turned off. And therefore to me this is the first stage. Now, the reason for it is this: it is to urge one, to drive one, to make one work purely in the visual and not rely upon words at all, because I'm still a purist, and I do believe that film, being the newest art of the twentieth century, is a series of images projected on a screen, and this succession of images create ideas, which in their turn create emotion, just as much as in literature, words put together create sentences and so on and so forth.

FORBES: *Do you think, at that stage, do you think in black and white, or is your preference for color? I mean, do you find yourself thinking in terms of black-and-white images?*

HITCHCOCK: Not at all, no. The color, the color is part of the structure. In other words, you restrain color, bring it in when it's necessary, but don't orchestrate it so loudly that later on you may use it, and, in a word, to mix metaphors a moment, you've exploded your gunpowder.

FORBES: *Yes, I mean there was something behind that question, because if I may be so bold, I thought there was only one of your films which leaps to mind which I thought would have been better in black and white, and that was* The Birds. *I don't know why; this is only a personal preference. I would have preferred to have seen that film in black and white. I wondered why you opted for color.*

HITCHCOCK: Well, strange enough you should ask that. I opted for color because the birds were black and white, so that the faces of the people involved would be separated from the birds.

FORBES: *Yes, my question was really more technical, because I felt the technique of the birds, the phony birds, would have perhaps been less obvious to me if they'd have been in black and white. That was the only thing that I . . .*

HITCHCOCK: Well, we actually used real birds. There were no mechanical birds used at all.

FORBES: *There were one or two wooden ones, or stationary ones, weren't there?*

HITCHCOCK: We hope that it deceived the eye. But that was purely a matter of quantity, rather than quality.

FORBES: *Would you as a generalization think there's any validity to the fact that thrillers such as you are associated with, do you think they benefit by color or do you think the old original black and white? To me, film is still a medium in black and white. I confess that in the film's I've made in color, I had a sort of personal dissatisfaction with them.*

HITCHCOCK: Well, I think that color should be reduced and desaturated down, until the only thing left on the screen is the flesh color of the face, so that you can go and desaturate the color as much as you wish.

FORBES: *Yes, the sad thing is that you and I might aim for that on the studio floor, and then we see our films out in release, we wonder what we shoot them in, because they appear to be shot in some nameless process, don't they, once they leave our hands?*

HITCHCOCK: Well, that is true up to a point, but on the other hand remember that what you give the camera, so it will record, and I think the attention has to be paid to set decoration, costume, and all those things that, if I may say so, defy the efforts of Technicolor.

FORBES: *Yes, well I won't comment on that. When you say you start with the script, how many—I mean, I know my own case, the amount of, as it were, stillborn children one has—how many times do you think in your career have you started off with what hopefully you thought was something that was going to excite you and, alas, have had to abandon it?*

HITCHCOCK: Oh, many times. In the last two years, I've abandoned two projects. And the point is you get so far and you realize it's not going to work out, so it's better to lose $150,000 or $200,000 than two million. Just dump it, and let it go.

FORBES: *I've often found myself, and perhaps you've had the same experience, that although we dump things, certain things, part of the egg remains, and continues to gestate, and we pull them out of a drawer, out of our subconscious, in years later, and use them again in a different context. Does that happen to you?*

HITCHCOCK: No, it doesn't happen to me. The only thing that I pigeonhole are certain ideas that belong to a certain genre picture: the adventure film, for example. You store up an idea and you put it away, and one day it will come out. For example, in a picture like *North by Northwest*, I've waited about fifteen years to put Mount Rushmore on the screen. So you keep it back in your mind. Unfortunately, it doesn't always work out, because storing the scene up and having the pleasure of anticipating the use of it, the Department of Interior step in, and say, "You mustn't have any character climbing over the faces of the presidents." You say, "Why not?" They say, "Oh, because this is the shrine of democracy. You must only have your characters sliding or chasing between the heads." And I was completely defeated, because I had a lovely idea which I thought of: Cary Grant sliding down Lincoln's nose and then hiding in the nostril.

FORBES: *It's a Kleenex ad.*

HITCHCOCK: And the man in search of him is in the vicinity, but unfortunately Cary Grant, hiding in the nostril, begins to have a sneezing fit. And I was never allowed to do it. Actually, while we're on this particular subject, I think it would be of interest somewhat to know that if I have an adventure film of this nature, and I have a background, I make it almost a must that the background must be incorporated dramatically. For example, in the same film, Cary Grant was trapped in an auction room. Now the question was, how could he get out? There's only one way he could get out, is by bidding, crazy bidding. So therefore, it isn't just the background, but it's the use of it that you must make. And that's why I was rather defeated in Mount Rushmore.

FORBES: *I think you and I share, talking of actors, we share, shall we say, a certain lack of pleasure at the thought of directing Method actors, don't we?*

HITCHCOCK: Well, the Method actor is all right in the theater, because he has a free stage to move about. But when it comes to cutting, and the face and what he sees, and so forth, there must be some discipline. And I remember discussing with a Method actor how he was taught and so forth, and he said, "Oh, we're taught improvisation. We're given an idea, and then we're turned loose to interpret it the way we want to." I say, well that's not acting, that's writing, and that's why your Method actor today always arrives on the set with a new script.

FORBES: *It's a very selfish form of acting anyway, on the screen. It's very selfish . . .*

HITCHCOCK: Well, I don't believe in it at all.

FORBES: *. . . because you only pay lip service to the other actor, because they're off in some private world . . .*

HITCHCOCK: Well, that happened to me once. I can tell you, I was doing a film with Montgomery Clift, who was that type of actor, and he turned up on the set one morning with the scene completely rewritten. All I said to him, I said, "Has it has occurred to you that there's another actress in the scene?" And I wouldn't let him do it.

FORBES: *I believe we're going to see one of your own acting performances in another clip which is coming up, which must be the despair of Method and non-Method actors.*

HITCHCOCK: I hope it's short, so that I am not shown suffering the indignity of being an actor for too long.

FORBES: *Well, I believe the clip we're about to see is a clip from* Blackmail, *I believe, a test from* Blackmail, *I think I'm correct in saying. If we could have that now.* [clip of Hitchcock directing Anny Ondra in a sound test for *Blackmail*]

FORBES: *I see your range goes from Method acting to low comedy, I can see that.*

HITCHCOCK: Yes, yes.

FORBES: *How many years ago was that?*

HITCHCOCK: That was 1929.

FORBES: *And who was the lady?*

HITCHCOCK: Anny Ondra. She's now married to Max Schmeling, the boxer. Very nice woman, charming. She's Czechoslovakian, actually.

FORBES: *Does she still act? No, presumably not?*

HITCHCOCK: Oh, no, no.

FORBES: *Well, shall we invite some questions from the audience on what we've discussed so far?*

HITCHCOCK: Yes, let's do that.

FORBES: *We'll take the first one down there, sir.*

QUESTION: *When are we going to see* Topaz?

HITCHCOCK: About in the middle of November.

QUESTION: *Mr. Hitchcock, you said that the screen should always be charged with emotion. Do you have any particular rules or techniques that help you to achieve that?*

HITCHCOCK: Charged with emotion do you say?

QUESTION: *Yes. I saw the quote in the Truffaut book.*

HITCHCOCK: Well, the point is that pure film is montage, which is the assembly of pieces of film, which in their turn must create an emotion in an audience. That's the whole art of the cinema, the montage of the pieces. So it's merely a matter of design, subject matter, and so forth. I mean, you can't generalize about it; you can only hope that you produce ideas expressed in montage terms that create emotion in an audience. After all, I suppose you've got to go back to the early days of Griffith, where you have the ride to rescue the man from the guillotine, and the crosscutting from one to the other, which creates the emotion in the audience. That's the most elementary form.

QUESTION: *Again, in the Truffaut book you mention at one point, or Mr. Truffaut mentions, that re* Psycho, *there is virtually no one character in the film with whom one can identify, to which you reply it wasn't necessary. Surely the almost physical impact of that film is due to the fact that it is the supreme audience-identification film. You involve us so much with Janet Leigh and Anthony Perkins that the impact of what happens is considerably larger than what it would have been previously.*

HITCHCOCK: Well, you're involved up to a point. I don't really think it applies to a picture like *Psycho*. It would apply much more to a picture like *North by Northwest,* where you're involved with the adventures of the hero, you see, and that's why sometimes the star of a picture, in that type of picture, is much more helpful, because you worry about him, whereas an unknown you wouldn't worry about him. So it's like, you know, when you walk through the streets and you see a man lying there waiting for an ambulance due to a car accident, and you look at him and you say, "Poor fellow." But if you take a double look and find it's your brother, you can see the difference in the emotion. So the identification really boils down to are you a hundred percent anxious about that particular star? The lesser-known the person, I think sometimes your interest is slightly lessened.

FORBES: *Well I think that your genius in that film for me was the way in which you squandered Balsam, what's his name, Martin Balsam, because I think that was absolutely a supreme stroke for me. I mean, to take a character—and I was intensely involved in his character, hoped he was gonna go on for the whole picture—and bang, you killed him off in the most marvelous sequence.*

HITCHCOCK: Well, that's the whole point, is that it's killing off the leading lady as well: it was a reversal of all the usual processes.

FORBES: *Well it's marvelous, absolutely marvelous. Sir, you were next.*

QUESTION: *Mr. Hitchcock, in the past you've been at odds with the head office over the story line of your films and have been overruled, notably with* Suspicion *and* Secret Agent. *Nowadays, now that the studio uses your name as the main selling point of the film, do you find you have more freedom in the making?*

HITCHCOCK: Yes, I have complete freedom, but that of itself is in a way a handicap, because one enters into the field of financial ethics, and no doubt one can do whatever one wants, but you become restrained by a kind of responsibility. In the cases you mentioned, the earlier one like *Suspicion,* for example, with Cary Grant, well, basically he should never have been in the picture to start with, because you run into this problem: you cast a man who is suspected of murder, and then you have to compromise, which is the bad thing. And a propos of that picture, I remember the head of RKO came back from New York, and they'd just appointed a new head of the studio, a man called Lesser, and with a big grin on his face, he said to me, "Oh, you should see what Lesser has done to your film *Suspicion.*" I said, "What?" He said "Well, wait and see, but it's now only fifty-five minutes long." What this man had done, he had gone through the film in my absence and taken out every touch or scene that would indicate the possibility that Cary Grant was a murderer. So there was no film existing at all. Well, that was quite ridiculous, but nevertheless, I had to compromise on the end. The thing I wanted to do with the end of that picture was that the wife was aware that she was going to be murdered by her husband, and so she wrote a letter to her mother, saying she was very much in love with him, she didn't want to live anymore, she felt he was going to kill her, but society should be protected. So he brings up this fatal glass of milk, she drinks it, and before she does so she said, "Will you mail this letter to Mother?" and she drinks the milk and dies. And then you have just one final scene of a cheerful Cary Grant going to the mailbox and popping the letter in. But it was never permitted, you see, because of the basic error in casting.

FORBES: *I can't seduce you to come back to Elstree for me and remake it, can I?*

HITCHCOCK: Well, it wouldn't be difficult.

FORBES: *Can I seduce you anyway: there's no chance of you coming back to England and making a picture over here, preferably for me?*

HITCHCOCK: If it's the right story, you know. I mean, I've always said when one goes inside a studio, you can be anywhere, so it would have to be a story that relates to the atmosphere and background of London or England, you know.

FORBES: *I think it would be marvelous if you did, because I'm sure you'd see London, so-called "swinging London," with new eyes.*

HITCHCOCK: Yes, and then I'd be back in the studio that I started a contract in 1927 . . .

FORBES: *At ABC?*

HITCHCOCK: Yes, with a picture called *The Ring,* with Carl Brisson.

FORBES: *Edgar Wallace subject, wasn't it?*

HITCHCOCK: No, no, it was an original.

FORBES: *It was? It sounds like an Edgar Wallace, doesn't it?*

HITCHCOCK: It was a boxing picture.

FORBES: *I'm thinking of the ring around . . .*

HITCHCOCK: You're thinking of the ring, yes. You're tied up with washing machines.

QUESTION: *Mr. Hitchcock, you mentioned a moment ago the question of remakes. Why, in fact, did you remake* The Man Who Knew Too Much? *Was it, in fact, dissatisfaction with the original? And ultimately, which version did you prefer yourself?*

HITCHCOCK: It was remade because I was short of a subject, and I thought, of all the pictures I had made, this would suit the American public: it had a certain amount of woman emotion in it, the kidnapped child, and so on and so forth. The version's different. The first version was more spontaneous, contained less logic, less reason. But, you see, there's a thing that the big public has, which doesn't always please one, and that is what I call moronic logic. And I also feel sometimes, in certain stories, logic is dull.

FORBES: *There's usually an illogicality about your logic, I think. That's what separates it from the herd.*

HITCHCOCK: Well, you know, if everything's explained and ironed out, you lose the bizarre and the spontaneous.

FORBES: *The gentlemen in the center, I think, had his arm up. Or somebody here, just before the last. All right, we'll take the young lady with white sweater on, please. Yes, you. Well, the lady with the white sweater did put up her hand, then the green lady stood up. Would you like to fight it out amongst yourselves?*

HITCHCOCK: Change sweaters.

QUESTION: *I wondered, had you ever been tempted to step outside the sort of thriller limitation and do something completely different, or is it the attraction, you know, is the limitation the attraction to do something new?*

HITCHCOCK: Well no, it's not for me, it's the public, you see. If I made, for example, a musical, the public would wonder, when will the moment come when one of the chorus girls will drop dead . . . and what from?

QUESTION: *Mr. Hitchcock, apart from self-satisfaction, Mr. Hitchcock, what is your basic motive for making the films that you do make?*

HITCHCOCK: Basic motive?

QUESTION: *Yes.*

HITCHCOCK: Money. There's an old expression, which says, "All work and no play makes jack."

QUESTION: *Mr. Hitchcock, I'm amused by your olfactory dilemmas at Mount Rushmore. You said that you have in your mental bottom drawer a series of bizarre locations or scenes or backgrounds which you hoped to make use of one day. Could you tell me what is the one you most want to make use of and have not yet had the opportunity?*

HITCHCOCK: Well, I once had an idea that I would like to open a film, say, at the Covent Garden opera or the Metropolitan or the Scala in Milan, and Maria Callas is on the stage singing an aria, and her head is tilted upwards, and she sees in a box way up a man approach the back of another man and stab him. She is just reaching a high note, and the high note turns to a scream, and it's the highest note she's ever sung in her life, the result of which she gets a huge round of applause. She would then be horrified to see the body falling out of the box into the auditorium. Panic ensues, the curtain is lowered, Callas is in a state of hysteria, is helped off the stage into her dressing room, cries to be left alone, and people go out and leave her. She immediately locks the door and goes over and dials a number on the phone. I don't know the rest.

FORBES: *Make that one for me. I'll buy that.*

QUESTION: Mr. Hitchcock, in view of the way things have changed—today we have space travel, the landing on the moon, we have nuclear explosions—do you think, has your own concept of what is terrifying changed over the years, and if it hasn't radically, do you think it will in the future, as we face more and more horrifying things?

FORBES: *Two questions: Have your concepts of horror changed with the changing times, such as the advent of moon travel and the nuclear bomb, and what frightens you?*

HITCHCOCK: Policemen frighten me.

FORBES: *Not English policemen, surely?*

HITCHCOCK: Oh, the worst. Because they're so polite. I don't think you can bring the element of nuclear bomb into it, because you'd have to know the people who would be involved in it. You see, when you bring in elements like that, they are rather actually external from the story, unless it's about, you know, a scientist involved in it, or what have you.

FORBES: *Do you know who frightens me is the priest who blessed the first H-bomb. He really frightens me.*

HITCHCOCK: Oh, yes.

QUESTION: *Mr. Hitchcock, in the film* Marnie, *there is a lot of criticism about the art direction, particularly the street scene in the harbor.*

HITCHCOCK: I agree with you. It was a bad scene.

QUESTION: *Can you tell us something about your toleration of Bernard Herrmann, as he composed the music for [your films]?*

HITCHCOCK: He composed music for a lot of films.

QUESTION: *To what extent do you collaborate with the soundtrack composer on your films?*

HITCHCOCK: There's never any chance. You see, the musician always has it his own away, and very often I've been invited by the musician to come down and listen to the score, and then when one has expressed some dissatisfaction, he said, "Well, it can't be changed now, it's all been orchestrated." And that always happens with the musician. The only time I've ever heard perhaps some themes played was before a picture, *Spellbound*, by Rósza, and recently by Maurice Jarre, in the last picture. But really, you're quite helpless, because then you say, "Well, can't I hear some of the music?" They say, "Well, how can we? We can't; it's no good playing it on the piano. You have to hear it with full orchestra." So really, they always have their own way.

FORBES: *That's funny you say that. My experience has been rather happy. I may entirely agree with you, but I've been lucky working with John Barry, and he gets involved much earlier on, and he's very flexible and will change, because otherwise wouldn't you agree that a composer can sometimes take a hard picture and make it diffuse and sentimental . . .*

HITCHCOCK: Oh, yes, it's true.

FORBES: *. . . just by his score, and completely corrupt your intentions.*

HITCHCOCK: Well, I found on one picture that I heard the first day's work on a picture, then had to wash up the whole thing. I said finish, cut it out, no good. Because of this particular reason. One hadn't had a chance to hear it before.

FORBES: *Well, that's the economics of the film industry . . .*

HITCHCOCK: Yes, it is.

FORBES: *. . . because to record the music is fantastically expensive for a film, and it all has to be done really to the fine cut, because it's got to be orchestrated . . .*

HITCHCOCK: To be timed.

FORBES: *. . . literally to a metronome and literally down to the last frame of film. I mean he has to bring the baton down on the last frame. I'll take one more question, then we'll have a break and see another film clip.*

QUESTION: *Mr. Hitchcock, you seem to have a very nice sense of humor, which you obviously had before you established yourself as a thriller, directing thrillers. How come you've never had any comedies?*

HITCHCOCK: But every film I make is a comedy.

FORBES: *Well, that leads us very nicely into the clip, because it's one of my all-time favorite films. I can't tell you how many times I have seen it. I saw it recently on television over here. It's a clip from The* Lady Vanishes *and stars the upper-class Rowan and Martin of yesteryear, that marvelous comedy team Naunton Wayne and Basil Radford, who were supreme, weren't they?*

HITCHCOCK: Yes, yes.

FORBES: *Their timing was absolutely supreme. And I believe I'm right in saying that this particular screenplay was written by an old friend or two old friends . . .*

HITCHCOCK: Gilliat and Launder, yes.

FORBES: *Yes, Sidney Gilliat and Frank Launder. What a marvelous screenplay, too.*

HITCHCOCK: Yes, it was.

FORBES: *Absolutely beautifully observed. So let's with pleasure look at a clip from* The Lady Vanishes.

[clip from *The Lady Vanishes*: the maid changing her clothes in the room shared with Naunton and Radford, followed by the long-distance phone call that they disrupt]

FORBES: *So what I find so fascinating about that: I think not only is their timing impeccable, but I think your timing is impeccable, because I think you don't fuss, you let the actors like that, who have their own instinctive timing, you don't mess about with it in the cutting room. So many films are ruined because a false sense of timing is put on to a comedian . . .*

HITCHCOCK: Oh yes, you can't do that.

FORBES: *. . . and if his ear is good, like their ear was impeccable . . .*

HITCHCOCK: Oh, yes, that's true.

FORBES: *. . . that you didn't mess around. That I find an object lesson.*

HITCHCOCK: That has to be left to them.

FORBES: *Isn't it a pity that comedy teams like Radford and Wayne and indeed Laurel and Hardy, they don't seem to happen these days in that sense, do they?*

HITCHCOCK: No, no.

FORBES: *Gag men do, but not acting comedy teams.*

HITCHCOCK: Not character people in teams.

FORBES: *You never worked—and forgive me if I've got it totally wrong—you never worked with Laurel and Hardy in any shape or form?*

HITCHCOCK: No, not at all, no.

FORBES: *Would you have liked to have done, because of all the sort of old-time comedians, they're the people I think I admire most.*

HITCHCOCK: I don't think I could have done, because I was already Hardy . . . in size.

FORBES: *But does that type of humor attract you as an individual?*

HITCHCOCK: Oh yes, it does. Oh yes, no question.

FORBES: *What makes you laugh?*

HITCHCOCK: Oh, I think one of the funniest films I ever saw was Laurel and Hardy in a film called *Bonnie Scotland*. Do you remember that? And the longest take I've ever seen on the screen, when the two of them are standing on a Scottish bridge, and I think it was Laurel who was taking snuff, and he sneezed, and he sneezed right into the snuff box, and all the snuff blew into Hardy's face. There was the longest take before anything happened I've ever seen, and finally this long sneeze came, so big that it tilted him back into the river below. And then Hardy was left on the bridge, and nothing came up but water and fish, every a few seconds like that. [Hitchcock gestures.]

FORBES: *Yes, marvelous scenes. Can I have another question please, over there.*

QUESTION: *You mentioned earlier two abandoned projects. Was one of these* Mary Rose? *If not, can we expect to see* Mary Rose?

HITCHCOCK: Well, in *Marie Rose*, I have that on one side, and I'm trying to attack it from a science fiction angle, because I'm sure the public will want to know, where did a girl go when she disappeared for twenty-five years and came back as young as she was when she disappeared? And I think it's going to come when we find the solution about the body being atomized, which it will be in some years' time: there'll be the power to atomize the body, and move it away elsewhere, and reassemble it again.

FORBES: *In the eternal cutting room.*

HITCHCOCK: Um hm.

QUESTION: *Mr. Hitchcock, there's a great deal written about your cinema films, but some of your TV work is also excellent. I know some of the episodes that Robert Stevens directed got Emmy Awards. Could you tell us a little about these? Are there any which you remember with particular affection? And, for instance, how do you select directors for those episodes which you don't do yourself?*

HITCHCOCK: Well, you know, after all, when that series started, it was actually based on the English short story. It was essentially the short story that inspired the series, and we had lots to draw upon, and I think we used most of them that were ever written, because in the early days in the twenties, most of our important litterateurs always went in for the short story, whether it was Galsworthy, Hugh Walpole, or Mrs. Lowndes. There were a whole lot of people, a tremendous lot. And I made one once, which took me just two days to do. I think it was a Roald Dahl story, called "Lamb to the Slaughter." And this was a story of a young wife, played by Barbara Bel Geddes, and she was preparing dinner, and of course in America, you know, they can take food out of the deep freeze and put it straight into the oven, because when you buy a cooking oven, the brochure that comes with it tells you the timing for frozen food or nonfrozen food. Anyway, she's preparing dinner and her husband, who's a chief of police, comes home and tells her they're all washed up, there's another woman. And she's rather stunned by this, and she, almost in a trauma, goes out to the garage and takes a leg of lamb, which is frozen, out of the deep freeze and comes back, and she finds her husband rummaging through the desk drawer. And she says, "What are you doing?" He says, "I'm getting my things together." She says, "You're not going tonight?" He says, "You try and stop me." And this thing infuriates her that she goes up behind him with the frozen leg of lamb and kills him, hits him on the back of the head. And still in a daze, she goes and puts it in the oven, turns the gas on, and prepares the rest of the meal, and she comes back and realizes she must do something about this dead body. So she wrecks the room, as though there were a fight, and calls the police. And she's acquainted with all of them, and very soon the whole rigmarole is going on, the photographer, the fingerprint man, and the doctor. And the chief detective is saying, "Well, doc, what instrument was used?" He says, "Well, as far as I can see, examining the body, it's that shape, like that." [Hitchcock gestures.] He says, "Its narrow, because the hand must hold it, and yet the bruise is very flat." And the investigation goes on, and they're searching for the weapon and can't find it, and finally two of the men go in the kitchen, and here's this leg of lamb sizzling away, and they come back and they say to her, "Look, you've forgotten your dinner." "Oh, fellows," she says, "I can't be bothered with a dinner after all that's happened here. Why don't you have it, all you have it," you know. And finally, you end with all the detectives and police sitting around the table, just having finished the leg of lamb, and one of them says, "Well, I don't know, for all we know it may be under a our very noses." And that's the end of the story. Of course, when you make that kind of TV film, the censor must step in, because there's a need for what is called the retribution clause: she cannot get away with it. So I come on in a supermarket at the end, wheeling the usual basket, and I stop and I say, "You know she married a second time, but the second time she forgot to turn on the deep freeze." And that was the payoff.

QUESTION: *I'm struck by your film* Rope, *particularly with its fluid camera movement, the brilliant lighting which you used, and the absence of the usual cutting. Are you contemplating a return to being a theatrical director?*

HITCHCOCK: Not necessarily. That was devised because it was a theater piece, and I thought that because the subject played in its own time, you see, it started at 7:30 and ended at 9:15. I devised the flowing camera technique to give that sense of lack of interruption in time, but I don't think I would do it again unless it were called for.

QUESTION: *Do you find time to see other people's films? For instance, do you find as much pleasure in Truffaut's films as he finds in yours?*

HITCHCOCK: Of course.

QUESTION (continued): *What sort of films do you like watching?*

HITCHCOCK: Oh, I don't mind. I have pretty broad tastes, you know. I see them, you know, privately, in the projection room. Some of the Italian films I like, you know, Fellini and those fellows.

FORBES: *I saw an interesting Czech film the other day which would I think possibly interest you if it ever comes your way. It was called* Murder Czech Style, *by a director called Jiri Weiss, whose work I hadn't seen before, which it really did impress me, a most engaging black comedy, you know.*

HITCHCOCK: Yes, I did enjoy the Czech film *Closely Watched Trains*. That was a very good picture.

QUESTION: *Mr. Hitchcock, is there any film you wish you had never made?*

HITCHCOCK: Lots of them. I can't particularize, really, but there are several.

QUESTION: *Mr. Hitchcock, have you ever thought of combining, say, two or three short stories in different moods in one cinema film?*

HITCHCOCK: Not really. I think it's very hard to expect an audience to look at a film and then take a pause and then start all over again. That's why the motion picture as we know, in its best form, is more akin to the short story. It's the only medium, apart from the short story, where we expect an audience to sit down for two hours and watch a thing continuously without a break. I don't really think there have been many successful films that have been broken up in that way.

QUESTION: *Mr. Hitchcock, could you tell us when you first had the idea of appearing in all your films? I think it started with* The Lodger. *And could you tell us why, because I don't know of any other filmmaker that does it.*

HITCHCOCK: No, in those early days, we ran out of actors. That's really true.

FORBES: *Have you ever bothered to join Equity?*

HITCHCOCK: No, but I think they pay a stand-in for me.

FORBES: *Are they after you?*

HITCHCOCK: Oh yes, yes.

QUESTION: *Would you agree that your films have been influenced by German cinema?*

HITCHCOCK: Oh, very much. Well, you see, I worked as a writer and as an art director in the UFA studios, at the time when Murnau and Lang and Jannings were working there. As a matter of fact, I was working on the UFA lot, having written a script, and was designing the sets, at the same time that *The Last Laugh* was being made. Oh yes, sure. The first film I made in England, *The Lodger,* had a very Germanic influence, both in lighting and setting and everything else.

QUESTION: *Mr. Hitchcock, which of your films gave you the most personal satisfaction, and why?*

HITCHCOCK: Well, probably two films. The first one is a picture called *Shadow of a Doubt,* which I wrote with Thornton Wilder, and this was one of those rare occasions when suspense and melodrama combined well with character. And it was shot in the original town, and at that time they were shooting an awful lot on the back lot. So it had a freshness. The other film is *Rear Window,* because to me that's probably the most cinematic film one has made. And most people don't really recognize this because the man is in one room and in one position. But nevertheless, it's the montage and the cutting of what he sees and its effect on him that creates the whole atmosphere and drama of the film. In other words, the visual is transferred to emotional ideas, and that film lends itself to that.

FORBES: *Would you say, Mr. Hitchcock, it'd be a fair comment to say that your films have never really been concerned with social consciousness, as we now bandy around the term? You haven't really taken note of your own times; you've plowed your own furrow, as it were.*

HITCHCOCK: That's true. Samuel Goldwyn once said, "Messages are for Western Union." [laughter and applause]

FORBES: *Yes, I don't think the applause is actually well-placed, because not all films that fall into that category are necessarily bad films, and Goldwyn was getting a cheap laugh, really, which has echoed down the years and may bury him. But what I meant was, a subject came my way, which is an American subject, and would seem to me on the face of it to be ideally suited for you. It's a true life thing; it's called* Witness to a Killing *and is based on that New York murder, where fifty-six people saw a girl stabbed to death in the street and did nothing about it. Would that sort of subject attract you at all?*

HITCHCOCK: Yes, except that it is an objective approach, and it would be very hard to get an audience involved in that.

FORBES: *That's interesting.*

HITCHCOCK: It would be objective from an audience point of view. They would be examining the behavior pattern of the people who witnessed it, and therefore the comment would be, "Can you imagine how irresponsible people are when it comes to being involved?" They'd rather not be involved. But the comment would come from the onlooker, rather than provide them with any particular emotion.

FORBES: *Do you get any of your ideas or stories from headlines or from newspapers?*

HITCHCOCK: Sometimes. I made a picture, *Wrong Man*, once, which was a recounting of an actual case of wrongful arrest. I shot it in the actual places where everything occurred. Even I was allowed to photograph the trial in the same courtroom, with the judge sitting beside me as technical adviser. And the people keep coming up and whispering to me, saying, "The judge is wrong. The judge is wrong." And we had to wait until the judge went out of the court to put things right.

QUESTION: *Mr. Hitchcock, what do you think of the current trend in the cinema towards nudity and also towards frank love scenes, and how will it affect you in the future in your filmmaking?*

FORBES: *Or your own appearances.*

HITCHCOCK: Do you mean in the nude?

FORBES: *Yes, when can we expect your first nude appearance?*

HITCHCOCK: Never. I think that's a passing phase. After all, how far can you go with nudity, or sexual relations? You know, it would seem that we're all waiting for that zoom in to a close-up of the sexual act and how close can we get to it? Once you've reached that point, then where do you go? After all, it makes no difference to me, because that scene I've already done: I did it in the end of a picture called *North by Northwest*, where I showed Cary Grant pull a girl into an upper berth, and then I cut to the phallic train entering the tunnel.

FORBES: *Next tunnel? You sir.*

QUESTION: *Of your latest films, I feel that* Torn Curtain *perhaps is the least successful. First of all, do you agree, and do you think it might be slightly miscast?*

HITCHCOCK: It was totally miscast. Sure. I should have had in that film a singing scientist.

QUESTION: *Mr. Hitchcock, about* Torn Curtain. *Could I ask you how you got political permission to shoot exteriors in East Berlin? And also how you managed to control the color in the exteriors so well?*

HITCHCOCK: We never shot in East Berlin.

FORBES: *And he also asked how did you manage to control the color?*

HITCHCOCK: Well, you can always control color, by desaturation. You see, Technicolor have a very wide range, and they can desaturate color, and wash it out almost as you can on a TV set. You know, in a color TV set, you can twist that knob until you get practically black and white if you want it. And Technicolor can do the same.

QUESTION: *Do you find casting the films more difficult now that actors such as Cary Grant and James Stewart are getting older.*

HITCHCOCK: Well, there are no stars anymore. I mean they're diminishing all the time. And the reason we don't get stars is because there aren't enough films being made. You see, you have to remember these men you're talking about were made stars by a tremendous number of films in which they appeared. We always had a saying that a star is made by appearing in a quantity of hit pictures. That quantity is no longer with us. Instead of a company making fifty-two pictures a year, the average company in Hollywood only makes twenty. So therefore the opportunity of getting sufficient talent going is no longer with us, so that we're getting fewer and fewer stars. But on the other hand, you are getting lots of successful films, without stars.

FORBES: *Do you find the current trend of taking so-called nonstars—take, for example, Jon Voight in* Midnight Cowboy, *I don't know if you have seen that film . . .*

HITCHCOCK: Not yet, no, no.

FORBES: *It was a remarkable performance, I mean a remarkable achievement on Schlesinger's part to have got the performance. Do you find that attraction: to take someone really totally unknown . . .*

HITCHCOCK: Oh, yes, of course. After all, the best casting man is the novelist. He can describe his character down to every facet of the mind. We don't have that opportunity in films. We have to compromise very often.

FORBES: *Am I right in saying, talking of the novelist, you've never worked with or Graham Greene has never written for you?*

HITCHCOCK: No, never, no.

FORBES: *Do you regret that?*

HITCHCOCK: I don't know. It's very hard to say, until you put this sort of thing into practice. Very difficult to tell.

FORBES: *I think he's got so many affinities with you, that I'd love to see you come together, because I think he's such a superb craftsman . . .*

HITCHCOCK: Oh, yes, he is.

FORBES: *. . . and he writes on the page, he visualizes, all his first sentences just grip you, you know: "Murder meant nothing to Raven." Everything leaps off the page in an image with Greene. I'd love to bring you together. If you ever come to ABC, it's you and Graham Greene.*

QUESTION: *Mr. Hitchcock, did you have a tightly worked script in* Lifeboat, *or did you improvise, or do your actors fill in the final . . .*

HITCHCOCK: No, tightly worked script. Impossible to improvise in a picture where you're spending fourteen weeks of back-projection. There's no chance to improvise there.

FORBES: *Except to improvise your own early demise. Fourteen weeks of back-projection?*

HITCHCOCK: Yes.

FORBES: *Frightening.*

HITCHCOCK: Yes, it is.

FORBES: *Frightening.*

HITCHCOCK: Storm included.

QUESTION: *Mr. Hitchcock, in your film* Under Capricorn, *you deal with a subject which one wouldn't usually associate with you. Can you tell us why you made this film and how you feel about it now?*

HITCHCOCK: The film was done more or less for the benefit of Ingrid Bergman. That was a case of trying to find a subject to suit the star, which I don't believe in. So it was really a compromise. And also, of course, the bad thing for me was that it was a costume picture, which to me have no appeal, because I've never been very good at it, and to me no one in a costume picture ever goes to the toilet.

FORBES: *On that sanitary note, should we have another clip, from a film we've been talking about,* Torn Curtain.

[clip from *Torn Curtain*: the killing of Gromek]

FORBES: *One of the interesting things about that sequence is a few years ago that would probably have been saturated with music, wouldn't it?*

HITCHCOCK: Oh yes, yes.

FORBES: *As the knife came, there'd have been [imitates music sound], you know, there'd have been the old . . . I mean I applaud the fact that there is no music.*

HITCHCOCK: No music, yes.

QUESTION: *Mr. Hitchcock, may I ask you, how did you hear about Wolfgang Kieling, and how did you cast him in this film?*

HITCHCOCK: I saw him in Frankfurt. He's now in East Berlin. Yes.

QUESTION (*continued*): *You didn't know that then?*

HITCHCOCK: That he would go to East Berlin? No.

QUESTION *(continued)*: *I played with him in Amsterdam before he left . . .*

HITCHCOCK: Why did he to go to East Berlin?

QUESTION *(continued)*: *Because he saw me.*

QUESTION: *Mr. Hitchcock, some people would accuse you of a lack of taste in that last sequence. The blood particularly, and the rather sort of gratuitous violence of the scene is utterly unlike anything you've done before. It seems to surpass even* Psycho *in its stomach-turning, nauseating quality. I think it's a master film direction, but it strikes me as still a little bit tasteless. Would you comment on that?*

HITCHCOCK: I would say that the demonstration of the scene is intended to show how difficult it is to kill a man. It is a messy business. It is a horrible business, and it should be a deterrent, because it's not all that easy. They usually show the killings on the screen very simple: a gunshot, and bang, you're dead. But if you don't have a gun or can't use a gun, it just shows you what a horrible, awful thing it is to kill someone. Especially, as you see at the end, in Auschwitz.

QUESTION: *In the light of that, were you surprised when people laughed at that sequence just now?*

HITCHCOCK: That's the usual reaction.

QUESTION *(continued)*: *Are you pleased with that kind of reaction?*

HITCHCOCK: Of course.

QUESTION *(continued)*: *You are?*

HITCHCOCK: Yes.

QUESTION *(continued)*: *That means it's money in the box office?*

HITCHCOCK: Well, I wouldn't say that, but you know . . .

QUESTION *(continued)*: *No, I mean do you care why people enjoy your sequences?*

HITCHCOCK: Yes, because that's the emotion emerging.

QUESTION *(continued)*: *Why do you prefer people to laugh at something like that?*

HITCHCOCK: Because that's a release of tension.

QUESTION *(continued)*: *But it's not funny.*

HITCHCOCK: No, but it is a relief. People who want to find relief will find their own ways. In a scene like that it was impossible to give them the relief from the tension all the way through, because of the nature of the scene, the need to have to kill the man. Usually, when you're setting up a tense sequence, it behooves you to make sure that you get the moments of relief from the tension. Sometimes you can do it, sometimes you can't. Here's a case where it didn't provide the opportunity.

FORBES: *Can we just pursue, before I take another question, can we just pursue this, because it's a very interesting topic? We've discussed how far nudity has gone, can go, should go. Would anybody else like to comment further on the question of violence in the cinema, and as applied, not necessarily as Mr. Hitchcock applies it, but ask him how other directors apply it? I mean, taking your question and your question, sir, you said, you know that, no somebody over there, said how tasteless it was. I mean, where do you think violence on the screen should begin and end, as it were? Would anybody like to phrase a question or comment on that? You, sir.*

QUESTION: *I'd like to pursue this particular sequence and the questions that were raised. In fact, we've seen that sequence out of context. But an audience, had an audience seeing the film from the beginning to the end, who would laugh during that period of time? I think the tendency is that people with certain sadistic tendencies would laugh, whereas I think if we had seen it in context, then we generally would not laugh, as we have here. I think we were predisposed to laughing at the sequence. But would an audience having seen the film from the beginning laugh at this particular time?*

FORBES: *Would a sadist like to comment on that? Will one of the laughing sadists, would they like to reveal themselves? Are you a laughing sadist, madam?*

QUESTION: *No. But this is how he has explained it. It is a release of tension. I've come out, you know, laughing, and saying brilliant, marvelous, how he got round it, you know, terrific scene. But it's definitely a release of emotion.*

FORBES: *Do you normally laugh when you're terrorized in real life?*

QUESTION (continued): *I am a sadist [giggling]. No. Again, I think it is this release of emotion.*

FORBES: *Do you think people in real life laugh when they're terrorized?*

HITCHCOCK: Well, they always come off the scenic railway giggling. They scream while they're on it. Or people at the fairground come out of the haunted house: they've paid money to be scared, but when they come out, they're giggling, always. I think the prime example is when it all began, when a three-month's-old child is held in its mother's arms, and the mother says, "Boo!" And the child suddenly is startled, gets the hiccups, and then it laughs, and mother laughs, and all seems to be satisfied. Why mother says "Boo!" to the child, I don't know, but they're still doing it.

FORBES: *I agree with you. I had a real-life experience this week, because my wife and I were going to bed in a strange room, and just before we went to bed, she said, I know you think I'm going to make this up, but I've just seen a rat cross the room. And so I knew something was demanded of me, a degree of courage which I didn't possess. So I armed myself, and sure enough, a rat then ran up the wall, and my wife indeed at one point did start laughing, although she was absolutely terrified out of her mind.*

HITCHCOCK: Sure. Well, there are people who do . . . sometimes the laughter takes other forms. It takes the form of humor about the situation. I remember years ago they used to have at Islington here, they called it the World's Fair, and it was a sort of merry-go-rounds and sideshows and that sort of thing. And in one of the tents, which only cost about a few pennies to go in, no forms to sit on, just stand there. And on the platform—and the rat gave me the idea—there was a man biting the heads from live rats. On the whole, people were sort of petrified at this exhibition, but there were two char ladies at the back, and one of them, naturally to relieve *her* horror and tension at this, she called out with clenched teeth, she said, "Don't you want any bread with it?"

FORBES: *Have you ever witnessed, which I believe was quite popular in sideshows some years ago, regurgitation acts, where people swallowed live rats and then regurgitated them? There was a man called Dan Mannix, who wrote a book about it. Did you ever see one of those?*

HITCHCOCK: No. I never saw that. Why regurgitate it? Why not let it stay down? Who wants the rat back?

FORBES: *Well, he used to, the climax of his act was to swallow two rats, who then proceeded to fight in his stomach, and he ended up by swallowing large quantities of water.*

HITCHCOCK: Oh, I thought you were going to say that the rats fought and he burped.

QUESTION: *I think we can take it that that sort of laughter is tinged with hysteria. We might as well face the fact that violence is an integral part of the cinema and always has been. As you said before, Mr. Hitchcock, practice makes perfect, but nevertheless we who've come to the National Film Theater know that many stars were stars almost from their first films. And today you don't get people like James Cagney or Humphrey Bogart; you don't get women like Greta Garbo and Bette Davis in her day. So, to cut it short, do you think the cinema has seen its best days or more or less had it?*

HITCHCOCK: Well, in that type of star-studded film, to some degree, yes, but a new thing is taking over, and that is the casting of films realistically, without compromise. That's the difference. But the star system can't come back, because we don't make enough films, as I said earlier. You only make stars by quantities of successful films, so that the woman or the man who is the potential star gets the biggest possible exposure, and that we don't have today.

QUESTION *(continued)*: *Would you say the momentum has diminished?*

HITCHCOCK: Yes, it has. After all, remember, the days of the big stars were a product of showing films twice a week at the cinema. Program changed Mondays and Thursdays. That's gone.

FORBES: *There's also the double feature . . .*

HITCHCOCK: Yes, four pictures in a week, sure.

QUESTION: *I just had a comment about what this gentleman said, about the laughter being tinged with hysteria. I thought in fact the laughter was directly related to the point that you're trying to get across, i.e., this woman's desperate attempts to find a solution. It was the character's attitude to the violence that you are laughing at, not the violence itself. And I think when you were saying about what are the limits of violence, to what violence can be treated: there are no limits, provided you are also interested in the attitude, the feelings of the character, and not just a blur.*

HITCHCOCK: That's fine, that's true. [whispers to Forbes: Well, I think we've had it, don't you?]

FORBES: *I'll take three more questions. I think Mr. Hitchcock has given, as usual, more than value for money, and I'll take three final questions from people I haven't taken questions from before.*

QUESTION: *You seem to anticipate your audience's reactions to your films pretty exactly. Do you derive any pleasure or power from this . . . the way you manipulate?*

HITCHCOCK: I think that's very important. I think that comes in devising the film, to anticipate what the audience reaction's going to be. The audience won't know it, because they haven't seen the film, but in watching each scene, you have to say to yourself, "What are the audience thinking now?" And one does that in the creation of a script.

QUESTION: *You like being frightened up to a certain point, thinking that it's good for us? But have you ever had to stop too short, thinking something would be too frightening?*

HITCHCOCK: No, never, no.

FORBES: *Right, our final question's at the back there, that gentleman.*

QUESTION: *As regard to the question of the relation between the filmmaker and the audience, you seem to see your role as being a very passive one. In other words, you give the audience roughly what they will want to come back here to see again. Are you happy with this situation, in the sense that, are there things that you'd like to do, the kind of films you'd like to make, which you can't make, because the taste of the audience has suppressed it?*

HITCHCOCK: Well, after all, somebody once said, years ago, a play is not written or complete without an audience. You can have a play, for example, you can rehearse it, you can have a complete run-through, but until that audience witnesses that play, the whole thing is incomplete, and the same thing to some extent applies to a film. In other words, there's no satisfaction in having a big auditorium like this, and having one seat in the center, and then showing the film. It's the collective audience, and their reactions, that is of interest and must promote your endeavors.

QUESTION (*continued*): *It makes no difference to you what kind of audience you've got. It doesn't matter, does it?*

HITCHCOCK: The bigger the better, especially if you have a Japanese audience to worry about. After all, what greater satisfaction can a filmmaker have, to know that a given scene that he's devised in a film, to know that on the same evening in Tokyo, West Berlin, London, and New York, the audience are all reacting in the same way? And that's the power of the cinema. Theater doesn't have it, literature doesn't get the chance to have it, but we are able, by the manner of copying films and placing them in movie houses all over the world, and that is the greatest satisfaction one can have.

FORBES: *Well, Mr. Hitchcock, on behalf of this collective audience, I'm sure they'd wish me to thank you for your usual inspired and urbane performance. For myself, I can't say I've actually sat at the feet of the master, but in years to come I can say I shared a sofa with you, and I'm very privileged. Thank you very much.*

INTERVIEW: ALFRED HITCHCOCK

R. Allen Leider

"Interview: Alfred Hitchcock" was published in basically the same form in both *Good Times,* June 1978, 46, 51, 76, and *Elite,* September 1978, 27–30. I reprint the latter.

ELITE: *Do you enjoy making people frightened, scaring them?*

HITCHCOCK: Oh yes. Fear is a basic emotion. People like to be scared if they can control it. That's why people go on the fast rides at amusement parks and to movies like mine. They want to be scared for some inner emotional reason. They don't want to be scared in a real sense, though. They want to be scared of non-existent things like monsters and theatrical characters. Imagination plays an important part in what I do, the way I scare people.

ELITE: *You do not believe in explicitness in your technique?*

HITCHCOCK: Not in the terrifying scenes. Only for the expositions, the setting up of the stage, so to speak, so people know all the facts, so they can be frightened the way I want them to be frightened. Explicit violence is never as good as people can make violence in their heads. In *Psycho,* I never show the knife touching the girl, for example. It's all suggested. In *Frenzy,* the nude girl is dumped from the truck in a bikini of potatoes wired to her body, but the mind fills in the nakedness. I never take a chance at offending anyone. That would spoil their enjoyment of my films. I usually allow the editing to do the suggesting. Again in *Frenzy,* I let the murderer take the girl to his room and then I pull the camera away, allowing the audience to listen and imagine what is taking place in the room above. All they see is a window. My films are largely reaction films. I never do whodunits.

ELITE: *Why not?*

HITCHCOCK: Because whodunits are not emotional experiences. Murder mysteries are intellectual puzzles and most of the audience wants to experience, not think. Thinkers don't function well if they get emotionally involved. In that scene in *Frenzy,* the murderer takes the girl upstairs and says to her, "You know, you're my kind of girl." Now we know from previous events that he will kill her. When the camera retreats down to the street and we see the window, the audience is automatically clued to think "he is killing her, but no one will hear it."

ELITE: *Did you have a strict upbringing yourself?*

HITCHCOCK: Oh yes. I was brought up a strict Catholic. The Jesuits at the schools I attended were very, very authoritarian. It enhanced my fear of authority, like police. I had most of my schooling under these Jesuits until I went to a vocational school.

ELITE: *What was your early ambition?*

HITCHCOCK: I intended to go into some form of engineering. I attended a school for engineering and navigation studies. I took all sorts of interesting courses: metal work, drafting, even blacksmithing. I had my first job as an estimator for an electrical company.

ELITE: *It doesn't sound very artistic.*

HITCHCOCK: It wasn't, but I was making money. I kept up an interest in art with a course I was taking at the University of London. I finally wound up with courses in fine arts, painting and more mechanical art. I was promoted into the advertising department at the electrical firm. I designed ads and did layouts.

ELITE: *How old were you at this time?*

HITCHCOCK: About 19.

ELITE: *How did the Jesuit training affect this new line of endeavor?*

HITCHCOCK: I learned professionalism, dedication to goals, and discipline to one's own routines. Many people in the arts lack this discipline and it shows in their work. I have a system for what I do and I never waver from it. It works because it has inflexible rules.

ELITE: *When did you decide to leave the electrical business?*

HITCHCOCK: It wasn't easy. I had heard about a job at a local Paramount office in London and applied for it while I was working at the electrical company.

When I got the Paramount job I worked both positions until I made a decision.

ELITE: *How did you get started making films?*

HITCHCOCK: I was working in the advertising department of a studio in England. I was what they called a layout man and I pasted up the parts of the advertisements on big sheets of paper. I also hand-lettered the title cards for the silent films we made in those days. I was working as a writer later on and someone asked me if I had given thought to directing a film. I was shocked at the time. Me? Direct a motion picture? I did it anyway, three times. They were interesting experiments. They showed a lot of influence of the German theater which was very fashionable at the time. I didn't get overexcited about them, though.

ELITE: *What do you think was your first good film?*

HITCHCOCK: *The Lodger.* It was about Jack the Ripper. I was very pleased with the way I used shadows in the film. Too many directors overlight their sets. Shadows are equally important. I was taught at art school that only light and shadow exist and that lines were imaginary things. I, therefore, use shadows to show people pictures.

ELITE: *Some people have called you a ghoul. How do you react to that?*

HITCHCOCK: I think it's meant as a compliment. I certainly hope so. I do know when the audience is going to scream, and I must say I enjoy it. But the scenes that people often say are my most shocking are not the ones I pick myself as the most terrifying. I think *The 39 Steps* is much more effective than *Psycho,* for example. My own favorite is the part where Robert Donat is being entertained in a man's home and he is describing the master spy he is tracking. All he knows about the spy is that the little finger is missing from his right hand and when he says this, his host holds his left hand, minus pinky and says, "You mean left hand." That is shocking.

ELITE: *Do you think people really enjoy being jolted that much?*

HITCHCOCK: Yes. They get much of this enjoyment from their childhood. That is their reference bank for their emotions at movies. Many of these people live rather hum-drum lives and without the movies and TV to give them some emotional jolts they would crack up from boredom, I should think.

ELITE: *Imagination is the key then?*

HITCHCOCK: Yes, like in the days of early radio. The audience decided what the room, the characters and costumes looked like. It was all sounds and suggestions. That wonderful experience was destroyed forever by television. It spelled it out. I try to restore some of that lost imagination by getting my audience to fill in the blanks and fill their heads with images they create. In *Psycho,* the bathtub scene was set up to allow the most terror possible without showing graphic violence. It did it without color, too, because a good director knows that color destroys part of the viewers' attention. Black and white is much more nightmarish. The knife moves up and down. We fill in the stabs. We never see them. We do the violence based on our memories.

ELITE: *Why do you persist in making a single genre of film? Is there a criminal element or experience in your own past that has put you on this single track?*

HITCHCOCK: Not really. The British are a very crime-oriented people to begin with. Just look at our tabloids with their lurid details of murders, rapes, and the like. They thrive on it. There exists a crime mystique in England and it rubs off on everyone. I would imagine that being a creative, theatrical sort of person makes me a better user of this mystique than the layman.

ELITE: *Is American crime worse or better than British crime?*

HITCHCOCK: Much worse because you use guns. We have no guns to speak of in Britain. The police don't carry them and it's a matter of courtesy that criminals don't either. You can knock people out or tie them up, but you don't shoot them. Even knives are rare as weapons. Here people get blasted all over the place. I prefer my own style.

ELITE: *But doesn't the repetition of themes and techniques make for a weakening product?*

HITCHCOCK: No. Not in the slightest because I do it differently each time. Most good directors do it, too. I am not alone in this respect. I use the "wrong man" theme a lot because it is something everyone can identify with easily. Each of us has at one time or another been wrongly blamed for something we were innocent of. Most of the times there was no evidence or circumstantial evidence. Children are most frequently the victims of this sort of thing, breaking a vase or window. The universality of the experience makes a successful movie theme. The "wrong man" in the movies just has it worse off. He didn't break a vase, he is accused of murder or some heinous crime and is chased by the police or by other criminals. That's terror.

ELITE: *Have you ever been wrongly accused of something?*

HITCHCOCK: Of course. Once my father went so far as to have the local constable lock me away in a jail cell for a few hours so I would know what it was like to be imprisoned. I was terrified, even though I knew it was not real. I have always been shy of police since then.

ELITE: *What frightens you personally, other than policemen?*

HITCHCOCK: Cars. I never drive cars. If I don't drive I can't get a ticket. Police-men and the law are my basic fears. I try to avoid them. Policemen are very powerful. They can come to your home or stop you on the street and question you. They can arrest you and lock you up. That is awful.

ELITE: *Do you worry a lot?*

HITCHCOCK: No. But I think about it from time to time.

ELITE: *Do you have a sense of humor?*

HITCHCOCK: Certainly. In fact, I love practical jokes of any kind. I play them on my friends constantly. I once gave a dinner party and called my friends to a very posh restaurant where I had arranged for all the food to be dyed *blue*. It really shook them. Sometimes, I'll have close friends for dinner and I will tell one couple or so that it is a fancy dress and the others that it is casual and they come in very contrasting modes of attire. Or perhaps masquerade costumes when everyone else is in tuxedos. I like to laugh, sure.

ELITE: *What don't you like?*

HITCHCOCK: I don't like the bedroom wrestling matches we see in films today. It's too much and it's unneeded. I never use nudity or sex unless it is vital to the plot and then I suggest it. Explicitness kills the whole illusion you start to build.

ELITE: *Explicitness, then, must be another of your dislikes. Is there another thing, like police, a personal thing that also makes you cringe?*

HITCHCOCK: Yes. Many. I hate eggs in any form. I used to get them when I was young. They always smelled bad. The smell of hard-boiled eggs is the most horrible thing I can think of. It makes me sick to my stomach. I also distrust bottled dressings and gravies. I like my sauces made fresh. I distrust bottled sauces of any type.

ELITE: *That covers smell and sight. Is there a sound that frightens you?*

HITCHCOCK: Yes. It really doesn't frighten me, but it grates on my nerves like chalk squeaking on a blackboard. I hate hearing a person spanking the bottom of a bottle, like a catsup bottle. They hit it violently and some red ooze comes out of the top. It looks like blood. It also is prepared, bottled sauce so it covers two dislikes. This ooze then glops over some delicious food like potatoes and lies there like residue over the innocent vegetable. It's disgusting.

ELITE: *You make it sound very poetic.*

HITCHCOCK: That's one of the reasons I seldom have food scenes in my pictures.

ELITE: *I understand that film making is expensive and profitable, even for the early days of the business. Have your films made you exceptionally rich?*

HITCHCOCK: Not really.

ELITE: *Do you have backers for your films or do you produce them yourself?*

HITCHCOCK: I'd never invest my own money in films. I believe that the profits from one film should dictate the next film, but the risk involved in self-investment is too great. I'll tell you why. When you make a film and edit it, you have control over what it is. Then it goes to a distributor and you never see it again, nor do you have control over where it will be shown and how it is promoted. These things can destroy a good film. You are helplessly in the hands of sales people, publicists, and others. Once the germ of the film is conceived and translated into a motion picture and turned over to the distributors it becomes *their* film. The most foolish thing I could do, therefore, is to invest my own money in a picture.

ELITE: *I see. Why did you leave television? Yours was a very successful program.*

HITCHCOCK: It still is. It's in reruns, syndication all over the country. We ceased producing new shows because we were in the production of the program for ten years. I made 273 half-hour programs and 90 one-hour programs. That's a lot of story material. If I made any more, I would be competing with myself in some markets. Besides, I don't think there is any quality in television films, nor in any of the recent theater cinema I have seen recently either.

ELITE: *What about the new wave directors?*

HITCHCOCK: I don't think that they have really learned the business of making motion pictures. I think to really know the motion picture industry one must go backwards to the silent films and learn how to tell a story visually. These new people spend most of their time copying each other. It gets boring watching scenes of out of focus flowers and faces in the foregrounds. Art is supposed to create emotion and most of the new wave directors fall short on this point. They sacrifice story and visual rhythm for gimmicks.

ELITE: *You once were quoted as saying that "actors are cattle!" Can you elaborate on that point?*

HITCHCOCK: I was misquoted for one thing. That statement was part of something else I was discussing. I said that actors had to be treated like cattle in that to direct actors you must guide their every movement, their looks, their total physical presence in front of the camera.

ELITE: *Then you do like actors?*

HITCHCOCK: Of course. Actors are people first and performers second. They have to be treated as people, although I don't think that acting is a very dignified profession. You have to wear funny clothes sometimes and put all that paint on your face. I don't see that as work. I would never be an actor.

ELITE: *Do you have favorite actors?*

HITCHCOCK: Yes, and I use them again and again, if possible.

ELITE: *Have there been some who didn't work out?*

HITCHCOCK: Yes. When I get a difficult actor, I simply remind him who is paying him and that most often solves the problem. I remind them that their salary is not endless. I do demand a lot from them, though, for that money. I demand professionalism. They have to know their lines, all of them. They also must define and know their roles, the germ of the character they play. The problem is that many people, actors, directors, crew people, are entering the business nowadays with a total lack of knowledge of the business. They have desires and goals, but no foundation for a solid, professional career in motion picture-making, which is an art form, not a money-making venture exclusively. I have done everything: lights, sets, camera, editing. Few, if any, of these new people have done more than acting of one sort or another. It shows in their performances.

ELITE: *I understand that you forbid television stations to edit anything from your movies when they are telecast?*

HITCHCOCK: It's my cardinal rule. They can destroy months of planning and work with a single snip of their scissors and my name is on that film. It would hurt me, so I prohibit them from doing it when the picture is rented to them. When *Rear Window* was first telecast, I only allowed a few small breaks for legal station identification. Other films have designated spots for the commercials, so the rhythm of the action is not broken into by toothpaste or mouthwash. But I NEVER allow any scenes to be deleted. That would be real murder!

ELITE: *People often think of a movie director as a monster who shouts and yells at everyone. Is this true?*

HITCHCOCK: There must be some like that. I'm not one of them. I am very placid. Ingrid Bergman once told me that I was a man who never fought because once I walked away from an argument with her on the set of a film we were doing. I dislike arguing so I don't argue. I avoid confrontations. That's another fear I have, I guess.

ELITE: *Is that a common problem with people today—avoiding confrontations?*

HITCHCOCK: Communicating in general is a cause of most of the world's problems. Years ago we had no TV or radio. Just newspapers, and dull ones at that. Today people are bombarded with information from all sides, messages that they cannot comprehend because they get so much from all sides. They can't handle it. Then you have the situation where people copy TV behavior. Crimes are copied and other violent acts.

Years ago there was a Rod Serling film on TV about airplane hijackings just like the one on the television. That is what too much communication does. It does not allow for thinking about the information received. I once had a similar situation that I still regret to this day. It was in *Foreign Correspondent*. It was made years ago with Joel McCrea. There was a big scene wherein a politician was assassinated by a man posing as a photographer. It's in the middle of the street in a crowd. The photographer had a gun in the left hand and the camera in the right. As he took the picture, he shot the politician dead and ran off in the confusion. Not long after the film was released, the same crime was committed that way in Teheran. I was stunned and I still regret it.

ELITE: *Why do you think people look for crime films? Do they admire the criminals?*

HITCHCOCK: No. Only sick people do that. Most people look at the crime and the criminal and think, "There but for the grace of God go I." But they don't often emulate the good that is demonstrated in films because there is not as much satisfaction in that. They see the man accused wrongly of the crime or chased by the police or the enemy and think, "Thank God it's not me." He's always being shot at or something, and they don't want to identify with him. They want to feel safe or in control.

ELITE: *What do you look for when you approach a script for possible production?*

HITCHCOCK: I tend to gravitate towards a situation where an innocent man is pulled into a bizarre series of events. In *North by Northwest,* for example, a businessman is mistaken for a superspy. In *Rear Window* a convalescing man witnesses a murder across the courtyard via binoculars while peeping on the neighbors. People can easily identify with these situations and they are totally believable. They could happen.

ELITE: *Is it hard to plan fright in a film?*

HITCHCOCK: It takes time. First, you have to know what audiences are afraid of. Second, you have to know how they feel about certain things and how to make them feel these things. It's all design and pre-production planning, so that when the finished film is shown, they react as you intended them to.

ELITE: *Do you think that many of the successful horror films and suspense films that are on the screens today are too frightening in an explicit manner?*

HITCHCOCK: Yes. They throw it at you in globs instead of letting it develop within you. They also repeat the killings over and over again. It's overkill in many different ways. In *Frenzy,* I only had one killing, one act of violence, but the other killings in the mass murder plot were only suggested. The single act served as a model for the audience's imagination to fill in the details of the latter, "suggested" murders.

ELITE: *Does television influence the public's taste in cinema? Or in violence for that matter?*

HITCHCOCK: Oh yes. Certainly. There have been many TV shows, news programs, documentaries that practically glorify felons. They revel in violence, especially the news shows during the Vietnam war. They overdid it with the battle footage. It was carnage without a message. It was entertainment and such things should not be entertaining without a message, a moral point. Even in World War Two the newsreels had moral messages about war.

ELITE: *What is the most frequently-made mistake made by today's suspense film-makers?*

HITCHCOCK: The most frequent mistake that bothers me is that I never get to know the victims. That personal information makes the crime that much more horrible because you identify with a person, not just a body being shot up or hacked to pieces. You can relate to the effects the murder will have on their relatives and the lives of others.

ELITE: *But often in your films, the objects of danger are total unknowns.*

HITCHCOCK: Only in mass-terror situations. For example, in *The Birds,* there is a scene in which a young girl watches a single bird. In the background is a jungle gym with a single bird on it. When she watches the bird land on the gym, it is filled with ravens. The audience is shocked. We know they will attack the girl, and because she is a child it is horrible. There is little we have to know about the girl, but the fear of hundreds of birds attacking a child is enough.

ELITE: *You also seem to favor women as the victims. Why?*

HITCHCOCK: Because they are traditionally the victims, although men, too, have been victims of other types of crimes. Ladies have been victims only in domestic plots.

ELITE: *Your women also never seem to be overtly sexy. Is that due to the Jesuit schooling or to British reserve?*

HITCHCOCK: I never analyzed it. I have myself never been fond of the type of woman who walks around advertising how sexy she is. You know, the woman with her sex appeal hanging around her neck like expensive jewelry. The large-bosomed ladies just don't evoke the same type of emotional reaction that the ladies I use do. I let the sex appeal come from the acting. Eva Marie Saint in *North by Northwest* was modestly dressed, and acted rather conservatively, yet she was very seductive and sexy by virtue of the performance and the story. Ingrid Bergman is another very sexy lady, but only because of an inner beauty, an inner sexiness. Sex is not an overt display. It is an inner magnetism, an energy that is transmitted by actions.

ELITE: *Have critical notices ever affected you in any way?*

HITCHCOCK: It depends. I never got overly upset about it, but I do get concerned when they get out of line, when they criticize the content instead of the technique. It's like looking at a landscape painting and criticizing the scene instead of the way the scene was painted. Besides, I sometimes wonder about the qualifications of many of these film reviewers and critics. Many have not the slightest idea of what their function is. Many of the critics I read are not cinema students at all. They have no background in the field they work at. Often they get promoted from some other department, like books or restaurants. It's a gift—free movies—from their editors.

I never get riled by a bad review from an experienced critic who is doing a professional job with knowledge and opinions. But inexperienced people bother me. Non-professionalism in any form really bothers me. I remain on good terms with many critics who have disliked some of my films or have printed poor notices, because I respect them as journalists, as professionals, and they still respect me as a director even if they didn't like the last film.

ELITE: *Have you a new project in mind for the future?*

HITCHCOCK: I always have new things under consideration, but I never disclose them. I leave that up to the distributor. It's his job to promote and make noise about it.

ELITE: *Will you ever consider a new form of expression like a major TV movie or something like that? The three- and four-part TV novels are now the vogue.*

HITCHCOCK: No. I'd never do that because the quality in television is not too good and it would take the same effort to make a good theater picture. That's what I do.

ELITE: *Well, we'll look forward to your next endeavor. Thanks for the time.*

HITCHCOCK: They say a murder is committed every minute. This interview has spanned ninety murders. Think about that!

SELECTED BIBLIOGRAPHY

Auiler, Dan. *Hitchcock's Notebooks: An Authorized and Illustrated Look Inside the Creative Mind of Alfred Hitchcock.* New York: HarperCollins, 1999.

Bergstrom, Janet. "Lost in Translation? Listening to the Hitchcock-Truffaut Interview." In *A Companion to Alfred Hitchcock,* ed. Thomas Leitch and Leland Poague, 387–404. Malden, MA: Blackwell, 2011.

Bogdanovich, Peter. "Alfred Hitchcock." In *Who the Devil Made It: Conversations with Legendary Film Directors,* 471–557. New York: Knopf, 1997.

"'Dangerous Lies' Is Coming to Utica." *Utica Morning Telegram,* December 3, 1921, 9.

Freeman, David. *The Last Days of Alfred Hitchcock.* Woodstock, NY: Overlook Press, 1984.

Gottlieb, Sidney. "Brand Hitchcock." In *39 Steps to the Genius of Hitchcock,* ed. James Bell, 72–77. London: British Film Institute, 2012.

———. "Hitchcock in 1928." In *Hitchcock Annual,* ed. Sidney Gottlieb and Richard Allen, vol. 16, 1–22. New York: Columbia University Press, 2010. (Introduces Hitchcock's essay "An Autocrat of the Studio," reprinted on 22–28.)

———. "Hitchcock Interviewed in *Filmindia.*" In *Hitchcock Annual,* ed. Sidney Gottlieb and Richard Allen, vol. 15, 242–49. New York: Columbia University Press, 2006–7. (Introduces and reprints an interview with Hitchcock not included in the present volume.)

———. "Hitchcock on Griffith." In *Hitchcock Annual,* ed. Sidney Gottlieb and Richard Allen, vol. 14, 32–49. New York: Columbia University Press, 2005–6. (Introduces and reprints Hitchcock's "A Columbus of the Screen.")

———. "Hitchcock on Truffaut." *Film Quarterly* 66, no. 4 (Summer 2013): 10–22. (Introduces and reprints "Hitchcock on Truffaut.")

———, ed. *Hitchcock on Hitchcock: Selected Writings and Interviews.* Vol. 1. Berkeley: University of California Press, 1995.

Kerzoncuf, Alain, and Charles Barr. *Hitchcock: Lost and Found.* Lexington: University of Kentucky Press, forthcoming 2015.

McGilligan, Patrick. *Alfred Hitchcock: A Life in Darkness and Light.* New York: HarperCollins, 2003.

Spoto, Donald. *The Dark Side of Genius: The Life of Alfred Hitchcock.* Boston: Little, Brown, 1983.

Truffaut, François. *Hitchcock.* Rev. ed. With the collaboration of Helen G. Scott. New York: Simon and Schuster, 1984.

Vest, James M. *Hitchcock and France: The Forging of an Auteur.* Westport, CT: Praeger, 2003.

ACKNOWLEDGMENTS OF PERMISSIONS

The Hitchcock Estate has very kindly granted their permission to reprint all the pieces in this volume. Original publication information appears below the title of each article, story, or interview. Additional permissions are as follows:

"Lights! Action—but Mostly Camera!" is reprinted with the permission of Simon and Schuster, Inc. All rights reserved.

"Introduction" by Alfred Hitchcock, copyright © 1943, copyright renewed 1970 by Alfred A. Knopf, a division of Random House LLC; from *Intrigue* by Eric Ambler. Used by permission of Alfred A. Knopf, an imprint of the Knopf Doubleday Publishing Group, a division of Random House LLC. All rights reserved.

"'It's the Manner of Telling': An Interview with Alfred Hitchcock" is reprinted by permission of F. Anthony Macklin. Copyright © 1976. All rights reserved.

"Interview with Alfred Hitchcock," from *Antaeus,* is reprinted by permission of Daniel Halpern. Copyright © 1973. All rights reserved.

"Hitchcock Speaking," previously published by *Cosmopolitan* magazine, October 1956. Reprinted with permission of Hearst Communications, Inc. Copyright © 1956. All rights reserved.

"Alfred Hitchcock Resents" article © SEPS licensed by Curtis Licensing, Indianpolis, IN. All rights reserved.

"John Player Lecture" is reproduced with permission of Curtis Brown, London, on behalf of the Estate of Bryan Forbes. Copyright © The Estate of Bryan Forbes 1969.

"Interview: Alfred Hitchcock," from *Good Times,* is reprinted by permission of R. Allen Leider. Copyright © 1978. All rights reserved.

INDEX